Dr. Bailey has a truly gifted and exciting 

of love and grace to the nations.

Pastor Bill Winston
Living Word Christian Center
Forest Park, Illinois

Pat Bailey came to Victory World Missions Training Center in 1983 as a young, single-parent mother. She vowed she would go to the mission field if no one else in her class went. Since then her travels have taken her to minister in over 80 nations.

Her writing comes out of living it. The truth has been proven under pressure. You will gain valuable insights from this book. You may decide to get your passport. Get ready!

Billy Joe Daugherty, Pastor
Victory Christian Center
Tulsa, Oklahoma

I knew when Dr. Daisy and I first met you that God's hand was upon you and you were destined to carry His message and share His love abroad. That is happening in a formidable way, for His glory. I commend you for your grit and courage in ministering to so many people in the most difficult areas of our world, in areas and situations almost impossible to contemplate, with the message of Christ's love and compassion.

Dr. T.L. Osborn
OSFO International
Tulsa, Oklahoma

I am convinced that Dr. Patricia Bailey offers the Body of Christ a gold mine filled with nuggets that are life-changing truths. What a sharp tool God has chosen to give us *Finishing Touches*.

Bishop T.D. Jakes, Sr. Pastor
The Potter's House of Dallas, Inc.
Dallas, Texas

It has been our privilege to know Dr. Patricia Darlene Bailey and to receive from her God-given, insightful depth and passion for the harvest consistently for more than a decade.

To my wife, children, and Apostolic Team, she is a Kingdom Ambassador extraordinary. A woman of proven character and uncommon spiritual endowment. She is teachable, transparently clean, and accountable.

This book is straight from the heart of the Father, and it is authored by one who is experienced. Pat's passion for mission is contagious. She is a bridge-builder across the nations and denominational boundaries.

In the course of her mission pursuits, she has oftentimes hazarded her life and that of her team for the sake of the Gospel. Patricia Bailey is a 21st century Sister Phoebe, and we gladly commend her as Paul did in Romans 16 verse 1.

This book in particular is recommended strictly for those willing to give "their utmost for His highest."

Dr. Tunde Bakare, Apostolic Leader
Global Apostolic Impact Network (G.A.I.N)
Founder: The Latter Rain Assembly
(End Time Church), Lagos, Nigeria.

FINISHING TOUCHES

GOD'S MASTER DESIGN TO DEFINE YOUR PURPOSE, MATURE YOUR SOUL, COMPLETE YOUR CALL

by

Dr. Patricia D. Bailey

Harrison House
Tulsa, Oklahoma

Some quotations from the Scriptures contain words emphasized by the author. These words are not emphasized in the original Bible versions.

06 05 04 10 9 8 7 6 5 4 3 2

FINISHING TOUCHES: God's Master Design To Define Your Purpose, Mature Your Soul, Complete Your Call
ISBN 1-57794-617-0

Master's Touch Ministries International
P.O. Box 3175
Alpharetta, Georgia 30023

Published by Harrison House, Inc.
P.O. Box 35035
Tulsa, Oklahoma 74153

DEDICATION

I wish to honor the people who have helped in shaping and molding my life the most by dedicating this book to them. As I follow God on the path of destiny He has for me, I continue to benefit from the life skills I developed and godly counsel I gained from these important people in my life.

To my Father and Mother, for chastising me even when I didn't feel I deserved it, thanks. Dad, your "baby girl" in looking back appreciates all you did to train me!

To my Pastors, Drs. Fred and Betty Price, for correcting me even when I thought I was right. The aim of my heart is to make you proud of me.

To Bill and Veronica Winston for encouraging me in molding a new image of myself, and for your belief in me.

To Tunde Bakare and Mrs. B for allowing me to cry on your shoulders when nobody believed me.

And last but not least, to my son, Karim Israel, my family, and to my staff for all your continual sacrifices. May God richly reward you for your labor of love.

CONTENTS

FOREWORD

In *Finishing Touches,* Dr. Patricia Bailey, a mover and shaker in the Kingdom of heaven, lays out a road map of directions for the fulfillment of God's purpose and plan for your life. The journey begins in helping you discover the unique destiny God has for your life. "I know the plans that I have for you, declares the LORD..." (Jer. 29:11 NASB). In that secret place of intimacy with God, you find who He is, who you are, and where He wants to take you in life.

Dr. Bailey's expert guidance will help you identify specific areas of stagnant immaturity in your life where you trust your own ways, your own strengths, and your own abilities. These areas of weakness can hinder your destiny.

You are then ready for the journey into maturation where Dr. Bailey gives a clear and exciting presentation of spiritual principles which God has set in motion. By applying the precepts in *Finishing Touches,* you will discover how to live out of your spirit man as led by the Holy Spirit. The counsel of the Holy Spirit always brings you to the place of trusting in God's power, not in your own self. Take an essential step to a level in your Christian walk where you die to self and walk in the supernatural power of the God of this universe who can do exceedingly abundantly above all that we ask or think.

Pastor Paula White
Without Walls International Church
Tampa, Florida

INTRODUCTION:

DESTINED BEYOND YOUR EXPECTATIONS

God designed a way for man to enter into His realm of living here on the earth. God wants us to allow Him to orchestrate our future. God's design for our life, if we follow it, will protect us from the domination and manipulation of man, even if the "man" dominating and negatively affecting your future is *you!*

Some people feel trapped by behavior patterns their life has set for them or feel limited in what they can accomplish by behavior patterns defined as personality traits. Some people hide behind their challenges, without attempting to excel beyond them. Other people who in their own strength create the type of future they think they want often discover living in the reality of that future does not provide the fulfillment they thought they would find. In any case, these people are denying themselves from experiencing the best God has for them.

God created us to fulfill a destiny that will exceed the expectations of any we could plan for ourselves. He provided us with the means to complete our call through His Son Jesus. When we accept Jesus as the Way the Father provided for us to form a kinship relationship with Him, we receive the same benefits of sonship that Jesus has.* We cannot create the type of future we want without the Father and Jesus.

* To learn how to form a relationship with the Father, see the prayer at the end of this book.

God wants to show Himself strong on behalf of those whose heart is His. "For the eyes of the Lord move to and fro throughout the earth that He may strongly support those whose heart is completely His..." (2 Chron. 16:9 NASB). What God has planned for your life is uniquely orchestrated for you alone. He wants to make your destiny come true. But above all, He wants your heart. He passionately wants you.

When God begins a good work in us, as He does in all who have formed a relationship with Him through His Son Jesus, He will also complete that work as we continue to yield to Him. God is the One to orchestrate our destiny, not man! Our part is to cooperate with Him. He works with our willingness to yield and makes the finishing touches on the rough edges of our character.

People who feel trapped by their own limitations have found they cannot transform themselves. Our activities of self-help, which do bring a degree of success, have disillusioned our need for sole dependency upon God if we cross the line to place the reliance on ourselves, rather than on Him, for bettering ourselves. It's all about depending on Jesus, not on ourselves. God wants us to draw on Him to turn our weaknesses into strengths. The Bible tells us that God's strength is made perfect *in* weakness. (2 Cor. 12:9.)

Some of us familiar with the scripture cited above know that God wants to help us but don't know how to let Him. How do we allow God to turn our imperfections, the very areas holding us back, into strengths? How do we reach the point of allowing God to orchestrate our destiny?

We learn the answers to these questions by building an intimate relationship with God, learning more about who God is, what He is capable of doing and wants to do for us, and how to let Him work with us and for us. Developing a deep relationship with God takes time, as does any relationship, and it is a process of growing and maturing spiritually.

A BIGGER AND BETTER PLAN

When I was twenty-one years old, I saw God's demonstration in my life of His orchestrating events to propel me into fulfilling the particular destiny He had for me. Before then, determined to be the next black anchorwoman covering Capitol Hill, I was progressing toward the future I had planned for myself. After I surrendered my life to God, I was catapulted into a different kind of new life.

In spite of the obstacles before me and with a small son, I stepped out in faith to attend Bible school and later missions school. I was discovering and building a relationship with a God who lived beyond the inner city and surely beyond the four walls of my church back home. I had a passion then, as now, to bring people to Jesus for them to experience God's love, wisdom, and protection.

It was when I met missionaries T.L. and Daisy Osborn that God began moving in a way that changed the entire course of my life. As I was sitting on the second row in the packed auditorium of the missions school, T.L. called me out of the crowd. "I can see nations in you," he declared. I didn't even know what he meant. I pictured a globe spinning around inside me like the globe on one of those daytime soap opera programs. And then his wife, Daisy, did something neither had ever done before. In front of the entire auditorium, she extended an invitation to me, a total stranger and novice student, to join them in an upcoming crusade to Kenya, Africa.

As the time neared for the crusade, I received a call from the Osborns' ministry office. "We have learned that the area where we were to minister is in a period of major elections. It has been our policy to never go into a country to do crusades during political elections, and so we are redirecting the outreach to West Africa."

I had already purchased my nonrefundable ticket! It was all the faith I could muster, at that time in my early faith-walk, to believe for the $2,100 to buy it. I wondered why God allowed me to purchase it knowing that the crusade would be canceled. But since

I already had my ticket, I determined that I would go to Africa with or without the Osborns, little realizing that this had been God's plan all along!

In a miraculous turn of events, our church was hosting a guest speaker the following Sunday from Kenya. I could hardly wait until he finished his message so that I could meet him and share my situation. "Oh, that's not a problem," he said without hesitation. "We'll arrange some meetings for you."

I provided him with the dates of travel along with a small passport photo, the only recent picture I had available on such short notice.

When I arrived in Kenya, I walked off the plane to find a delegation waving banners and posters. Plastered on them, as well as on billboards advertising the upcoming meeting, was my picture! It was that small passport photo blown up. Beneath it were the words, "Miracle Crusade—come receive your healing—blind eyes open, deaf hear, lame walk—with a woman of faith and power, Patricia Bailey from the USA"!

What woman of...? I thought. I had never held a crusade in my life. I was there to minister at a few meetings and see what Africa was all about. I prayed silently as I thought, *God, what have I gotten myself into?*

When my son was three months old, his father abandoned us. We didn't see him again for two decades. At twenty-one years old, I was a single mother raising my son alone. But God had not abandoned us, and His hand was on my life.

I had prepared myself to fulfill the calling God placed on my life as much as I could in natural ways by going to school. I prepared myself spiritually by building my relationship with God through reading His Word, learning more about Him and how He tells us to operate in life. I experienced His provision by stepping out in faith and obedience to what He told me to do, trusting Him. But that day in Africa, my first reaction was anything but feeling prepared for the way I was launched into my ministry! And true, it was beyond what *I* could handle. I kept my dependence totally on God.

In spite of all the commotion, I couldn't deny the fact that deep within I felt an innate sense that this was where I belonged. Just hours before the meeting I began to earnestly seek the face of God. I had to remind myself of who I am in Christ Jesus and visualize Him using me to heal the sick and raise the dead.

When I arrived at the crusade site, I saw that the ads had effectively done their job—the tent was packed to capacity. People were everywhere, young and old, sick and well. As the meeting began, my translator was excited and ready to interpret for this woman of faith and power! Still anxious about my role, however, I was hoping that the tent had a back door for a speedy escape!

I preached a message of hope, faith, and power then opened the meeting for God's miraculous work. I had learned from the Osborns to demonstrate God's power before the call for salvation as miracles are the dinner bell for the unbeliever.

Faith rose inside me as the people flocked to the platform. The first person in line was blind. Immediately God opened his eyes. The next man had a tumorous growth on his body; it disappeared. Gaining confidence, I thought to myself, *This stuff really does work!* Healings began to take place in every part of the tent. Finally a madman was brought to the platform. Everyone knew him. He was a daily sight storming around the streets naked, hair matted, searching for food and eating from the rubbish bins. Before I could even question myself or allow fear to take hold, I leaped from the platform and straddled the madman, commanding the devil to come out of him in the name of Jesus! Instantaneously he was delivered and returned to his right mind.

After that meeting, I realized that God had another plan for my life—a plan that was bigger than anything I could have ever imagined. The open door of invitation from Daisy Osborn became more than an open door; it opened a new world to me, literally, *the* world. Since that day, God has guided and enabled me to take His deliverance and salvation to thousands and thousands of people in more than seventy nations. I have ministered in restricted areas closed to both women and the Gospel, the male-dominated Muslim regions of Sudan, Oman, Kuwait, and Algeria. Only God could open the door for a single black woman to take the Gospel into those areas. And He has done it.

When hard times come in my life, when people say, like from the beginning, "How can you ever minister in an Islamic region, in the Arab Peninsula as a woman, a single woman, a single black woman, a single black woman with a baby?" I know how to rely on God and His Word from the relationship I have built with Him. I know what He can and will do, and I know how to receive answers from Him.

When you know God, you know that He will provide. You also become familiar with His methods of operation. You know that many times He will use unexpected means that wouldn't occur to the human mind to accomplish something. People used to tell me, "You can't take a baby across customs!" Instead, God used the baby and the responses at customs to him of, "So cute!" to usher me in and out of the countries where God wanted me to be! It is important to learn how to hear God's voice and practice obedience, even when natural circumstances give the impression that another approach would be right.

In knowing how God operates, you also know that the provision does not always come when you think it should come, but it comes in God's timing, the right timing. From having already built a relationship with God, you know that the answer is coming and to expectantly stay in faith until it does come. You also know that when the answer comes, it will be worth the wait!

DO THINGS HIS WAY— DEVELOPING KINGDOM MINDSETS

The church of this century will face issues the early church never faced. Because the Bible foretells the times we are entering, we know what to expect and how to prepare. We are seeing the signs of the end coming to pass that Matthew 24 describes. This is a pivotal time in which God is instructing us. It is especially important today to keep ourselves receptive to Him as He leads us in new ways to handle new issues.

We can gradually become desensitized to His voice without realizing it. We may have begun responding out of habit in different areas of life rather than to His leading. God wants us to be able to hear His voice again in any area in which we have become desensitized. He wants to turn into strengths behaviors or traits which we feel limit us in reaching our destiny. He wants to help us grow in any immature area.

As we grow in Him and see Him lovingly bringing our destiny to pass, our desire becomes to please Him more and hear Him say, "Well done."

SUCCESS UNDER ANY CIRCUMSTANCES

If you have people under you, especially if you develop leaders, training leaders to be equipped to handle issues relative to our times is especially important. Prepare leaders to teach people how to live during these times and for introducing a large and diverse population to the One who can equip anyone to live successfully under any circumstances. Based on the chronological order of God, we are now in the epoch that is considered to be the greatest age of the harvest according to the prophets Isaiah (Isa. 2:2) and Joel (Joel 2:28,29). Another prophet, Micah, sounded an alarm in Micah 4:1-3.[1]

The migration of foreign ethnic groups to our metropolitan cities is multiplying daily as well as the historically large number of displaced, homeless, and refugee groups of people. Develop leaders who will prepare by putting in place an outreach strategy to accommodate and reap this new type of massive harvest, who will begin by becoming acquainted with the different cultures and life situations represented and with individual people. Teach leaders to be open to fellowshipping with members of the Body in other denominations to prepare for widening opportunities for effective ministry through combining strengths, should God direct. Unity among the members of the Body will be very important in ministering and in reaping the diverse and enormous end-time harvests.

If our practices have become rigid or merely traditions, if we have gravitated toward ritual worship, our leaders must allow God to show them how to return to an atmosphere receptive to His guidance and revelation.

OBTAINING AND MAINTAINING

Taking ground for God's Kingdom is one arena; but maintaining the ground taken is an entirely different arena. *Obtaining* a harvest, through planning and acting on a strategy, and *maintaining* the harvest are equally important areas. How do we train leaders to prevent losing the harvest they reap?

Building a ministry on character maintains the harvest and the ground we take for God. Purposing to live in a way that backs up the words we speak, whether a leader or a believer in any capacity, provides an example of godly character for the people we affect. A lack of moral integrity and character also affects—very negatively—the lives of those to whom we minister as leaders, or those whose lives we affect as believers. In order to properly care for the harvest obtained, all leaders must be vigilant to maintain integrity of character and never allow themselves to lessen their dedication to raising God's standard of excellence through the character-building aspect of leadership.

As we begin this century, our Father is instructing us as believers, beginning with our leaders, to put our house in order as preparation for moving ahead in the plan God has for each of us. As we develop individually, we become eligible for God to use us in a greater capacity corporately by our working with the other members of the Body of Christ to accomplish God's purposes.

If there are areas in your life which are holding you back from fulfilling your destiny, decide now to let God begin shining a light on them, and learn how to cooperate with Him to transform you. As you allow the light of wisdom to illuminate the dark places of your life, you will see that you no longer need to tolerate any area you thought was limiting you. You will realize that because you thought you were powerless to change, you and others were supporting those challenging areas with excuses that actually inhibited maturity and change! Just as Jesus with the woman at the well methodically removed every layer built around her heart by the hardships and disappointments of life (see John 4:3-30), He will free you with His light of truth and love.

God is methodical. He has a distinct way of doing things. He created us in His image to use His methods. He designed us to enter into His way of living by operating in His ways. By learning more about God and acting according to the ways He established for us (discussed in this book), you will establish excellence in every area of life and fulfill the future God has planned for you.

PART 1

DEFINE YOUR PURPOSE

CHAPTER 1

CONVERSATION SHAPES YOUR DESTINATION

Imagine the destiny of the person whose word is backed by God! When God finds a person who keeps their word and is a godly steward over their tongue, He will back that person's word. It is easy to imagine the impact on the destiny of a person whose word is backed by God! But again, rather than trying to control our tongue in our strength alone, we are to allow God to help us. The Bible tells us that to discipline the tongue requires the help of God. (See James 3:8.)

God created our mouth to reflect what is in our heart. When our mouth does not, it deceives and confuses our human spirit. A frustration takes place when a person tells something that isn't true. The reaction is so extreme it becomes physical: the person's heartbeat changes, their pulse alters, and for some people, even their palms become sweaty. The body is speaking, "You are not created for deception or lies!" We are created for truth, and God's Word is truth.

When we speak out of our mouth that which is contrary to our heart, we deceive our own heart. To deceive the heart is a dangerous matter. James tells us that if a man thinks that he is religious and bridles not his tongue, he deceives his own heart and *his religion is useless.* (See James 1:26.) He also says that the tongue has a powerful impact when left untamed. It defiles the whole body. (See James 3:6.)

The tongue when controlled, however, also has a powerful impact. When the tongue is tamed and speaks God's Word from the heart, it has the desired impact because God watches over His Word to perform it. (See Jer. 1:12 NASB.) The Bible says that out of the abundance of the heart, the mouth speaks. (Matt. 12:34.) To put the Word in our heart, we read it and meditate on it, and the Word begins to change us.

God is His Word; they are one and the same according to John 1:1:

In the beginning was the Word, and the Word was with God, and the Word was God.

We think that words only communicate, but words were originally designed to create and still do. God demonstrated this first with Himself. He said, "Let there be light" (Gen. 1:3), and immediately the following response was light. God spoke to the source before there was ever an eternally manifested tangible substance, but light was already an internal substance within Him. He called light out of Himself. That is why Paul wrote the church at Colossae and communicated his revelation inspired by the Holy Ghost according to Colossians 1:15-17:

Who is the image of the invisible God, the firstborn of every creature:

For by him were all things created, that are in heaven, and that are in earth, visible and invisible, whether they be thrones, or dominions, or principalities, or powers: all things were created by him, and for him:

And he is before all things, and by him all things consist.

John said it this way in John 1:3:

All things were made by him; and without him was not any thing made that was made.

As we are created in His image, we also must take on the substance that got its origin from the source—God Himself. That is why we have the authority to speak to things and they will obey, conform, and create. Words do more than communicate; God framed the whole world by something that proceeded out of Himself. Did He frame the world by His power, wisdom, or strength? No, He chose to use something that we could use also; He chose words to create and frame the world, and so can we! Hebrews 1:1-2 (NKJV) tells us:

> *God, who at various times and in various ways spoke in time past to the fathers by the prophets, has in these last days spoken to us by His Son, whom He has appointed heir of all things, through whom also He made the worlds.*

Psalm 33:6-7 (NKJV) also tells us:

> *By the word of the Lord the heavens were made, and all the host of them by the breath of His mouth. He gathers the waters of the sea together as a heap; he lays up the deep in storehouses.*

If God used words to create His world then we should use words to create our world. We are a result of the words that either we have spoken or words that have been spoken over us.

We are all created in God's class. God created every human being in His class, in His image and likeness, for a reason. He is a God who methodically does everything based on principle, and He never does anything without purpose. He thinks, processes things in His mind, and operates with foreknowledge and post-knowledge. And He is accountable to Himself by operating according to His principles. He could swear by no greater oath, so He, being the highest protocol of authority, had to swear by Himself. There is no one higher than He, because He is *El Elyon,* the Most High God,[1]—above Him there is none other.

This God we serve designed the Way for man to enter into His realm and way of living, His distinct way of doing things. His order is the principle that He lives by, and this principle is His Word.

The Word is the eternal thought of God, all the thoughts that He has had throughout time. What an awesome God! This controlling principle, whom He calls the Word, was uttered out of Himself. So God drew out of Himself, His eternal thought and predetermined counsel. These thoughts were in Him and already established in Him before time began. This is why the deep human spirit within us can call out to the deep Holy Spirit within God. He automatically backs and supports His sovereign will for our life because the will was first in Him. His will for us began with Him originally. It is His design; it is His counsel; it is His original thought. He expresses that thought by using words as His instruments to create and communicate.

When we read and speak the Word or speak in line with the Word, the Word carries the power to change because it is creative. God backs our Word when we speak in line with His Word.

Since this controlling principle, the Word, is the way God operates, let's define what words can do:

- Words create: John 15:7
- Words war for you: Daniel 10:12
- Words produce life or death: Proverbs 18:21
- Words justify or condemn: Job 9:20
- God's words are alive; therefore, they bring life: John 6:63
- God's words are spirit and life, again, bringing life: John 1:14
- Words of man are like deep water: Proverbs 18:4
- Words are eternal; they never die: Matthew 24:35
- Words framed the world: Hebrew 11:3
- Words reveal your heart: Romans 8:27
- Words stir anger: Proverbs 15:1
- Words pour out foolishness: Proverbs 15:2

God intended the heart and the mouth to agree. We believe therefore we speak, according to 2 Corinthians 4:13:

We having the same spirit of faith, according as it is written, I believed, and therefore have I spoken; we also believe, and therefore speak.

This great creative ability of the tongue demands responsibility for discipline. Man is the only living species that has the creative ability of the tongue because he is the only species created in God's image and class. A parrot can only respond to verbiage that it has heard. But the ability to arrange verbiage and increase vocabulary or define language, were all created by man. Man has the ability to develop one language out of another. For an example, Spanish and Italian were first derived from Latin, which is practically a dead language. There are dialects and vernaculars that are official languages and tribal tongues. Yet they are all comprised by words. Blessings or curses are brought into existence by words. You can see why it is important to be mature about this elementary lesson of the tongue. In the light of spiritual growth, leadership, or ministry, our words can build our destiny, our ministry, or destroy it. Proverbs 21:23 says:

Whoso keepeth his mouth and his tongue keepeth his soul from troubles.

Our soul consists of our mind, will, and intellect. We can keep our mind out of trouble by guarding our tongue. As we saw, James, the greatest instructor on the lesson of the tongue, gave us the powerful indictment to warn us of the danger of self-deception that follows not guarding or bridling our speech: If a man thinks that he is religious and bridles not his tongue, he deceives his own heart and his religion is useless. It would be extremely hazardous to overlook this powerful warning.

Learning to discipline our tongue is a basis for our growth in any area. This is why a wise man thinks twice before speaking. He has to take time to ponder and check in with his heart. Leaders especially need to be on alert to guard their speech because once that word is released, it is eternal. This is exactly why the Word of God tells us that we are ensnared or trapped by our words. Jesus said it is not what goes into a man that defiles him, but what comes out.

Truly, discipline over our tongue as believers, and especially for those in leadership, is an imperative lesson. Our words locate us: Once again we see the correlation between the mouth and the heart.

James continues to give us even more clarity about the little member of the body that is so important, *your tongue.* We can find this in James 3:2-12.

> *For in many things we offend all. If any man offend not in word, the same is a perfect man, and able also to bridle the whole body.*
>
> *Behold, we put bits in the horses' mouths, that they may obey us; and we turn about their whole body.*
>
> *Behold also the ships, which though they be so great, and are driven of fierce winds, yet are they turned about with a very small helm, whithersoever the governor listeth.*
>
> *Even so the tongue is a little member, and boasteth great things. Behold, how great a matter a little fire kindleth!*
>
> *And the tongue is a fire, a world of iniquity: so is the tongue among our members that it defileth the whole body, and setteth on fire the course of nature; and it is set on fire of hell.*
>
> *For every kind of beasts, and of birds, and of serpents, and of things in the sea, is tamed, and hath been tamed of mankind:*
>
> *But the tongue can no man tame; it is an unruly evil, full of deadly poison.*
>
> *Therewith bless we God, even the Father; and therewith curse we men, which are made after the similitude of God.*
>
> *Out of the same mouth proceedeth blessing and cursing. My brethren, these things ought not so to be.*
>
> *Doth a fountain send forth at the same place sweet water and bitter?*
>
> *Can the fig tree, my brethren, bear olive berries? either a vine, figs? so can no fountain both yield salt water and fresh.*

This is quite a bit of Scripture to read, but in this passage lies the formula and answer to all of life's challenges. They all begin with our words. The tongue is such a small member that it is easily overlooked or taken for granted like the bit in the horse's mouth or the rudder to a ship, which determine direction. Our tongue determines our direction in life. We go where our words go. Our life follows our words. As God himself watches over His Word to perform it, then we should surely be responsible enough to guard our own words.

Oh, how powerful is this member, the tongue! The religious leaders of the day asked Jesus to call down fire like Elijah, but He told them that they didn't know what Spirit He was of. They didn't understand the power of His words. He said the Son of man came to save the world, not to destroy it. The tongue can truly kill physically and spiritually!

Often people in leadership damage people under them with their words. This is why the tongue is referred to as sharp and able to cut asunder. Many people in life have been scarred during their childhood because of words. Women are sometimes afraid to marry again because of the words spoken of them by a previous husband. Those words, though the women may be divorced, are holding them in bondage simply because of the power of the words that were spoken.

Lastly, James compares the tongue and its function to a small fire. When kindled and left carelessly it can start a forest fire. Do you remember, years ago, the commercial about the prevention of forest fires? Smokey Bear would say, "Only you can prevent forest fires." How true this fact is! Only we can prevent that which we say out of our mouth.

Words set on fire the entire course of nature. The Bible says that the tongue is set on fire by hell. Smokey Bear would hold up a match. The intent was to show where the neglect begins that causes forest fires which sometimes result in the loss of lives. That one match is like the tongue; the strike of a wrong word can redirect our course in life.

We cannot be separated from our words, just as God is never, ever separated from His words. He backs His own Word and hastens to perform it, as stated in Jeremiah 1:12. The Bible says that when we say something we should swear to our own hurt and change not. (Ps. 15:4.) This means even if we end up profiting less, we should not change what we said we would do and keep our word. We should keep our word even if it is to our own hurt or loss because God honors such integrity. We must learn to swear by our own hurt and change not.

In developing leaders, a person should not be promoted in leadership until they have proven that their words reflect their character. The most dangerous thing one can do is to put someone in leadership who has never been taught about disciplining the tongue, or who has the knowledge but never practices it. This is why I believe that it should be a prerequisite for all leadership to practice bridling their tongue. If a man's word is no good, he is not good. We are the worth of our words.

If you keep your word and practice the discipline of bridling your tongue to speak in line with God's Word, which you have put in your heart, your words will reflect your destiny. And God will back your word.

CHAPTER 2

AUTHORIZE YOUR SUCCESS

Some people have a challenge with believing that God will keep His Word. They have trouble believing this because their human spirit has never witnessed the discipline in their own life of honoring their own words. This is a vicious cycle of deception of the heart.

Thinking before speaking is a discipline that is not easy to learn. The easiest thing to do is to let words slip. I observe people in leadership positions, business people, ministers, and public figures speaking freely without thinking about the consequences of their words. I listen carefully to what comes out of their mouths, because if we listen for a few minutes, we can tell where they are in their spiritual maturity in Christ. It takes time and it is not an easy effort in the beginning because we have to retrain our tongue not to speak and say what it wants to say.

Some people say, "I speak whatever is on my mind." There's the problem: An unrenewed mind and an untamed tongue is a disaster going somewhere to happen! In training leaders, teaching the power of the tongue should be mandatory. If we leave our leadership to themselves without ever being brought into accountability for their words, we will always have immature leadership.

Paul said when he was a child he spoke as a child. Our conversation reflects our immature or mature state. We can tell the level of maturity in our leaders (or any believer) by their words. This is not meant to place people in bondage; it is simply God's plan to afford His people the opportunity to move from where they are to where they want to be. Whether or not we move is all governed by our words. It begins with the little things we say, like "I'll see you next week," or "I'll call you back in five minutes."

When a person's consciousness is seared, they graduate to: "I'm going to give you that $50.00 that I owe you next week." What is next is bad credit—not keeping their word with creditors. Why do you think it is called credit? A credit means belief or confidence in the truth, sound character, reputation, honor, and distinction in another's character. Have you ever noticed what they call the acknowledgements after a movie is over? The credits! They publicly honor a job well done. Your credit is your total worth. Credit also means to be trustworthy.

We get the word *accountability* from the language of accounting. The word *credit* means to make good, to enter a worth to award credit. From *credit* we get the words *credible* and *credibility.* Our words should reflect our destiny, and if there is any word that should describe a leader or ministry, it should be the word ***credibility.*** Some leaders in ministry have been shady! To be a man of credibility begins with our words, which begin with our tongue.

Let's start by calling ourselves into accountability. Moses demonstrated this with God: Moses protested when God wanted to destroy Israel. When we practice keeping our word as a way of life, it will intensify our prayer life. We will have faith in our words to God because we will value words as more than a communication vehicle.

Finally, let's observe how Jesus the Savior handled words. One of the greatest illustrations of how the Savior viewed faith and its connection to spoken words is found in Matthew 8:8-9:

> *The centurion answered and said, Lord, I am not worthy that thou shouldest come under my roof: but speak the word only, and my servant shall be healed.*

For I am a man under authority, having soldiers under me: and I say to this man, Go, and he goeth; and to another, Come, and he cometh; and to my servant, Do this, and he doeth it.

Jesus marveled at this man. (See v. 10.) The centurion had two things going for him. He understood authority and submission, and he also understood how the words of a person of authority accomplish great things. He seems to understand how the function of the sent word accomplishes an assigned task. The type of word that he was making reference to was the *logos* word. The Greek for this word used here is *logos,* a spoken word of command, advice, or decree.

As a centurion, he knew that when he wanted something done he didn't have to go and do it himself. The authority he possessed in his position backed up his spoken command. Not only did he not see it necessary for Jesus to come to his house, he was not worried at all that the words of God would not accomplish what they were sent out to do. So his request was simple. Speak the word only. If we could ever learn to speak the word over every circumstance, we would accomplish more in our life and, as leaders, in ministry.

To be consistent and disciplined in speaking only the Word over circumstances, we must train our tongue and walk by faith and not by sight. This supersedes psychological reprogramming; this process comes only by meditating upon the Word. As twenty-first century believers we must train ourselves to speak only the Word over every circumstance, and our leaders must teach the people the power of the Word of God. Hebrews 1:3 declares that God upholds all things by the "word of his power."

THE TONGUE REVEALS THE HEART

Jesus opened up the understanding of the functionality of the tongue. The tongue indicates verbally and openly what is stored away in the unseen heart of man. He so skillfully illustrates this revelation to the people of God in the parable of the fruit tree. I find it absolutely astounding that He uses the fruit tree as a parable, because the end result of every believer is to bear fruit. The mature stage of leadership is bearing fruit that remains. We were ordered and chosen by God to do so according to John 15:16:

> *Ye have not chosen me, but I have chosen you, and ordained you, that ye should go and bring forth fruit, and that your fruit should remain: that whatsoever ye shall ask of the Father in my name, he may give it you.*

In Matthew 12:33 Jesus says:

> *Either make the tree good, and his fruit good; or else make the tree corrupt, and his fruit corrupt: for the tree is known by his fruit.*

He immediately transitions the conversation into a lesson that reveals what is hidden in their hearts. Earlier in the same chapter, verse 25, Jesus discerned their thoughts and their hearts. He proceeded to say in Matthew 12:34:

> *O generation of vipers, how can ye, being evil, speak good things? for out of the abundance of the heart the mouth speaketh.*

He addressed them as a "brood of vipers" (NASB). This term spoke of their offspring and their forefathers. Jesus said that they were a mirror of their wicked ancestors of hypocrisy by speaking one way with their mouth and hiding another matter in their heart. God is always after the matters of the heart, which cannot be seen or heard.

What strong terms to use: a "generation of vipers," a "brood of vipers"—a generation of snakes! The very nature of a snake is deceptive and full of guile. He explained that a tree produces after its kind, and if it is a bad tree, it will produce bad fruit. The fruit is an indication of the substance of the tree. Likewise, the tongue indicates what is in the heart. For out of the abundance of the heart, the mouth speaks.

Learn to listen to what people say as an indication of what is in their heart. Within a few minutes you can locate them. The tongue will expose them every time. It is especially important for leaders to do this. The parable in Matthew 12:35 becomes crystal clear:

> *A good man out of the good treasure of the heart bringeth forth good things: and an evil man out of the evil treasure bringeth forth evil things.*

If we are ever in question of what is hidden in our own heart, we need to do a checkup from the neck up. We should observe what is daily coming out of our mouth. We may need to change our conversation. It may also be necessary to separate ourselves from the people whom we have grown accustomed to talking with.

In Matthew 12:36, Jesus begins to bring closure to the subject matter with an explosive, sobering word.

> *But I say unto you, That every idle word that men shall speak, they shall give account thereof in the day of judgment.*

At this point, their plot to ensnare Jesus with their words has boomeranged against them, and they are now looking inwardly at the deception that is stored up in their own hearts. According to the previous scripture, there is a day of judgment when every word will be tried and accounted for. Jesus uses the word *account,* which is comparable to the word *accountability.* We can clearly see that accountability begins with the tongue. Believers, I charge you strongly to learn to discipline your tongue. If you have ever questioned the importance of your own words, then Matthew 12:37 will be a sobering verse for you to read and should snap you back into reality:

> *For by thy words thou shalt be justified, and by thy words thou shalt be condemned.*

Here we see once again the importance of training our tongue and the importance with which Jesus views words. Our words can truly make us or break us. They condemn us or justify us.

LIFE-TO-LIFE RESUSCITATION

Jesus helped them understand that the substance of the words that He spoke were life. Words are containers or capsules that house the substance of what is contained inside. One word for the breath of God in Hebrew is *Ruach.* Life is God's breath. In the Lord's "...hand is the soul of every living thing, and the *breath* of all mankind" (Job 12:10).[1] That same life of God that is His breath is what created the heavens and the earth. "By the word of the LORD were the heavens made; and all the host of them by the *breath* of his mouth" (Ps. 33:6).[2] The breath of God houses His will, intent, and sovereign plan. The very mind of God is transmitted into man through the breath of God.

Genesis 2:7 tells us "the Lord God formed man of the dust of the ground, and breathed into his nostrils the *breath of life;* and man became a living soul." Another Hebrew word, *Neshamah,*[3] is translated "breath" in this verse. God imparted His breath into man, and life began to take place. Man became a *living soul.* That same breath also houses God's Word, His uttered thoughts imparted into man. Words are living components that produce life. Words act as life-to-life resuscitation for man.

In the act of CPR, the mouth-to-mouth technique is used to revive, recover, and resuscitate life. Air is blown into the person to fill the lungs and the pumping of the chest is done to jumpstart the heart. The Word of God is a life-to-life resuscitation aid. The Word can bring back to life dead marriages, dead situations, dead dreams, and dead hopes. The Word of God can jumpstart the life of those who have lost their zeal and passion for life. The *rhema* Word of God is the living Word of God. When we utter the *rhema* Word of God, we produce life to our circumstances.

This section on the power of words is extremely important. Please do not casually read through this section of the book. If need be, put the book down and begin to ponder your words. Think about your daily conversation. Think about what you are saying on a consistent basis about your present situation. Examine what has been coming repeatedly out of your mouth. Jesus called an undisciplined mouth a perverse mouth.

He said to His disciples that His words produced life for they were spirit and life. In this particular occasion, Jesus also addressed His disciples about mutiny and abandonment. He even said that some of them did not believe in Him. As He confronted them concerning this subject, many of His disciples walked away. The passage doesn't say a "few," but "many."

Some didn't believe that one would betray Him, and many of the Pharisees sought an occasion to entrap Him with His words, giving them a valid reason to put Him to death. They failed to realize that Jesus knew that the power of life and death was in the tongue. Therefore, He pondered His words before He spoke. He knew that His death was for an appointed time and that no one would kill Him prematurely if He kept His tongue in order.

He asked the remaining ones whether they wanted to depart also. Peter spoke up boldly; thank God he opened his mouth this time with words of truth and revelation. Isn't it amazing how undisciplined Peter's tongue was in his early years as a disciple? However, he grew to a place of maturity and finally learned to think before speaking. This time he spoke something very profound: "Lord to whom shall we go? You have the words of eternal life." What a powerful statement!

How relative are Jesus' words in our life today? How important is it to you, as you read the last lines of this chapter, to examine your speech? Is it really possible that we can be in certain situations in our life due to the door that we opened to the enemy by not guarding our mouth?

CHAPTER 3

THE COMPASS TO YOUR DESTINY

Words are the connection between our present and our future, and are the marvelous God-breathed utterances that shape and give form to possibilities. A possibility will remain dormant until the possibility is spoken. And once spoken over and over, life attaches itself to it, and it begins to manifest itself through the vehicle of our words.

Job 12:11 tells us:

Does not the ear test words and the mouth taste its food?

Once God formed man from the foundation of the earth, He breathed into man's nostrils the breath of life. He released Himself into man, and from that moment, man had a built-in divine compass to his destiny. God spoke and brought forth life. He built into man the same ability to speak forth life. As we have seen, our words must mirror our destiny.

Just as the entrance of God's Word brings light and understanding even to the simple, our words bring light and understanding to our future. We cannot be separated from our words; they go and possess for us what we cannot obtain for ourselves in the natural realm. The word *tsavah* means to fetch, to send with command and to order into being. We should *tsavah,* send out our words, to constitute our destiny and to affirm our prophetic promises.

To allow God to orchestrate our destiny as He desires, we must be responsible to speak only what He commands of us and utter His counsel only. We cannot *tsavah* anything that is contrary to His Word because there are specific guidelines to the privileged promise. Because God operates by a controlling principle, and we speak in line with it, we cannot carelessly covet what is not predestined for us.

This is why the enemy battles to control our tongue. Solomon said that the man who guards his mouth keeps himself out of trouble. If our mouth can keep us out of trouble, then our mouth can create our destiny. Life and death are in the power of the tongue (see Prov. 18:21)—the tongue has unseen power.

Job 12:11 (NKJV) states, "Does not the ear test words and the mouth taste its food?" Another translation (NASB) words this a little differently: "Does not the ear test words, as the palate tastes its food?"

The revelation from this proverb is extremely powerful in showing us a very important way to guard our heart against receiving, then meditating on, words not in line with God's Word. We know to guard our heart and to keep it with all diligence, because out of it springs the issues of life. (See Prov. 4:23 NKJV.) We know that God backs the words we speak from the abundance of our heart when we keep it filled with His Word, which carries life and the power to change.

Our palates are the members of our body that register to the brain the desire to taste. Why is it that we can look at certain foods or drinks and know that we do not like the taste even though we have not tasted what has been placed before us? Once our brains record the taste in the archive of our memory, recall comes into place. Recall stores it away until the moment we see the particular food or drink that we like or dislike. The memory we have of the food or drink will determine whether we will want to eat or drink what we see.

Why do you think culinary students have to pass several tests of tasting different food items prepared before they can graduate? To determine the quality, content, blend, and whether the food meets the standards for approval. Likewise, our ears test words to determine the quality, content, blend, and whether or not they meet *the* standard of approval. When our ears hear something that is contrary to our destiny, recall kicks in and says, "REJECT • REJECT • REJECT! • NO MATCH • NO BLEND!"

Just as we can acquire an appetite for something that was originally distasteful to us, so can our ears become conditioned to reject what is distasteful because it contradicts God's Word. To restate this, if we continue hearing something over and over again that contradicts the original program, we will disengage the original order, begin to repeat it ourselves, and begin to meditate upon it.

But just as the palate for the taste of food can be reconditioned, so can the ears be retrained to test words. Our ears are the gateway to our souls (as are our eyes). This is why Jesus said, "Take heed how you hear" (Luke 8:18 NKJV). Solomon said in Proverbs 4:20-22:

> *My son, attend to my words; incline thine ear unto my sayings. Let them not depart from thine eyes; keep them in the midst of thine heart. For they are life unto those that find them, and health to all their flesh.*

If you are well acquainted with the power of words and are living in the destiny God has for you, which you have been speaking, as you are reading this book you are probably nodding in agreement and thinking, *How true this is.* Someone else reading this book may be thinking, *I wish someone had taught me about the power of words ten or twenty years ago!* and someone else, *I did learn this ten or twenty years ago, but I didn't remain disciplined in this area of my life.* Another reading this book may be thinking, *Oh, come on, how important can words really be?*

If we do not learn to change our conversation, our life will never change! Our conversation is the compass to our destination.

Just remember this: One day we said out of our mouth a few simple but powerful words, "Jesus, come into my heart." If we really meant those words that we spoke, they changed the course of our life. By speaking those words and meaning them, the reality of what they mean came to pass in us: God didn't rest salvation upon works; we are righteous because He has made us righteous; we don't make ourselves righteous through our accomplishments in life, but by believing in our heart and confessing with our mouth, we receive salvation.

Here again we see the connection between the mouth and the heart. Our confession is made unto salvation, and the words that come out of our mouth take us from a destiny of hell to a destiny of heaven.

On a wedding day, a man and a woman stand face to face; she says words out of her mouth, and he says words out of his mouth. When they exchange these words, according to the Bible, they are no longer separate entities; in the spirit realm the two have become one simply from the words exchanged during their vows. Words of marriage produce matrimony. God always begins a creating process in seed form. Our words are seeds, and to receive a harvest, we must plant words. Jesus said:

> *..."Do you not understand this parable? How then will you understand all the parables?*
>
> ***"The sower sows the word."***
>
> Mark 4:13,14 NKJV

When our "word seeds" mature, they will produce after their own kind. In other words, if we plant words of defeat, then that is what we will reap. If we plant words of victory, then that is what we will reap.

If we are not planting "word seed," then we are leaving the door open for the enemy to sow weeds in our life. Even our Creator Himself used words to create the world in which we daily operate: Notice the Creator's use of words in Genesis 1:3, 6-7, 9 and 11 (NKJV):

Verse 3:

> *Then God said, "Let there be light"; **and there was light.***

Verses 6-7:

> *Then **God said,** "Let there be a firmament in the midst of the waters, and let it divide the waters from the waters." Thus God made the*

firmament, and divided the waters which were under the firmament from the waters which were above the firmament; ***and it was so.***

Verse 9:

Then ***God said,*** *"Let the waters under the heavens be gathered together into one place, and let the dry land appear":* ***and it was so.***

Verse 11:

Then ***God said,*** *"Let the earth bring forth grass, the herb that yields seed, and the fruit tree that yields fruit according to its kind, whose seed is in itself, on the earth";* ***and it was so.***

God had to speak forth words in order to create. This action is the word *amar,*[1] which has as one meaning, "think use [speech], utter": in other words, to utter a thought. Because God had been thinking of light, He said it and it came forth! So we see that this process began first with God Himself as a divine act. This word also means to "command," "declare," "demand," "determine," "desire," "require."[2]—it simply means to speak what we desire. It is now decreed as a divine act. When we speak what we desire, something comes alive on the inside of us. The word *amar* was the first sound ever uttered. It also means to "certify" and "avouch."[3] It is now legislated as a divine act. The word *avouch* means "to prove: establish," "affirm," "to take responsibility for," "to acknowledge one's responsibility for"[4]; "to vouch for."[5] *Vouch* means "to give assurance, affirmation, or a guarantee," "to uphold by demonstration or evidence"[6]; "to give personal assurance."[7] It means to take responsibility.

Therefore, we can certify a guaranteed new way of life by altering our words and becoming more responsible and conscious of the words we speak. There are very practical ways to start the process. Let's start by putting our hands over our mouth when we know that we are about to utter words that are contrary to our destiny. Our determined destination should be reflected in the words that we speak; let's not abort our prophetic destiny by using negative words that don't line up with the promises for our future that God's Word contains.

Let's determine within ourselves to speak these words on a daily basis: "I can have what God says I can have; I will do what God says I can do; I will be what God says I can be; I am destined for greatness because of the words that I speak!" We must train our mouth to say this statement to speak forth the destiny God has for us, and *say it; say it; say it!*

Another type of uttered speech God uses is the word *tsavah,* which means to "appoint," to "send," or to "enjoin."[8] It also means to prohibit by command, to forbid by decree or to send forth a word to accomplish a specific assignment. The Bible tells us that God's Word is like rain that comes down from the sky and doesn't return; it waters the earth and brings forth a bud to give seed to the sower. Isaiah 55:10-11 (NKJV) states:

> *"For as the rain comes down, and the snow from heaven, and do not return there, but water the earth, and make it bring forth and bud, that it may give seed to the sower and bread to the eater, so shall My word be that goes forth from My mouth; it shall not return to Me void, but it shall accomplish what I please, and it shall prosper in the thing for which I sent it."*

The phrase "...but it shall accomplish what I please..." means that God sends His Word to accomplish a mission. God's Word has been given a command to never return to Him void; His Word will never return as a failed mission.

In Matthew 8:5-10 (NKJV), a centurion soldier approached Jesus concerning his sick servant:

> *Now when Jesus had entered Capernaum, a centurion came to Him, pleading with Him, saying, "Lord, my servant is lying at home paralyzed, dreadfully tormented."*
>
> *And Jesus said to him, "I will come and heal him."*

> *The centurion answered and said, "Lord, I am not worthy that You should come under my roof. But only* ***speak a word,*** *and my servant will be healed.*
>
> *"For I also am a man under authority, having soldiers under me. And I say to this one, 'Go,' and he goes; and to another, 'Come,' and he comes; and to my servant, 'Do this,' and he does it."*
>
> *When Jesus heard it, He marveled, and said to those who followed, "Assuredly, I say to you, I have not found such great faith, not even in Israel!"*

The centurion was a man of wisdom and knowledge. He insisted that Jesus "only speak a word," or "speak the word only" (KJV) because he knew and understood the power of words. He felt that if his words produced what he said, then how much more would the authority of the uttered words of Jesus Christ produce what Jesus said!

PART 2

MATURE YOUR SOUL: THE PETER PAN SYNDROME

CHAPTER 4

ACCEPTING THE GIFT

In our stages of growth we should become more conscious of our righteousness as opposed to our sin. Practicing a consciousness of our state of righteousness is a journey in maturity. This growth process of maturity does not have to be painful. Under the law, man was conscious of his sin continually; but under the New Covenant God desires for us to focus more on *who* we are and *what we have* in Christ Jesus. Our own righteousness is filthy in His sight; however the righteousness of God in Christ Jesus is our new identity.

As we honestly grow in Christ our desire increases to please Him. As we grow to please Him, we become more aware of our new creation realities. These realities are more powerful than the bonds of sin because sin is no longer our master. We are not under the law but under grace according to Romans 6:14 (NKJV):

> *For sin shall not have dominion over you, for you are not under law but under grace.*

Does this mean that we will not miss the mark because we are under grace? By no means! It simply means that we must practice a lifestyle of walking in our redemptive rights. To refuse to grow up and walk in God's truths is to refuse to accept what Christ has made available to us. It cost the Father the blood of Jesus for us to live this life in its totality. We appropriate this life by grace. For if this growth and acceptance of righteousness came by our own works or by the law, then Christ died in vain according to Galatians 2:20-21 (NKJV).

> *"I have been crucified with Christ; it is no longer I who live, but Christ lives in me; and the life which I now live in the flesh I live by faith in the Son of God, who loved me and gave Himself for me.*

"I do not set aside the grace of God; for if righteousness comes through the law, then Christ died in vain."

His death is not in vain in our life when we recognize that we are in Christ Jesus. Maturity sets in when we meditate on the fact that Christ lives in us and we become God-inside minded. This is by no means a formula that makes us flawless, but rather creates an awareness of our purchased possession. In other words, we have more working in us internally than we have working against us externally. First John 4:4 (NKJV) tells us:

> *You are of God, little children, and have overcome them, because He who is in you is greater than he who is in the world.*

We can see the process of the stages of maturation in 1 John 2:12-14 (NKJV):

> *I write to you, little children, because your sins are forgiven you for His name's sake. I write to you, fathers, because you have known Him who is from the beginning. I write to you young men, because you have overcome the wicked one. I write to you, little children, because you have known the Father. I have written to you, fathers, because you have known Him who is from the beginning. I have written to you, young men, because you are strong, and the word of God abides in you, and you have overcome the wicked one.*

In the beginning of the scripture, the author, recognized to be John, addresses them as his little children. We can see the Master portrayed as an endearing Father. We can easily interpret the inspired love of the Father. First John 2:1 (NKJV) tells us, "My little children, these things write I unto you, that ye sin not. And if any man sin, we have an advocate with the Father, Jesus Christ the righteous."

I find it very interesting that He assures us that we have an advocate with the Father in the event of our falling short.

As the maturity level develops in our life, it doesn't mean that we are free from the ability to sin or free from the enemy tempting us with sin. We must always remember that we have an advocate with the Father, our high priest Christ Jesus, and it is through Him only that we are more than conquerors and triumphant in living this Christian life. We are assured of this because Christ Jesus is the propitiation for our sins and He is our righteousness. This righteousness is our purchased possession. Jesus died to provide this for us and now we must possess the provision and walk in our covenant entitlement.

The Father is ever pursuing the heart of man, and it is He who orchestrates the change. He knows exactly how to unlock the combination to our heart and how to align circumstances in our life that will cause growth and maturity. He is a perfect Father who wants to see His children grow in the fullness of His Son Christ Jesus.

CHAPTER 5

THE TRANSMISSION OF TRANSPARENCY

Just as the transmission of a car allows the vehicle to shift gears for maximum performance, it is also vital to learn how to shift gears to transition into a lifestyle of transparency. The transmission is the conduction process that prevents the gears of a car from locking up. Many believers operate with locked gears because they refuse to transition into maturity. The most vital step is to be transparent. The transmission transmits power from the engine to the wheel. The engine is the heart of the car. The wheels are the feet. The process of transmitted power from our heart to our destiny requires transparency. Without it we operate with locked gears that stagnate our growth process. Transparency propels us into our God-given destiny and maximizes our potential.

The Word of God tells us that we already are the righteousness of God in Christ Jesus. How do we mature into an awareness of this righteousness? We must practice a mindset of rehearsing what Christ has done for us and embracing the substitution sacrifice. This should make us very patient with others who have not yet accepted the work of grace and righteousness in our life.

Sometimes it seems too good to be true. Could Christ really be the propitiation of all of our idiosyncrasies? Could God really desire to use us in spite of our imperfections? We must be willing to grow up and become transparent. Often people make it hard for us to be transparent because they expect us to be perfect, especially when we are in leadership positions, but as we share the victories and defeats, it becomes easier for us to accept the grace that God has freely given us to overcome our struggles. As we become more and more sentient of this act of righteousness, we become aware of our sonship. Galatians 4:3-6 (NKJV) tells us:

> *Even so we, when we were children, were in bondage under the elements of the world. But when the fullness of the time had come, God sent forth His Son, born of a woman, born under the law, to redeem those who were under the law, that we might receive the adoption as sons. And because you are sons, God has sent forth the Spirit of his Son into your hearts, crying out, "Abba, Father!"*

Maturity helps us to walk in our sonship privileges. If we never mature we will never reap the benefits of sonship though we are heirs of the Father. Immaturity keeps us under a slave-ship mentality and blinds us from our covenant rights through entrapment and bondage. As we increase in the awareness of our status of sonship, we can better appropriate what is rightfully ours.

The greatest thing any believer can do is to teach others how to walk in their covenant rights as believers. Especially as leaders, we can no longer refuse to walk in our covenant rights. We see a beautiful illustration of leadership being restored to covenant position in the life of Peter.

In John 21, Jesus shows Himself to His disciples after His resurrection. Redemption has now been fully purchased through His death, burial, and resurrection, and righteousness is now unattainable without the subtitutionary sacrifice. Though we already know these things we must rehearse them in our minds over and over. Like Peter, we feel that we love the Lord and we would never forsake Him. It's amazing how pressure brings out things inside of us that we never knew existed.

In the eighteenth chapter of John, Peter denies the Lord three times. Jesus foretold what would happen as Peter was positioned under pressure. He was so confident that he could never deny his Lord and Savior. After all, Peter is the one who was willing to cut off the ear of the high priest's servant as they were attempting to capture Jesus. Peter had some growing up to do. As leaders there are many areas in our life in which we are confident and secure, but how do we respond when we are placed under pressure? When an orange is squeezed, under pressure, apple juice does not flow out. Only orange juice can come from an orange because the juice is the substance of the content.

After Peter's denial, he condemns himself and runs away from his purpose instead of clinging to the promise of Christ's return. He returns to his former way of living. This state of immaturity is often played out in the life of believers when we disappoint our Lord and ourselves. Sometimes the tendency is to run away from God. But as we mature we learn that He is already present at the place of our hiding. There is no escape from His presence. At the Sea of Tiberius, Jesus said to His disciples, "Children, have you any food?" (John 21:5 NKJV). He then proceeds to tell them where their next meal is, which demonstrates His paternal love that keeps Him always watching over us! Jesus takes this time to restore Peter and to also teach His disciples a powerful lesson on restoration, righteousness, and maturity.

He invites them to have breakfast with Him. The Risen Savior is concerned about their physical needs. Immediately after breakfast Jesus (as we continue reading in John 21) said to Peter, "Do you love Me?" Can you imagine the mixed emotions and thoughts that were running through Peter's mind? Peter had to be overwhelmed with guilt and joy all at the same time. Jesus addresses Peter not as Cephas, the rock and the stable one, but He addresses him the same way He addressed him at their first meeting, as Simon. He took Peter back to his origins as if to say, "Let Me take you back to the beginning." When we miss it, we must immediately put things in proper perspective by taking things back to the beginning. We must go back to the beginning of our walk with Him, to our initial encounter, to the place where we first met Jesus. Before things got complicated, before there were expectations, before we knew the Greek, the Hebrew, the motivational gifts of our vocation and our calling.

Our first encounter with Him is a love encounter. "Simon," He calls Peter, before he became the rock, the stable one, even before Peter received the revelation from on high about the Messiah. Notice He invites Peter to examine his love once again—the same love, which he felt would never fail. Our love is not predicated upon our ability to never miss it. It is predicated upon our response to His love. Peter responds, "Yes, Lord, You know that I love You." The most unexpected response now comes from Jesus, "Feed My lambs." He restores Peter's apostolic position by entrusting him with an assignment that is the most precious and sensitive to the Master's heart: His young, His most immature flock—His lambs. Isaiah 40:11 (NKJV) tells us:

> *He will feed His flock like a shepherd; he will gather the lambs with His arm, and carry them in His bosom, and gently lead those who are with young.*

The very people who cost Him His life are the people who are the focus of His resurrection, His lambs. He entrusted them into the care of Peter, the one who had forsaken Him. What an awesome Savior. Jesus addresses Peter again, but this time as Jesus questions Peter's love, He says to him, "Tend My sheep." The sheep are the ones who are a little more mature than the lambs. The sheep need tending; they need someone to watch over them, to oversee their lives. In Acts 20:28 (NKJV) we are instructed:

> *"Therefore take heed to yourselves and to all the flock, among which the Holy Spirit has made you overseers, to shepherd the church of God which He purchased with His own blood."*

Paul said, "After I depart wolves will creep in and not spare the flock." (Acts 20:29.) The Lord said to Peter, "Care for My flock for Me"; in so many words, "You have a new opportunity to demonstrate your love for Me." (Author's paraphrase.) God cannot be separated from His people. Matthew 25:40 reminds us that whatever we do to them we do to Him. To forsake them would be to forsake Him. What a challenge of maturity and restoration: the Risen Lord entrusting us with His flock. What a vocation, what a calling, what a humbling experience and a privileged opportunity to represent the very Christ.

For each denial Peter was given an opportunity of threefold restoration. The most mature stage in our life as leaders is to acknowledge that we are to represent Christ to the world. We are His under-shepherds and stewards to His flock. The flock belongs to Him, yet He entrusts us with such a task to care for His most prized possession. Maturity settles in when we realize that it is not about us. During the three times that Jesus questioned Peter's love, the disciples were there to witness the dialogue and examine their own lives as well. When Jesus questioned Peter for the third time, Peter was grieved and didn't respond with revelation as he did in the previous inquiries; his persona of annoyance surfaced before Christ.

Can you picture this? Peter is in the presence of the Prince of Peace and has an annoying attitude! Peter should know that he is in the presence of Jesus Christ—the omniscient and all knowing God. The all knowing nature of God was questioning Peter's love, not because He did not know the answer; He was questioning Peter so that he could locate and realize his level of commitment. Jesus was using the present situation to restore Peter and to also teach the other disciples a valuable lesson. When the Lord is equipping us for maturity in life, it is never for ourselves alone. It is ultimately for the sake of the Body. We are being equipped to do the work of the ministry, and growth is mandatory for us as leaders. The first step of maturity is being willing to admit that we need to mature in the underdeveloped areas of our life.

We don't have to pretend when we come before our Father. We don't have to hide or be fake. He knows everything about us. He knows us better than we know ourselves. (See Ps. 139.) His ultimate purpose for uncovering our frailties is to equip us for greater dimensions of ministry.

Next, the Lord makes a shift so smooth that Peter and the disciples can hardly sense the transition! Jesus restores Peter by commissioning Him to do the work, which speaks of maturity. Next, Jesus shifts the price He will now pay to finish the work, which will require a higher level of maturity. Suffering for the sake of the work is the area where many leaders fail. It is vitally important to know that the suffering is not God placing sickness or disease upon someone for the sake of His Kingdom. It would be ridiculous for the Lord to plague us with an illness and then die upon the cross to purchase our healing. The sufferings are the consequences we go through for the sake of the Gospel. This is not a negative confession; it is just the truth! The Bible tells us in 2 Timothy 3:12 (NKJV):

> *Yes, and all who desire to live godly in Christ Jesus will **suffer** persecution.*

The Word of God never told us that we *may* suffer persecution. But the Bible uses a stronger and more affirmative word; it states that we *shall* suffer persecution. This is beyond a possibility of persecution; this is a fact. The work of feeding the sheep is not void of persecution, afflictions, and opposition. But we can be of good cheer because John 16:33 (NKJV) tells us:

> *"These things I have spoken to you that in Me you may have peace; in the world you will have tribulation; but be of good cheer, I have overcome the world."*

In John 21:18 (NKJV) Jesus tells Peter:

> *"Most assuredly, I say to you, when you were younger, you girded yourself and walked where you wished; but when you are old, you will*

stretch out your hands, and another will gird you and carry you where you do not wish."

When Jesus spoke to Peter concerning his covering and clothing, He was speaking in a language that Peter understood. He also taught Peter and the other disciples a powerful lesson. The clothing for the males in the East during this era consisted of an undergarment called a girdle. Fishermen removed their outer garments as they launched out into the deep, away from the shore and the visibility of women. Men themselves did this girding as they decided to go fishing. Peter made a decision to forsake the promise of Christ and return to the revenue of his former career.

Peter's years of maturity would be nurtured under the rule of Nero for forty years—the number of judgment. Jesus spoke of the future circumstances that Peter and the other disciples would have to suffer as they committed to the call. Now Peter's girding would prove in the future to be his chains and cords. His outstretched arms would be tied and bound to the cross upside down. They would later carry Peter where he didn't wish to go: to an open death of honor through crucifixion. It was a death of humiliation and shameful reproach; but to the believers of the early church it was an honor to glorify God even unto death according to Revelation 12:11 (NKJV) which states:

"And they overcame him by the blood of the Lamb and by the word of their testimony, and they did not love their lives to the death."

Though his flesh would not agree with that form of death, his hidden, mature man of the heart would soon learn to never forsake the Lord again and to join with the fellowship of the sufferings of Christ. As Peter identified himself with Christ in His death, he will also reign with Him in His glory.

CHAPTER 6

DEVISING YOUR OWN WAY

This is maturity—to lay aside your own selfish ambitions, fears, and hidden agendas for the cause of Christ. Jesus foretold of Peter's death and He made references to growth stages. The young man goes and does what he wishes, and the seasoned, mature man is led to the course of denial.

We cannot impart these truths into the lives of others until we meditate on them ourselves. We can't give people what we don't have and we can't lead people into a spiritual place that we have not gone ourselves. Yet the paradox and mystery is that we are all works in progress. None of us have arrived in our perfection and we all seek daily to walk in what has been freely given to us through the death of Christ. This walk is a work of grace that is unearned, and our final destination from this labor is to enter into the rest of redemption.

Hebrews 4:3 (NKJV) says:

> *For we who have believed do enter that rest, as He has said: "So I swore in My wrath, they shall not enter My rest," although the works were finished from the foundation of the world.*

We grow into this, and it's not an overnight, microwave, thirty days same as cash deal. We will spend the rest of our life growing in grace, and it is imperative that we choose to mature and not seek refuge in our unconfronted issues. When we become transparent in the areas in which we are falling short of the goal, we will see the strength of God work in our life according to 2 Corinthians 12:10 (NKJV):

Therefore I take pleasure in infirmities, in reproaches, in needs, in persecutions, in distresses, for Christ's sake. For when I am weak, then I am strong.

Paul also said in 2 Corinthians 12:5 (NKJV):

Of such a one I will boast; yet of myself I will not boast, except in my infirmities.

Why? Because it's God's grace that is sufficient for us. There is no reason to refuse to mature because the Lord is our enabler. An enabler, in the positive sense of the word, is God's inner working, His grace, His empowerment and enabling ability both to will and do His good pleasure. Therefore we can assume our position in righteousness with boldness. This is what the Father desires to see in the life of His children.

It's amazing how many of us in leadership refuse to put forth any effort that will inconvenience us or require us to go beyond the call of duty. We reject accountability and commitment. We interpret commitment as confinement and rationalize it as being boxed in and a hindrance to our free flowing spirit. This is a prime example of immaturity and lack of sobriety. Graveness is a missing attribute in today's leadership arena. When many leaders are not elected for a position or allowed to do things as they wish, they conveniently hear a prophetic voice from God instructing them to cruise to another church! Their migratory pilgrimage keeps them on a never-ending cycle.

The Bible tells us that those who are planted in the house of God shall be blessed. Planted denotes roots and people who are rootless become fruitless. We can never bear any type of fruit without some type of roots. The enemy deceives us in leadership positions and creates illusions of freedom. When in actuality the greatest liberty and freedom is found in submission to Christ. This is a hidden mystery and a paradox to the Kingdom—if we hold on to our life we will ultimately lose it, and if we give our life for the sake of the Kingdom we will gain it. To the immature and carnal mind it is not an easy task to be perceived.

The selfish act of immaturity is what actually sets the stage for our entrapment. How can there be liberty in becoming a bondservant for Christ? Our union with Christ frees us from the bondages of sin and death. Now that's ultimate liberty! The devise of the enemy is to always make us go after something that we already have. Satan began this process in the Garden with Eve. Both Adam and Eve already had what they compromised to get. They were already operating in the role of dominion and created in the image and likeness of God. Therefore the devil did not offer them something that they did not already have!

Some time ago I was pleading with a nationally renowned Christian leader to try and consider reconciliation with his wife. His response to me was, "It will cost me more money to keep her than to let her go; after all, God wants me to be happy." My unasked question was, "What is the cost or price of your happiness?" I don't mean to ever instigate any condemnation to those who have suffered a divorce; however, in this case the leader openly told me that he felt tied down and felt as though he married the wrong woman and needed his space. These are all indications of immaturity.

The Peter Pan Syndrome is growing at an alarming rate in the church today because leadership refuses to grow up. If leadership refuses to mature, where does that leave the laity? As leaders there are some things that we must endure for the sake of the Gospel.

SPIRIT-LED LEADERSHIP IS VITAL

In every organization and institution there is a portion of leadership that refuses to mature and develop. The unfortunate dilemma that these types of people create is a model of substandard living for others. I have coined a title for those who are in leadership and want to enjoy the benefits that come along with the position without the responsibility: I call it *The Peter Pan Syndrome.* Leaders who are plagued with *The Peter Pan Syndrome* are allergic to words such as: effort, sacrifice, accountability, responsibility, submission, commitment, endurance, stamina, and fortitude.

One of the common characteristics of a person in leadership who refuses to grow up is that they are always reminiscing about their past accomplishments. Generally, this type of leader is very noncommittal and at times they even manage to mature in the noncommittal area of their lives. In other words, they will face the challenges of maturity in a particular area as long as it doesn't require them to make a long-term commitment. They live their lives in a migratory cycle and never really complete any one assignment. Closure is usually a problem for them as well, simply because they refuse to commit to whatever it takes to bring closure to a particular situation.

It is dangerous to have someone like this in leadership because they refuse to mature and make their life accountable to someone by becoming transparent and allowing words of wisdom to be planted into their life. For such cases a spiritual impartation is needed. This is why Spirit-led leadership is vital in our leadership arena today.

Paul the Apostle visited an infant church in Thessalonica but was only able to stay through three Sabbath days (see Acts 17:2), about three weeks, to impart small nuggets of wisdom into the lives of the leadership in that region. He was forced to leave in order to save his life. Therefore the baby church was left to complete the work of advancing the Kingdom in Thessalonica solely on the last words of Paul. When the report came back to Paul as to how the church had increased and grown stronger, this is what he had to say in 1 Thessalonians 1:6-10 (NKJV):

> *And you became followers of us and of the Lord, having received the word in much affliction, with joy of the Holy Spirit, so that you became examples to all in Macedonia and Achaia who believe. For from you the word of the Lord has sounded forth, not only in Macedonia and Achaia,*

but also in every place. Your faith toward God has gone out, so that we do not need to say anything. For they themselves declare concerning us what manner of entry we had to you, and how you turned to God from idols to serve the living and true God, and to wait for His Son from heaven, whom He raised from the dead, even Jesus who delivers us from the wrath to come.

He declared that it was apparent to the people what manner of entry he had into the church of the region. This entrance into their lives caused them to turn to God and brought illumination and understanding which resulted in them putting away idols and taking ownership of their assignment. The equipping and impartation made by the apostle brought the believers to a level of maturity and fullness in a short span of time.

The purpose of pursuing the process of maturity and perfection is for the work of ministry. Paul tells us in Ephesians 4:11 (NKJV):

And He Himself gave some to be apostles, some prophets, some evangelists, and some pastors and teachers, for the equipping of the saints for the work of ministry, for the edifying of the body of Christ.

The purpose of the fivefold ministry gifts is for equipping the saints for the work of the ministry. We should pursue perfection and sobriety to do the work because it demands our maturity. The lack of maturity will affect the work of the ministry. Therefore, growing up is not optional in the Kingdom; it is mandatory. Kingdom advancement hinges on our willingness to mature. It is more painful for us as leaders to examine our life and take inventory of the necessary areas of changes. In order for growth to come into fruition, change is inevitable and we must purpose to pursue maturity and acknowledge those difficult places of immaturity.

The easiest way out is the path of least resistance and hiding behind behavioral patterns that our life has set for us; sometimes defining them as personality traits to deny ourselves of the best that God has for us.

THE LACK OF EFFORT

Another observation that I have been privileged to make in examining leadership here in the West, as opposed to other foreign countries, is the lack of effort that we put forth for the Kingdom. In America, we do not want to be inconvenienced and anything that makes us have to go beyond the call of duty is a bother to us. When asked to go the extra mile, we see the underdeveloped attitude of immaturity surface. Let's observe the many ways that Jesus went the extra mile and beyond the call of duty for His flock. In John 4:3-5 (NKJV) we read:

> *He left Judea and departed again to Galilee. But He **needed** to go through Samaria.*

Jesus went through Samaria to get to Galilee. Looking at a map, you will see that Jesus went totally out of the way to go to Samaria. But Jesus felt that He had to go the route of Samaria to get to Galilee because there He met a woman at the well, and I am sure that woman was glad that Jesus went out of His way for her!

In the Beatitudes Jesus tells us to go the extra mile. The people that Jesus spoke to during this era were of an Eastern mindset and were familiar with the law concerning an eye for an eye. Interestingly enough in leadership today, we always want to live by the scripture that states, "An eye for an eye, and a tooth for a tooth." But Jesus tells us to turn the other cheek to those who have done evil towards us. (See Matt. 5:38-39.) Mahatma Gandhi and Martin Luther King demonstrated this in their lives of nonviolent resistance. Gandhi said that it triggers something in a man when you do not feed into his hate and anger; it causes a reaction that diffuses their hostility. He also said that it was amazing to him how men are sometimes honored by the humiliation of others.

The Word of God tells us that a soft answer turns away wrath and that if we love those who love us we are no different from the heathen. But to love those who hate you glorifies the Father and heaps coals of fire upon the heads of our enemies. Roman 12:20 (NKJV) says:

> *Therefore "If your enemy is hungry, feed him; if he is thirsty, give him a drink; for in so doing you will heap coals of fire on his head."*

In Matthew 5:46-48 (NKJV below), Jesus uses the word *perfect,* which is the same word for *mature.* He says we will be mature like our Father. In today's vernacular, Jesus would say, *"Grow up!"*

> *"For if you love those who love you, what reward have you? Do not even the tax collectors do the same?*
>
> *"And if you greet your brethren only, what do you do more than others? Do not even the tax collectors do so?*
>
> *"Therefore you shall be perfect, just as your Father in heaven is perfect."*

In Matthew 5:40-41 (NKJV), Jesus instructs us to go beyond the normality of society.

> *"If anyone wants to sue you and take away your tunic, let him have your cloak also.*
>
> *"And whoever compels you to go one mile, go with him two."*

What is it that operates in the life of a believer who hates to put forth effort? What is it at work in our behavior that resists inconveniences? Suppose this was the attitude of Jesus? He was really inconvenienced on the cross, and I'm sure that hell was a greater inconvenience!

The words *believe* and *effort* should go hand in hand in our life. If we are to be honest with ourselves, the lack of these two attributes in our life casts a neon sign over our heads that says: *Peter Pan Syndrome!* In life, growth comes through the crucibles we face. If we listen and watch the response of leadership when asked to give up something or go beyond the call of duty, we will surely see the substance that is on the inside—whether positive or negative. Unfortunately in leadership what surfaces the most is negativity.

It takes effort to co-labor with our fellow saints. Nothing less than a made-up mind to mature is what is mandatory and needed in today's leadership. The mature person always takes the low road first: It's the strong that bear up the infirmities of the weak.

The Lord ended His lesson with Peter by inviting him to follow Him. This time Jesus' invitation is not only to follow Him in the good times, but also to follow Him in the hard times. If we ever mature and embrace this concept in the Kingdom, it will automatically transfer into other areas of our life. Many marriages fail due to the refusal of two people to die to their own way of doing things. With God, the way *up* is *down.* If we could only learn to compete in serving one another and truly esteem others—our spouse, our neighbor, and our fellow believers—higher than ourselves, we would be well on our way to developing a mature inner man.

When Jesus told Peter to follow Him, He really said a mouthful! For the remainder of our life we journey to mimic Him in all of His ways: Following Him is maturity personified!

NECESSARY SEPARATIONS

When we purpose to mature spiritually, a time of separation is generally a necessity. Everyone around us has not made a decision to go to the next level just because we have made a decision to go to higher heights in Christ. Going to the next level will cost us great sacrifices. We must never assume that the people around us are willing to pay the price to get from where they are to where they desire to be. The process of *spiritual growth* does not come by osmosis, nor is it a magical encounter or a physical phenomenon. It is not mystical or spectacular; it is an on purpose, line upon line supernatural working that takes our effort. As we yield to the inner workings of the Holy Spirit, He will become our constant teacher who daily works in us both to do His will and His good pleasure. It pleases God to see His children mature.

God has assignments for us that require our maturity. Certain positions in ministry demand seasoned persons for the journey and God knows exactly what to feed us to sustain us for this life's journey. God gave the prophet Elijah food to sustain him for his upcoming task. (1 Kings 17:4.) The prophet's journey required him to eat a specific type of food that only God could give. God chose a kind of bird with a selfish nature, a raven, and went contrary to the nature of that bird, commanding it to feed the prophet. God will go out of the way to provide what we need, even as He did in the way He went contrary to the nature of that bird. If God did that for Elijah, He will do it for you and for all of us. God is well able to provide whatever we need for our assignment. Our God-given assignment requires us to mature, grow up, and develop in our character, because only mature believers can conquer the upcoming battles and oppositions.

As the church age comes to a close, persecution will arise like never before. This is not a negative confession; I am speaking the warnings from the Savior Himself. He gave specific signs concerning the end times, and each category represents opposition, hard times, and persecution. But we are continually more than conquerors and we triumph in Christ Jesus. But in order to triumph in Christ Jesus, we must grow up in Christ Jesus. Because of the infinite foreknowledge of our Lord, He can see what we cannot see. He sees our potential and He knows our abilities; He guards our destiny and His blood purchased our redemption. He has given us His Name and we have been privileged to be stewards operating in His authority. Such power and authority merits mature saints who reign as heirs instead of being oppressed as slaves. Galatians 4:1-3 (NKJV) tells us:

> *Now I say that the heir, as long as he is a child, does not differ at all from a slave, though he is master of all, but is under guardians and stewards until the time appointed by the father. Even so we, when we were children, were in bondage under the elements of the world.*

God never gives up on our ability because He has committed Himself to our growth. He is the author, the completer, the finisher of our faith. He works with our willingness to yield and makes the finishing touches on the rough edges of our character. Our work in the inner man is already finished and made perfect; but our outward man perishes daily. It's amazing how God can take imperfect people and work perfection in them during the process of transformation. A separation process is often necessary in order for the Holy Spirit and Christ to complete the work within us. Just as the caterpillar needs a little time, a proper atmosphere, and space to go through its metamorphosis, so do we in our spiritual growth process: space, time, and a conducive environment.

Oranges can't grow in Alaska and apples can't grow in the desert! Sometimes we need to change our environment and make a decision to go where we have not been accustomed to going. If we limit ourselves in the natural, we can easily become a product of our environment. The fish teaches us that this does not have to be so: We can take a fish that was bred in salt water, born in salt water, and caught in salt water and cook him, but we still need to add salt! Why? Because the fish lived in the salt water but the salt water did not live in him! Many times, if we change our position, God will change our situation. Nicodemus was too short to see the Messiah in the midst of the crowd. He could not change his physical stature, so he changed his position, or location, and climbed a juniper tree. The tree gave him the elevation that he needed to have the proper view he desired.

CHAPTER 7

RIGHT ASSOCIATIONS

In order to grow, we must be willing to change and make changes. It is possible to change and still not grow; but it is impossible to grow without change. Let's address separation for a moment; this issue is so difficult for some people. If the caterpillar never separated itself, it would never grow or change into the beautiful butterfly. When we make a decision to mature spiritually, people around us will attempt to pressure us to remain the same. As a matter of fact, our peers may accuse us and criticize us for changing. During this time, many of us will try to justify our change and explain our change through apologies. This is not necessary! The only thing that is necessary at that time is the change itself. Those who criticize us for changing will soon applaud us in succeeding and say, "I knew they always had it in them!"

It's all right to sever relationships or separate temporarily. Some people are in our life for a reason. Abraham refused to separate from Lot and it cost him and Lot dearly. God refused to talk to Abraham anymore until He separated from Lot. In our life there may be times of silence from the Lord. Could it be that there are some unnecessary Lots in our life? There are four categories of people in our life: adders, subtracters, multipliers, and dividers. We cannot choose our families, but we do have the prerogative to choose our associates. Associates cause associations and association causes assimilation.

Bad company corrupts good manners according to 1 Corinthians 15:33 (NKJV):

Do not be deceived: "Evil company corrupts good habits."

Paul the Apostle had to separate himself from Barnabas. The Bible reveals that they had a great disagreement concerning John Mark, with whom they had fulfilled a successful ministry. To disarm the entire problem, Paul could have easily reminded Barnabas of the prophetic words that they received in Acts 13:2 (NKJV):

As they ministered to the Lord and fasted, the Holy Spirit said, "Now separate to Me Barnabas and Saul for the work to which I have called them."

Paul and Barnabas both had received apostolic impartation and training from the Antioch church; they were both a part of the first apostolic deployment from Antioch. Not only did Barnabas introduce Paul to the early apostles, he also recruited Paul. Barnabas went to Tarsus to seek him out and continued to search until he found Paul. Paul had returned to Tarsus for a season; it was the place of his birth. But Barnabas brought Paul out of Tarsus into Antioch.

We must be sensitive to interpret the seasons of our life and relationships. The work that the Holy Spirit had for Barnabas and Paul was still in effect when they separated at the time of their great disagreement concerning Mark. Because of their separation, the work was about to face strong challenges. The journey ahead would require spiritual stamina and fortitude. Just because someone begins with us in our spiritual journey does not mean that they will be with us at the end of our journey. We cannot always see what people are made of nor can we accurately discern their motives. God holds us responsible for *our own issues!* Paul said in 1 Corinthians 15:31:

I protest by your rejoicing which I have in Christ Jesus our Lord, I die daily.

Paul had a dominant and strong personality. Speaking on behalf of himself in 1 Timothy 1:12-13 (NKJV) Paul states:

> *And I thank Christ Jesus our Lord who has enabled me, because He counted me faithful, putting me into the ministry, although I was formerly a blasphemer, a persecutor, and an insolent man; but I obtained mercy because I did it ignorantly in unbelief.*

Although Paul referred to himself as an insolent man, with an intensely arrogant personality and boldly disrespectful demeanor, he praised God for counting him faithful and placing him in ministry.

Things began to heat up within the apostolic team and between the leadership of Paul and Barnabas. Paul began to take the lead, operating with great boldness and authority. When they reached the island of Paphos, they were confronted by a Jewish sorcerer and false prophet named Bar-Jesus, who was a very intelligent man and a member of the proconsul, *Sergius Paulus.* Bar-Jesus sought after Barnabas because he wanted him to preach the Gospel to him. But another sorcerer who had been controlling and deceiving many people opposed Barnabas and Paul because he desired to lead the council back into his own erroneous doctrines and away from the faith. It was Paul, not Barnabas, who looked Elymas the sorcerer in the eye and rebuked him. Paul told him that he was full of deceit, fraudulent, and of the devil! Young John Mark was still with them during this time and witnessed the entire ordeal. But Paul didn't stop there; he went on to call the man an enemy to all righteousness and challenged him to stop perverting the way of the Lord.

Paul stood strong and pronounced judgment upon the sorcerer and decreed that the hand of God was against him and that he would go through a season of blindness. The manifestation of Paul's judgment was not delayed; immediately a dark mist fell on the sorcerer, and he went about the village seeking someone to lead and guide him by the hand. Needless to say, as the council observed this, they were astonished at the teachings of the Lord as they witnessed the demonstration of the power of God against those who were enemies of the faith and brought opposition to the Gospel. The entire council was converted and became believers.

Great opposition was ahead as Paul took a stronger lead role. In Acts 13:13 we see the departure of John Mark, and later in the chapter we can clearly see Paul being presented as the chief speaker for the group. From Paphos they traveled to Perga in Pamphylia. They departed there and came to Antioch in Pisidia. The rulers of the synagogue welcomed them and invited them to exhort them with some encouraging words. It was Paul, not Barnabas, who read the law of the prophets and encouraged the rulers of the synagogue. Paul addressed them strongly and with great boldness as he walked them through hundreds of years of prophetic promises of God and the countless many who had rejected the truth of the prophets. He brought them from the journey of Moses out of Egypt to the present burial and resurrection of Christ. The Gentiles were astonished, glorified God, and were appointed to eternal life, but the Jews were stirred with envy. Therefore Paul and Barnabas were expelled out of that region.

The next assignment for Paul and Barnabas was in Iconium where many Jews and Greeks believed, but once again the unbelieving Jews were poisoned with jealousy and contaminated the minds of the brethren against Paul and Barnabas. Fleeing for their lives, they went to Lystra where something very significant happened. God demonstrated the Word with signs following by healing a man who had been crippled from birth. Through the prayer of Paul the man stood to his feet and began to walk. The people of Lystra began to call Paul and Barnabas gods: calling Barnabas "Zeus" and Paul "Hermes" because Paul was the chief speaker. So we see from Acts the thirteenth chapter that although Barnabas introduced and recruited Paul, it was Paul who had the assignment of the more dominant role in leadership and eventually became the writer of two-thirds of the New Testament. Did this make Paul a better person than Barnabas? God forbid! It made Paul more responsible to remain humble. After all, Paul himself admitted to being an arrogant man before his conversion, not Barnabas.

It was in Lystra that the Jews from Antioch and Iconium tried to persuade the people against Paul and Barnabas. It is always the religious people who oppose the Name of God. The enemy is very strategic in his efforts and he does not waste ammunition. The people stoned Paul, not Barnabas, but I am sure that Barnabas was with him because earlier they were attempting to worship the two of them. Act 14:14 states:

> *Which when the apostles Barnabas and Paul, heard of, they rent their clothes, and ran in among the people, crying out...*

They were both extremely dismayed at the people idolizing them as gods and preached to them to turn to the living God. (See v. 15.) The enemy was after Paul as a primary target. They departed Lystra and went into Derbe. Paul's tenacity drew him right back into the place of fire when he began to strengthen the converts. Paul told the converts to be strong and continue in the faith and that his very presence among them should demonstrate the importance of never giving up or giving in to pressure. Paul said this because the last time they had seen him was when he was fleeing for his life. But he lived to return and make a powerful statement to them and the enemy that opposition does not mean that the mission has to be aborted. When the enemy recognizes that no matter what he brings our way, we continually get back up again, then he knows that we are persons to be reckoned with. Paul carried the apostolic anointing to persevere and he was determined to finish his assignment. He took no pleasure in those who turned back, like John Mark. Eventually Paul made it back to Antioch to report the progress of the missionary project.

The wisdom and counsel of God is beyond words. Maybe John Mark would have never been able to endure such persecutions. Paul and Silas remained in Antioch for some time, and Paul sensed that it was necessary to go and visit all of the churches that they had formally labored with because he was concerned about their welfare. Barnabas, being a peacemaker and restorer, insisted that he take John Mark with him. When Paul and Barnabas returned to

Antioch from their first journey, they had not seen John Mark since they departed back to Jerusalem. Time had passed and Barnabas, no doubt, had taken John Mark under his tutelage and restored his faith and confidence. He saw the potential in John Mark and worked to mentor him with patience.

Paul's persona and anointing was different from the other apostles. He was a no-nonsense, very confident, and direct person. He was a bottom line person with no room for gray areas. He was quite the extremist and very zealous. Paul operated from a different perspective and conviction than did the others. He was the one stoned and left for dead. There is an old Jamaican proverb once quoted by the late Bob Marley that says, "He who feels it knows it." Paul suffered the stripes, shipwrecks, and all of the persecutions for the sake of the Gospel. He viewed John Mark as one who fainted and abandoned them under pressure. Could this possibly have been the hand of God? In the beginning, the apostolic deployment was inspired by the Holy Ghost and hands were laid on Paul and Barnabas, and they took John Mark along with them. The Holy Spirit never said, "Separate unto me Paul, Barnabas, and John Mark." Sometimes in our journey we attempt to take people along with us who are not appointed for the journey.

It was this major contention between Paul and Barnabas that drove Paul to depart with Silas, and Barnabas to depart with John Mark. When Paul and Silas were in Derbe and Lystra, Paul met Timothy whom he began to mentor. Timothy's father was not a Jew and his grandmother spiritually nurtured him. Timothy needed a spiritual father to further develop in other spiritual areas of his life. He needed a father to help him overcome the spirit of fear and intimidation because of his youth.

Paul received a vision to go to Macedonia; therefore, he and Silas proceeded to go to Philippi, a small colony of Macedonia, where they were imprisoned. Could John Mark have endured the beatings with rods that Paul and Silas received, along with the brutality and suffering they had to go through? Yet, we see Paul and Silas worshipping God in prison to the point that an earthquake shook the prison's foundation. It shook so violently that the doors of the prison were opened! This prison experience allowed the jailer and his entire household to receive salvation. While all of this was going on, Barnabas was in Cyprus patiently tutoring John Mark.

MARK'S CONTRIBUTION

Mark allowed the Holy Spirit to complete a work in him. The portrayal of a somewhat timid novice grows into a man given to attention and accuracy as he recorded his Gospel. Barnabus, Mark's mentor, did not have a Gospel that he was entrusted to release but John Mark did. It is apparent that John Mark made a decision to develop in maturity. Paul addressed him in Philemon 23-24 (NKJV):

> *Epaphras, my fellow prisoner in Christ Jesus, greets you, as do Mark, Aristarchus, Demas, Luke, my fellow laborers.*

Paul referred to him as one of his fellow workers. However, we must look at the process that John Mark allowed God to take him through in nurturing him into maturation. We must first note that John Mark had to decide to grow. He could have drowned himself in guilt and consuming thoughts of failure. But instead he allowed Barnabus to mentor him. In 48 A.D., Barnabus took John Mark back to Cyprus; this was a familiar region to John Mark because he had served there before. Barnabus put him back on the horse, so to speak, in the area in which he was most effective, and from that place he patiently taught John Mark how to ride again.

John Mark did not give up on ministry. Perhaps Barnabus's entire assignment in John Mark's life was to pull out of John Mark his potential and to assure him that the Master was working a perfect plan in and through the lives of imperfect people. Barnabus taught him that there is hope for the fallen. This revelation became a part of John Mark's ministry and writings because it was John Mark who told us the words of Jesus in Mark 10:27 (NKJV):

But Jesus looked at them and said, "With men it is impossible, but not with God; for with God all things are possible."

John Mark learned this firsthand as he wrote his account that became one of the Gospels from the perspective of his failures. It was also John Mark who recorded Mark 11:23-24 (NKJV below), revealing how much he had matured through the tutelage of Barnabus.

"For assuredly, I say to you, whoever says to this mountain, 'Be removed and be cast into the sea,' and does not doubt in his heart, but believes that those things he says will come to pass, he will have whatever he says.

"Therefore I say to you, whatever things you ask when you pray, believe that you receive them, and you will have them."

It was John Mark who revealed to us how even the disciples were clueless when Jesus was imparting such prophetic truths. In John 4:32-34 (NKJV), Jesus talked to them about meat that He has that they did not know of, and the disciples thought He had already eaten something while they were gone to fetch food.

But He said to them, "I have food to eat of which you do not know.... My food is to do the will of Him who sent Me, and to finish His work."

John Mark was privileged to witness the inner workings of the early church because they often met in the home of his family. He was also privileged to be an assistant to both Paul and Peter. John Mark's life demonstrates to us the beauty of God's character and how he relates to His children in seed form. We are not born mature adults, and He does not expect us as seeds to deal in mature matters. The Father expects us to fully grow up in every area, but He doesn't expect us to be born fully mature, perfect. In Mark 4, John Mark gives us the parable of the mustard seed: the sower and the growing seed. We know that a seed needs time to grow, and this is exactly what happened in the life of John Mark. He grew up to contribute to us such a wealth of knowledge and spiritual insight concerning the parables and their purpose. Mark 4:10-12 (NKJV) tells us:

> *But when He was alone, those around Him with the twelve asked Him about the parable. And He said to them, "To you it has been given to know the mystery of the kingdom of God; but to those who are outside, all things come in parables,*
>
> *"so that, 'Seeing they may see and not perceive, and hearing they may hear and not understand; lest they should turn, and their sins be forgiven them.'"*

Look at the handiwork of the master craftsman Himself. The Father took John Mark's failure and used it to position him as the prime candidate for revealing the mysteries of the Kingdom. It is believed that, according to Papias of Heirapolis, John Mark ministered with Peter in Rome as his interpreter. Papias goes on to record that the authority of John Mark was very needful to the early church as he archived his account of the things that were done by the Messiah. John Mark is credited for establishing churches in Alexandria, where it is commonly believed that he was martyred.

He not only became useful to Paul, but he is still useful to the Body of Christ today. God sees in us what no man can see, and He is committed to completing the work that He has begun in us.

We see in Paul's final greetings to the church of Colossae that he made mention of John Mark after many tribulations and imprisonments later. Paul was much older, wiser, and patient. His perspectives had changed and he had matured in ministry. By then, he had been betrayed, persecuted, falsely accused, and abandoned time and time again. The first sign of any type of restoration towards John Mark is the mention of his name in Paul's letter to the church in Colossae. He made mention also of Aristarchus as his fellow prisoner, Onesimus as his faithful and beloved brother, and also Tychius as a faithful minister. John Mark he mentioned as the cousin of Barnabas and instructed the believers to welcome him if he came to them. Colossians 4:10 states:

Aristarchus my fellowprisoner saluteth you, and Marcus, sister's son to Barnabas, (touching whom ye received commandments: if he come unto you, receive him...).

Since John Mark was Barnabas's cousin, could this be the reason that he was determined to be so patient with him? We have to be very careful not to show partiality in leadership towards family members. We must exemplify the same with anyone that the Lord sends our way. Many years had passed since Paul had heard from Barnabas. The last time we see him mentioned is in Acts 15 when he departed with John Mark; it is as though he had disappeared out of the main stream of things. I am in no way implying that he was not still operating successfully in ministry. Many people work tirelessly in advancing the Kingdom incognito. We will never know the names of many of them until we meet them in glory. In Galatians 2:1-9, Barnabas is mentioned in the conclusion with Paul and Titus in the church of Jerusalem. They were extending the right hand of fellowship in Galatians 2:9:

And when James, Cephas, and John, who seemed to be pillars, perceived the grace that was given unto me, they gave to me and Barnabas the right hand of fellowship; that we should go unto the heathen, and they unto the circumcision.

We see that Barnabas was led astray when Peter was confronted by Paul of his compromise and hypocrisy in Galatians 2:13:

And the other Jews dissembled likewise with him; insomuch that Barnabas also was carried away with their dissimulation.

But concerning John Mark, Paul did a wonderful act of reaffirmation in 2 Timothy 4:11:

Only Luke is with me. Take Mark, and bring him with thee: for he is profitable to me for the ministry.

Prior to expressing his need for John Mark, he addressed those who had abandoned him. But by this time Paul had thicker skin, and he understood necessary separations and the importance of allowing seasons for growth. The abandoned apostle commanded young Timothy to be diligent to come to him because Demas had forsaken him "having loved this present world" (v. 10) greater. He instructed Timothy to advance when others retreated. Only Luke remained faithful to him. In the midst of abandonment he sent for the one who first abandoned him, just as Christ restored Peter after his denial and abandonment. Paul used very strong words in this letter. He told Timothy that he needed John Mark, and he openly decreed that he was now useful to him. There is no mention of Barnabas here.

God has done a sovereign work of growth in Paul's and John Mark's lives. Paul had learned to appreciate and understand that He who has begun a good work in us will complete it. In Philippians 1:6 Paul writes:

> *Being confident of this very thing, that he which hath begun a good work in you will perform it until the day of Jesus Christ.*

Paul also received the revelation that He who saved us has *also called us with a holy calling.* And that calling is not according to our own works or natural abilities, but rather according to His own purpose and grace that is imparted and given to us only in Christ Jesus before time began. (2 Tim. 1:9.) Paul at this time was seasoned and yet softened by Christ. He was more patient and fatherly because he had mentored other "sons." He had almost written the completion of the epistles and was in the last days of his life on the earth. Paul could look back over everything from the Damascus road to the prison cell and conclude that we are more than conquerors even in our imperfections and we are made strong when we yield everything over to God, purposing and earnestly desiring to mature spiritually.

When we learn to interpret the separations in our life as seasons, some temporal and some permanent, we will be able to rise up and move on to maturity. Our heart will begin to desire greener pastures. We will develop a carnivorous appetite for meat instead of milk. We will welcome reproof, correction, and instruction because we have learned that only a fool despises correction (see Prov. 15:5 NASB), and only a bastard lives a lawless life of unaccountability. (See Zech. 9:6.) We hunger and long to please the Lord.

From the prison cell Paul wrote with feeble hand to tell Mark that he needed him and that he was useful to him. John Mark had by now experienced a few challenges and afflictions for the sake of the Gospel. No one in ministry or the Kingdom of God is exempt from godly persecutions. The godly will suffer persecutions and remain strong. John Mark had walked into his own restoration process and, like an eagle, had grown oil-treated feathers that permitted him to endure in the eye of the storm. He had been through enough adversities to know that in the midst of the afflictions and abandonments, the Lord was able to deliver him out of them all. The Lord never leaves us when we are unfaithful; He always remains faithful to His promises. John Mark had the comfort to know that believers will reap in due season when we purpose not to faint. The race is never given to the swiftest runner, but rather to the marathon runner who endures to the end. Fortitude and stamina had become attributes of John Mark as he received an invitation from the chief apostle and author of what would become two-thirds of the New Testament.

Paul, the once impatient man, sent for John Mark. We see such a demonstration of spiritual maturity and leadership in Paul's writings. Hebrews 5:12-14:

> *For when for the time ye ought to be teachers, ye have need that one teach you again which be the first principles of the oracles of God; and are become such as have need of milk, and not of strong meat. For every one that useth milk is unskilful in the word of righteousness: for he is a babe. But strong meat belongeth to them that are of full age, even those who by reason of use have their senses exercised to discern both good and evil.*

Paul used the word *time,* which is interpreted from *chronos,* meaning "a space of time," a "season."[1] These Hebrews had an allotment of time of maturity and still were operating as babes. John Mark, Timothy, and other young sons were just learning how to endure.

I conclude this chapter with this thought: Paul upbraided the church of Corinth for their spiritual immaturity because they were carnal minded. Paul wrote to the Hebrews because of their Peter Pan Syndrome. They refused to grow up. They should have been teaching others; instead, they still needed teaching themselves. Paul counseled the Bereans to study the Scriptures themselves to prove and rightly divide the Word of truth. There is a vast difference between a zealous novice and an aged believer who refuses to grow up. God is more than ready as the perfect Father to take us into the next dimension of our life to conquer areas in which we have failed to mature and have hid and made excuses for ourselves. Our Heavenly Father, by the power of the Holy Ghost, wants to chisel away the hard places and make them new again. He longs for mature saints, and there is nothing hid from Him nor does He condemn us. He wants us to grow in that particular area more than even we desire to. The Father wants to place the desire in us.

Our Father is removing the nest twigs from our place of rest and making it uncomfortable for us to remain in stagnation. It's time to fly. If the ability were not available for us, He wouldn't require it of us. Our Father has so many open doors for us; we must lay aside the hindrances of our past that attempt to haunt us and be willing to make the necessary separations for growth. We shouldn't judge the people from whom He separates us because they are also in their season of separation. Let us rise up to our potential and allow Him to separate us for the work He has ordained for us. It has been already established, and everything we need to complete the assignment is within us. As we consecrate ourselves, we will discover an endless reservoir that He has placed in us that remains untapped. As we separate ourselves, we will discover things in us that we never knew existed.

It is time for the necessary separation—to disconnect the phone, turn off the television, and make the time and space to get alone with our Creator and allow Him to reveal to us what He has placed within us to take us *to our assigned place and purpose.*

PART 3

MATURE YOUR SOUL: NON-OPTICAL OPERATIONS

CHAPTER 8

LIVING FROM YOUR SPIRIT

In order to fulfill the destiny God has for us on the earth, we must understand the way God designed the universe and man to function in it, as we have seen. God designed our world to operate according to the *spiritual* principles He set in motion. Though these laws are not optical laws, the operation of these laws are vital components to the success of man.

Spiritual laws govern the arena of the spirit just as forcefully and effectively as natural laws govern the arena of the earth. Not only that, God designed the spiritual laws governing the arena of the spirit to also govern the arena of the natural realm!

The law of gravity cannot be seen with the physical eye; but nonetheless, it is a law that is definitely in effect. If you do not believe the law of gravity exists because you cannot see it, jumping off a building to test it is not recommended! You would go down, my friend, and then you would be able to see and feel the effects of gravity!

Although the wind itself cannot be seen with the physical eye, the *results* of the wind *can* be seen with the physical eye. Wind is a powerful force of nature in the earth. If you need proof, again, standing in the midst of a hurricane or tornado is not recommended! You would soon experience the power that exists in the force of the unseen wind and *see* its effects!

THE SPIRITUAL PRINCIPLES THAT GOVERN THE WORLD

At creation, God set in motion unseen spiritual principles that govern the world. It seems obvious that in order to live successfully, we should learn what those legislative procedures are and function accordingly! Because God originated and established them in heaven, even heaven itself has governing principles and procedures!

Matthew 6:10 (NKJV) tells us:

> *Your kingdom come. Your will be done on earth as it is in heaven.*

MAN'S SPIRIT IS DESIGNED TO DOMINATE

God created man as three parts and designed the spirit to dominate. Because we cannot see the forces operating in the spiritual realm with the naked eye, we cannot see the triune imagery of mankind.[1] Nonetheless, man is a *spirit* who has a *body* that houses a *soul.* In order for mankind to operate and function on the earth, an earth suit, which we call a *body,* is needed. The moment that the earth suit is nonexistent, so also is the functioning ability of man. The soul, housed within the body, as just observed, contains the mind, will, and intellect.

THE RETURN TO SPIRITUAL CONTROL

Originally, the spirit man within dominated; the mind and body were subject to the spirit. But when man sinned in the Garden of Eden, he lost the divine order of God's original intent. The love of God is awesome; He refused to abandon man in this state of disorder and chaos because man was never designed to be "flesh-ruled." The flesh can never be satisfied. In it dwells nothing good; it is sensual and carnal. After all, it was made from the dirt. But when the spirit has been renewed and is operating in its headship position, giving God-inspired instructions to the soul, then the mind, will, and intellect, are governed accordingly.

Before the fall, man operated with his spirit dominating his soul and body. After the fall, God provided a way to redeem man into returning to a place of operating with his spirit in dominion. It is imperative for us to learn how to allow our spirit to dominate our soul and body in order to relate to, approach, and develop in the Kingdom of God because the Kingdom is spiritual.

OPERATING FROM GOD'S SPIRITUAL REALM

God is a Spirit. The fruit of the *Spirit* and the gifts of the *Spirit* are considered *spiritual* because God is a *Spirit*. We are instructed to worship Him "in *spirit* and in truth" (John 4:23) because He is a truthful and *spiritual* God; therefore, His dealings with man are heart to heart and *Spirit* to *spirit*.

Does this mean that God is not concerned about our mind and body? No! It would be totally erroneous to think of God from that perspective because in 1 Thessalonians 5:23 the Apostle Paul writes:

> *Now may the God of peace Himself sanctify you completely; and may your whole spirit, soul, and body be preserved blameless at the coming of our Lord Jesus Christ.*

In preparing the disciples for their paradigm shift from operating out of their soul to operating out of their spirit, Jesus taught them concerning Kingdom concepts because he wanted them to understand that the Kingdom of God cannot be observed with the naked eye. Second Corinthians 4:18 says:

> *While we look not at the things which are seen, but at the things which are not seen: for the things which are seen are temporal; but the things which are not seen are eternal.*

Even though the Kingdom cannot be seen physically, it *does* exist, and it houses the principles we need for Kingdom living. The principles of the Kingdom are God's rules for living, His modus operandi.

Because we believers cannot see the spiritual principles that regulate the world around us, some of us do not operate in accordance with them. Whether the reason is that we are unaware of those governing procedures or the reason is that we do not understand the power behind them, those of us who fit in either category still expect godly results in life. In both cases, we do not experience the types of results we expect because, no matter what the reason, we are not living in accordance with the governing principles God set in place to bring about those godly results.

It is surprising, however, that some of us who are very aware of and do know how to operate in accordance with these principles that rule the world around us, form another category: There are those of us who choose not to live in accordance with these principles, by which heaven itself is legislated, and still expect godly results in our life!

We believers cannot afford to operate without following God's unseen ruling procedures. In order to gain proper understanding of how to live in God's spiritual realm and how to follow the leading of His Spirit as a lifestyle, it is necessary to understand how God created man and how God intends for man to function.

In Revelation 12:7-9 we see an example of heaven's governing procedures in operation. When Satan violated a spiritual law, he and the angels following him received an eviction notice from God. Satan as Lucifer in heaven felt that he would escape the judgment of God because he drew a crowd. However, he fell from heaven instead! (See Isa. 14:12-15).

GUARD YOUR HEART WITH DILIGENCE

Sometimes a believer, especially someone in leadership, falls into that destructive trap of pride. This may happen, and is important to guard against, when a person begins to experience successes and blessings that result from God bringing to pass the words they have been speaking out of the abundance of their heart in line with their destiny.

For example, if the person is using their gifts to help others, operating in the gifts of the Spirit, drawing a following of people, and experiencing increased financial blessing, they may look at these blessings as indications of being on the right track with God. Instead of responding to Him with gratitude, they allow pride to creep into the heart they once carefully guarded to keep completely His. If the person has neglected building and guarding godly character traits in themselves and seeing that task as equal in importance to obtaining and maintaining ground for the Kingdom, the person may move into becoming deceptive.

It is not safe to judge a leader according to the size of their church, or judge a leader, or any believer, by the accuracy of their gifts. Because someone is blessed outwardly and *appears* to be following God and doing His work does not mean the person's heart is completely God's or that the person is hearing and following the leading of the Spirit. Romans 11:29 (NKJV) states:

> *For the gifts and the calling of God are irrevocable.*

A person may continue to operate in their gifts and calling even though their heart has moved away from complete devotion to God. God gives us ways to recognize whether someone is operating according to His principles. For example, Matthew 12:33 tells us, "...the tree is known by his fruit." Outward appearance, in itself, can be deceptive. We do not want to be in a position of following the lead of someone who is not following God.

Erring in this area of pride is very subtle and deceptive. It is impossible to violate spiritual laws and not suffer the consequences. God delays His judgments because He is longsuffering and is not willing to see any perish (from both an eternal, for the non-believer, and circumstantial, for the believer, perspective), but *delayed* judgment does not mean *denied* judgment. The delay is simply God's sovereign mercy demonstrated towards man. He is always hoping that man will turn from their iniquity and obey Him. Proverbs 16:18 (NKJV) reveals one of the consequences of pride: "Pride goes before destruction, and a haughty spirit before a fall."

One of my mentors, Terry Mize, once said to me when I was twenty-one, "Pat, watch the spiritual laws—they cannot be violated." When we repeatedly and unrepentantly violate spiritual laws, it is only a matter of time before we fall. Needless to say, I followed my mentor's spiritual advice, and his words of encouragement and my obedience have preserved me to this day.

REPROGRAMMING OUR LIFE

An essential fact that we must not overlook is that God will not reprogram your life for you. He already did His part by providing a Way for us to escape out of our sin through the re-creation of our spirits by the Lamb that was slain before the foundation of the earth. God is so wise. He made provisions for man before the fall of man ever took place by providing a holy sacrifice. Therefore, the task of bringing our body under subjection and renewal of the mind is our job assignment. In Romans 12:1-2 (NKJV), let's look very carefully at the thing that God instructs us to do through Paul.

> *I beseech you therefore, brethren, by the mercies of God, that you present your bodies a living sacrifice, holy, acceptable to God, which is your reasonable service. And do not be conformed to this world, but be transformed by the renewing of your mind, that you may prove what is that good and acceptable and perfect will of God.*

BRINGING THE BODY UNDER SUBJECTION

It is interesting how easy it is to briefly read through these two verses and miss the process that Paul is trying to teach us. He first instructs us to present our bodies as a living sacrifice. A sacrifice is anything that you place on the altar that cost you something and is very dear to you. Our bodies are very much alive! If you do not believe this, leave your body unsupervised for a moment and allow it to rule your life and see what an unruly mess it will put you in! This is exactly why we are carefully warned to bring our bodies under subjection and to mortify the deeds of our bodies. Romans 8:13 tells us:

> *For if ye live after the flesh, ye shall die: but if ye through the Spirit do mortify the deeds of the body, ye shall live.*

And Colossians 3:5 states:

> *Mortify therefore your members which are on the earth: fornication, uncleanness, inordinate affection (passion* NKJV*), evil concupiscence (desire* NKJV*), and covetousness, which is idolatry.*

The word *mortify* literally means to "put to death"[2] or "subdue"[3] the deeds of our bodies. What are we responsible for in the area of subduing our bodies? Paul said we must present our bodies. The body belongs to us; therefore, it is our responsibility to present it! Remember, our physical bodies never partook of the renewal experience—only our spirit man. Our physical bodies are not saved. No matter how much we try to dress up our body on Sunday morning, it is still as unregenerate as it was the day we accepted Jesus. If we do not buffet it and chastise it, our body will begin to rule and guide us.

I have practiced an exercise of discipline over my body that has brought great results. I deny my body certain things in order to remind it that it does not rule me, but that I rule it. I have declared some weeks as "War on My Flesh Week," and I consecrate specific times of fasting for the purpose of keeping my body under subjection and reminding it that I am the *boss!*

Now that we see through the scriptures that we present our bodies as a sacrifice by buffeting the body and mortifying the deeds of the body, Paul then brings us into proper perspective by telling us that this is our "reasonable service." In other words, it is the *least* we can do: a demeaning service.

RENEWING OUR MINDS

Let's look at the renewing of our minds. God will never renew your mind without your participation. You may ask, "Why doesn't God just remove all of the preprogrammed rubbish that is the residue of our former life?" The answer is really quite simple, yet vital to our success in our Christian life.

When our Father created us in His image, we had the capacity to think just as our Father. Our thoughts will never elevate to the level of His thoughts because He is all knowing. He doesn't have *access* to knowledge as we do—He *is* knowledge Himself. Since we have the capacity to think, we also have the capacity to choose and deny. Most people entirely miss this attribute of God. He respects man's right of choice and gives us a clue in helping us to make our own choices as we see in Deuteronomy 30:19 (NKJV):

> *"I call heaven and earth as witnesses today against you, that I have set before you life and death, blessing and cursing; therefore choose life, that both you and your descendants may live."*

THE TRANSFORMATION OF A SELF-WILLED SOUL

It was as if God gave us the answer to the test of life. *Choose life*—life is far better than death. If God didn't want us to choose then why would He say, "I have set before you..."? We are free will moral agents, and this is what comprises our soul realm. If we control a person's soul, we control that person, and they will be no more than a puppet to us. God does not pull all the strings in our life as if operating a puppet. If He did, I am sure He would pull the most important string and get us to accept His salvation plan for mankind. God respects even our choice to reject Him. This does not mean that He agrees, because He said in His Word that He is not willing that any should perish according to 2 Peter 3:9 (NKJV).

> *The Lord is not slack concerning His promise, as some count slackness, but is longsuffering toward us, not willing that any should perish but that all should come to repentance.*

That round thing sitting on our shoulders contains our mind, part of our soul, that has to be *renewed!* We have the tedious step-by-step task of extracting everything that is contrary to the knowledge of truth out of our minds according to 2 Corinthians 10:5 (NKJV).

> *...Casting down arguments and every high thing that exalts itself against the knowledge of God, bringing every* ***thought*** *into captivity to the obedience of Christ....*

We are instructed in the Word to cast down "arguments and every high thing that exalts itself against the knowledge of God"—to pull each one down. When we have done our reasonable duty of sweeping our house clean, we are also responsible for replenishing the newly swept house with something else—the Word of God. Philippians 4:8 (NKJV) tells us:

> *Finally, brethren, whatever things are true, whatever things are noble, whatever things are just, whatever things are pure, whatever things are lovely, whatever things are of good report, if there is any virtue and if there is anything praiseworthy–meditate on these things.*

I beseech you reader, by the mercies of God, please do not omit this principle in your life. If you, as a believer, never confront the areas that you have not allowed God to transform, you will remain in bondage in that particular area. Psalm 119:130 (NKJV) declares:

> *The entrance of Your words gives light; it gives understanding to the simple.*

The light shines and exposes all the dark areas of our life. The light brings detailed exposure to our unregenerate way of thinking that is contrary to God's way of operating.

The process that Paul introduces us to in Romans 12:1-2 that teaches us how to allow our spirit to dominate our soul and body is guaranteed effective. Following this pattern planned by God will free us from the hindrances holding us back from completing our destiny with Him.

CHAPTER 9

TRANSPARENT BEFORE GOD

The King of endless mercy and infinite grace has a road sign to guide us into the corridors of His presence, and that road sign is called *worship.* God wants us to bring our struggles to Him for Him to forgive us, cleanse us, and restore us. When we bring our failures to Him to draw on Him to turn them into strengths instead of trying to hide them or cover them up, we are worshipping Him in truth.

We saw before that we worship God, who is a Spirit, "in spirit and truth."

> *"But the hour is coming, and now is, when the true worshipers will worship the Father in spirit and truth; for the Father is seeking such to worship Him.*
>
> *"God is Spirit, and those who worship Him must worship in spirit and truth."*
>
> John 4:23,24 NKJV

The foundation of a true worshipper who seeks to "worship the Father in spirit and truth" is to come clean before God. Sometimes the simplicity of this matter escapes us. The enemy makes it his goal to complicate this elementary matter and keep us in the dark so that we will live an unstable life of wavering in and out of fellowship with God. But the moment we look into God's glorious presence everything else becomes a shadow in the light of His mercies and glorious grace.

When we fall short, God wants us to run *to* Him, not *from* Him! He not only wants us to draw near to Him when we are in need of forgiveness due to a disobedient act, He wants us to draw near to Him so that He can continue to shine His light into closed areas of our life.

We all make mistakes and have growth issues. In truly worshipping the Lord, we must be honest and truthful with ourselves. God delights in sincerity. He alone is able to cleanse and forgive us of our every sin, through the work of His Son, when we divulge the sins through confession. The Word cleanses us. (See Eph. 5:26.) God has provided access to His throne. As we come into God's presence with sincerity and transparency, worshipping Him "in truth," He embraces us with forgiveness, empowers us, and renews our strength.

By *His* mercies, God wants us to present ourselves, our bodies, "...a living sacrifice, holy, acceptable to God," our "reasonable service" (Rom. 12:1 NKJV). As believers, many of us fall back into that old expectation of ourselves to live without error, and in pursuing this impossible goal, we double the impossibility by depending upon our strength rather than on God's strength to enable us to live as we desire, completely pleasing to Him. And for those of us in leadership—we have the distinct impression that our followers think we arrived on the earth fully mature at birth. In fact, we have a tendency to expect the same of ourselves!

When we judge ourselves, we are allowed by God not to be judged. If we try to cover up our issues which need to be confronted and hide our failings behind our calling, our anointing, our office in the Body of Christ, or even our reputation as a strong believer or leader, refusing to take a close look at ourselves, we will find that we will fall before the judgment seat of Christ.[1] The beauty of righteousness is that it permits us to come boldly before God's throne and stand on His righteousness; this is why our self-righteousness is filthy and unacceptable in His sight.

THE PATHWAY TO GOD'S HEART

David helps us tremendously in understanding the nature of true worship. He wrote more about worship than did any of the other writers of the Bible, and his psalms are prevalent among the songs we sing throughout the Body of Christ today.

He was a man who blatantly sinned. He lost his focus, yet, according to Psalm 51, through worship he found the pathway to God's heart. Penitent after convicted of his sin with Bathsheba and arranging the death of her husband, David runs to God and confesses his sin, worshipping God and appealing to His mercy. I can only imagine that while on his journey to the mercy seat of God's heart, David's conscience inside of him was screaming, "Help, I'm almost there!" If I could only cry out to God and say, "Lord, I cannot continue like this." There is a freedom in being able to be naked before God and not ashamed, to be able to say, "This is where it hurts, and this is where I need help." The beauty is in knowing that He is waiting and longing to meet my need for restoration before I even call. "I will provide for their needs before they ask. I will help them while they are still asking for help" (Isa. 65:24 NCV).

It is this psalm we reference after blatantly missing the mark. Almost every believer finds refuge, comfort, strength, and restoration in this psalm, especially fallen leaders, who are often expected to lead errorless lives.

HELP, I'M ALMOST THERE

In Psalm 51 David escorts us through the process of acknowledging our sin, repenting, and being cleansed from it. He then educates us on the process of restoration, showing us an example of God's mercy in blessing us in a way we know we don't deserve following the sin: renewed confidence, restoration back into service, and the grand finale—the new act of bona fide worship.

David begins the psalm by reminding the Father of His extending mercies. God's multiplicity of mercies endures forever and is available throughout a thousand generations. The purest form of God's mercy is His lovingkindness, and David uses this attribute of God to plead his case. He asks God not to deal with him according to what he deserves, but according to the wealth of God's lovingkindness.

David also knew that God's mercy was tempered with tenderness; therefore, he asked God to blot out his sins. He did not ask for his sins to be atoned; he asked for them to be remitted because he knew that he had been found guilty and the only One who could deliver him was God. David was exposed openly by the prophet Nathan; all the evidence was mounted against him. David was indicted, found guilty, and sentenced by God through the prophet Nathan.

In reading the account in 2 Samuel 12, we see the mercy of God in the midst of His judgment. Verse 8 (NKJV) relays God speaking to David through Nathan:

> *"I gave you your master's house and your master's wives into your keeping, and gave you the house of Israel and Judah. And if that had been too little, I also would have given you much more!"*

If the tremendous blessings God had given David were too little for him, David could have simply asked God for more. God would have given more tremendous blessings to David, *legally* satisfying David within the boundaries of the commandments.

David displays his remorseful shame and regret before God. (Ps. 51:13.) He acknowledges that his sin is not only against himself and all of Israel, but also against the loving God who took him from the shepherd pasture, positioned him in the palace, and defended him against the wrath of Saul's javelin. At this moment David was face to face with his pride, greed, arrogance, unaccountability, rebellion, and selfishness. In Matthew 15:19-20, we read that later Jesus described these types of attributes as being of the heart, revealing these are the things that defile a man:

For out of the heart proceed evil thoughts, murders, adulteries, fornications, thefts, false witness, blasphemies: These are the things which defile a man....

All of these reproachful contaminations were living in the heart of the king, the very leader of all of Israel. These are the things that defile not only a leader but any man.

We see God's mercy flagrantly displayed in 2 Samuel 12:12-13:

"For you did it secretly, but I will do this thing before all Israel, before the sun."

So David said to Nathan, "I have sinned against the Lord." And Nathan said to David, "The Lord also has put away your sin; you shall not die."

Although we see the wrath of God in verse 12, we immediately see His mercy displayed in verse 13! For David, this was God's first sign of His unconditional love towards him in such an awesome dimension. There was nothing shallow or effortless about God's demonstration of love bestowed upon David because it is His goodness that brought David to absolute repentance.

First Corinthians 15:26 informs us that the last enemy to be destroyed is death. David fell prey to this enemy by committing the very act that he himself deserved—*death.* But because of God's tender mercies, David found unconditional love that he knew he did not deserve.

David's situation is relevant to us today as likened to us having sinned before God and, immediately after repentance, God blesses us openly in a way that we know within ourselves we do not deserve. That sense of bewilderment and overwhelming gratitude pierces our heart and causes us to respond with renewed determination. It raises us from our fallen state and sends us running, panting, into His open arms of embracing forgiveness.

What makes God so willing to believe in us, forgive and restore us? These are the attributes and hidden components that make Him *God Almighty!*

The child conceived in David's selfish act of disobedience and deceit had to give its life as a ransom simply because of David's craving to satisfy his flesh. We can see how our disobedience often affects others and God's overall plan for generations. All sin is selfish and self-centered; notice that there is an 'I' in the middle of the words *sin* and *pride*. We need to confront and demolish the 'I' areas of our life as David did.

In the midst of David's self-centered lifestyle, he had overlooked the mysteries of God. He received a shock treatment when the prophet Nathan confronted him. Sometimes the hardest areas to overcome, especially for a leader, are pride and not acknowledging our challenges. God always gives us ample time to deal with our situations before He exposes us. David searched deep into the heart of God and saw the light that pierced through the opening of Jesus' side—the light of forgiveness, restoration, acceptance, and fellowship.

David discovered a place in God that God's children could gain access to Him. The access code is quite simple as are most of the mysteries of God. He wants us to acknowledge and confess our sins, and make our life "a living sacrifice," our "reasonable service," to God according to Romans 12:1-2.

David discovered that the road into the heart of God is paved with forgiveness. Worship as a lifestyle is our reasonable service to God.

CHAPTER 10

THE POWER IN YOU

God's intent is for man to be His temple. He wants to house Himself in man and delegate to man the use of His power and authority.

We might think that God would want to establish His dwelling in a majestic man-made structure or in any part of the splendor of His own creation in order to relate to man from the *outside* as Father, Friend, and Provider. When God, surrounded with thunders and lightnings, descended on Mount Sinai in a thick cloud and a fire to meet with Moses, the Israelites trembled at the sight of the mountain shaking and smoking. (Exod. 19:6-18 NKJV.) After that sight, the Israelites would have wondered if a structure on the earth existed or could be built with a foundation broad and sturdy enough to contain God! What edifice could possibly be built with the capacity to house God's presence and glory?

Still, the Most High God, *El Elyon,* the God who inhabits eternity, wants to live *in* man. And He wants to live with a person who has a contrite and humble spirit!

For thus says the High and Lofty One who inhabits eternity, whose name is Holy: "I dwell in the high and holy place, with him who has a contrite and humble spirit, to revive the spirit of the humble, and to revive the heart of the contrite ones."

Isaiah 57:15 NKJV

Other words for "contrite" are: "repentant, regretful, humbled, remorseful,"[1] "penitent."[2] The High and Lofty God dwells in the high and holy place with a person who repentantly brings their failures to Him! The above scripture again carries the message of the value that God places on the person with a contrite and humble spirit, the person who guards their heart.

God wants us to give Him our underdeveloped character and depend on Him rather than on ourselves, allowing Him to orchestrate the events around us in order for us to fulfill our destiny, as we saw especially in David's example. When God raised up David to be king, He said David was a man after His own heart, who "shall fulfil all my will" (Acts 13:22). In spite of David's great sin, David—contrite of heart, repentant, restored to fellowship with God—experienced consequences of his sin but completed his destiny as king of Israel and fulfilling God's will.

The pathway David revealed in Psalm 51 of restoration back to God through examining himself and acknowledging and confessing his sins to God to receive God's forgiveness, mercy, and restoration was exemplified in the Tabernacle long before David wrote that psalm.

OLD COVENANT RITUAL REPLACED WITH NEW COVENANT ACCESS

We read in Exodus 25:8-9 (NKJV) that the Lord spoke to Moses:

"And let them make Me a sanctuary, that I may dwell among them.

"According to all that I show you, that is, the pattern of the tabernacle and the pattern of all its furnishings, just so you shall make it."

For the first time since the time of Adam, God came down to live *among* man. God, who is high above all nations, whose glory is above the heavens, who through His Son Jesus, the image of Himself, created all things and is the power that ordained all other powers, who is Himself reality, for a season chose to pitch His tent among men and tabernacle with His people. Later in this distinct period of time, God continued to grant His children the grace of His presence and glory by embodying Himself in Solomon's Temple.

The Lord gave very specific instructions for constructing the dwellings on the earth that would be able to contain His presence enough to protect man from being consumed by the weaknesses which exist in every person. Besides giving Moses specific directions to follow in making the Tabernacle, God also gave Moses detailed instructions for consecrating the Tabernacle, its furnishings, and the priests before first using the Tabernacle. (See Exod. 29; 40.) He designated in detail how to select the priests, their dress, their consecration and how they would minister in the Tabernacle—manner of ministry, duties, and cleansing.

If God's instructions described in the Old Testament concerning the manner in which to approach Him were not followed exactly, the results were severe. In Exodus 19:21 we read concerning the people of Israel, "And the LORD said unto Moses, Go down, charge the people, lest they break through unto the LORD to gaze, and many of them perish."

Unless people were properly sanctified according to the Lord's instructions before approaching Him, they would perish! Even though the Israelites in the camp who saw Mount Sinai greatly quaking under the Lord's descent had followed the directions to sanctify themselves, they were afraid. They saw the effects of the overwhelming presence of the Lord. However, with the New Covenant, God provided the Way for man to again enter into His presence (if man chooses to accept the Way). Jesus, through His death on the cross and resurrection, took on the sin that separated man from God. "Christ came as the High Priest of the good things to come....with His own blood He entered the Most Holy Place once for all, having obtained eternal redemption" (Heb. 9:11,12

NKJV). At last, God with all His awe-inspiring power was able to move into the dwelling place He desired—man!

This New Covenant is "a better covenant, which was established upon better promises" (Heb. 8:6). In the New Covenant, we can "...come boldly unto the throne of grace, that we may obtain mercy, and find grace to help in time of need" (Heb. 4:16).

In the New Covenant coming boldly into God's presence is quite a contrast to the approach required of the Israelites under the Old Covenant!

OLD COVENANT EXAMPLE AND SHADOW OF HEAVENLY THINGS

Under the Old Covenant, God established a place for Him to dwell among men through the pattern for the Tabernacle and the instructions for the priests' ongoing ministry to cover the sin separating Him from man. This served as an example and shadow (Heb. 8:4,5) of heavenly things and the work that Jesus, our High Priest, would do to remove the sin in order for God to make man His habitation and for man to access God directly.

In Old Testament times the priests offered sacrifices to God for their sins and the sins of the children of Israel on the bronze altar, the altar of the burnt offering, in the court of the Tabernacle. (See Exod. 39:39; 30:28; 40:6 NKJV.)

Before the priests could go into the tabernacle of meeting (the place of meeting between God and His people) or approach the bronze altar to offer a burnt sacrifice to the Lord, God required them to wash their hands and feet with water from the laver, located between the Tabernacle and the bronze altar. As discussed before, the priests were to follow God's explicit instructions in detail "lest they die."

Then the Lord spoke to Moses, saying:

"You shall also make a laver of bronze, with its base also of bronze, for washing. You shall put it between the tabernacle of meeting and the altar. And you shall put water in it,

"for Aaron and his sons shall wash their hands and their feet in water from it.

"When they go into the tabernacle of meeting, or when they come near the altar to minister, to burn an offering made by fire to the Lord, they shall wash with water, lest they die.

"So they shall wash their hands and their feet, lest they die. And it shall be a statute forever to them—to him and his descendants throughout their generations."

Exodus 30:17-21 NKJV

The priests offered daily sacrifices on the bronze altar, and additional sacrifices on other occasions, for their sins and those of the people. (See Heb. 7:27; Exod. 29:38,39.) From its location in the court of the Tabernacle, the altar represented the beginning of man's approach to God. It also represented the one ultimate sacrifice Christ offered for the sins of the world forever, which brought to a conclusion the need for ongoing sacrifices. (See Heb. 10:12,14-18.)

The laver, filled with water, was made of the bronze mirrors of the women who served at the door of the Tabernacle. (See Exod. 40:7; 30:18; 38:8 NKJV.) The bronze laver represents a time of acknowledgment and cleansing of sins. As the priests cleansed themselves by washing with the water from the laver before approaching the bronze altar to offer a burnt sacrifice or entering the Tabernacle, it is likely they saw their reflection in the water. James 1:25 (NKJV) speaks of a reflection we are to view:

But he who looks into the perfect law of liberty and continues in it, and is not a forgetful hearer but a doer of the work, this one will be blessed in what he does.

As we look into "the perfect law of liberty," the liberty brought by the Spirit of the Lord in the New Covenant, and as we behold His glory in the glass, we change into His image, glory to glory, as we allow Him to transform us. (See 2 Cor. 3:6,17,18.)

The laver was positioned parallel to the brazen altar. This declares to us the two areas of equal importance in our approach to God: first, examining our life to cleanse ourselves from the sins that so easily bind us by giving them to the Lord and, second, offering our body as a living sacrifice to Him. The altar represents Jesus' offering Himself for our sin; the laver represents Jesus' cleansing us from our sin.

Cleansing in the bronze laver represents a time of heart healing, repentance, forgiveness, and absolution. The priests, required to wash in the water of the bronze laver before offering burnt sacrifices as discussed, washed at least twice daily because they were required to offer two burnt sacrifices daily: one in the morning and one in the evening. (See Exod. 29:38,39,42.)

Just as the priests were required to cleanse themselves before offering the frequent sacrifices to God, we are to "come clean" before God with as much frequency as is needed for an ongoing lifestyle of true worship. We cleanse ourselves by looking into "the brazen laver," examining our reflection to be honest with ourselves in identifying our imperfections rather than excusing them. We then take them to God for Him to become strength in our weaknesses, forgive our sins, and restore us.

God does not intend to examine our life for us or go against our will and offer our life for us to Himself. We must mature to a place of openness before God by training ourselves to be honest in acknowledging our sins and approaching Him with a humble and contrite spirit.

JESUS' REFLECTION IN THE PERFECT LAW OF LIBERTY

A common area of weakness today, especially among leaders, is not being honest with ourselves about issues to be confronted. Some leaders do have extremely valid and practical time- and money-saving reasons for owning or traveling in a private jet; some, when traveling to another city to speak at a church or convention, may occasionally be hosted by someone who wants to bless them and members of their party with limousine service between events. However, because we live in an era of superficial flattery, some leaders have let pride enter their hearts and allow themselves to be exalted above measure. They have an excessive number of body-guards, chauffeured stretch limousine service, and private jet travel, when the extent of their needs and good stewardship of the Lord's money would not warrant this type of service.

Before some renowned men or women of God will speak to a church and bless the congregation with the free Word of God, they require the church accountant and attorney to go over their contract with a fine-tooth comb. Some leaders who, in pride, refuse to be accessible to people, have forgotten that they are *servants* of the Most High God and not *stars* of the Most High God. We serve in the *Kingdom* not *Hollywood!* The leaders who have fallen into this category out of pride need to exchange the lights, cameras, and director chairs for the bronze altar and laver.

Does all of this mean that I am against nice things or do not believe that a workman is worthy of his hire? God forbid! Jehovah is not against us having nice things—He just does not want the things to have us! My point is that as we eat of the pleasures of life, we need to always remember that the Lord our God is the One who gave us the strength, ability, and wit to obtain the wealth of these things for the express purpose of reaching the people who do not know Him and establishing His covenant in the earth.

Looking into the perfect law of liberty is for the purpose of transforming more and more into the Lord's image by giving more and more of our struggles to Him and growing closer to Him in the process. Galatians 5:13 warns against us using the "liberty as an opportunity for the flesh" (NKJV) but instead to use the liberty to which we have been called to serve one another through love.

NEW COVENANT CLEANSING

Under the New Covenant, Jesus took the penalty of death for sin on our behalf and cleansed us by His blood. (See Rev. 1:5.) Because of Jesus' sacrifice, instead of needing to cleanse ourselves with the water of the bronze laver, we are cleansed by Jesus' blood. (Rev. 1:5.) We are cleansed with the washing of water by the Word of God. Ephesians 5:25-27 tells us that Christ:

> *...loved the church, and gave himself for it;*
>
> *That he might sanctify and cleanse it with the washing of water by the word,*
>
> *That he might present it to himself a glorious church, not having spot, or wrinkle, or any such thing; but that it should be holy and without blemish.*

The word *washing* in the above scripture is the translation of the original Greek word *loutron,* meaning "a bath, a laver...."[3] Bronze ("brass" KJV) speaks "of divine judgment as in the bronze serpent (Num. 21:9; John 3:14; 12:31-33)"[4]; therefore, the place where the altar and laver stood was a place of judgment and cleansing.

John 15:3(NKJV) states:

> *"You are already clean because of the word which I have spoken to you."*

Revelation 1:5-6 (NKJV) tells us:

> *...To Him* [Jesus] *who loved us and washed us from our sins in His own blood,*
>
> *and has made us kings and priests to His God and Father, to Him be glory and dominion forever and ever. Amen.*

NEW COVENANT PRIESTS

Jesus, the High Priest who offered the final sacrifice for sin that restored our relationship with God, made us, we who are believers in Him, priests to God. Instead of cleansing our hands and feet in the bronze laver before approaching God, we look into the reflection in the perfect law of liberty to identify our shortcomings for cleansing through Jesus' blood and the washing of the water of the Word.

Please remember that the purpose of the bronze laver was not to leave man in a condemned state of depression but for renewal of strength, empowerment, and restoration of fellowship with God as in the life of David. The laver filled with water, which is ultimately the Word of God, fills us with God's presence and aids us in crucifying the deeds of our flesh as we present our bodies as living sacrifices in order to experience the fullness of God's power and fellowship without limitations in life.

Under the Old Covenant the priestly attire was of fine material—robe, sash of beautiful tabernacle colors, headgear—and the high priest's attire, more distinctive, was highly symbolic spiritually of the "greater and more perfect tabernacle, not made with hands" and Christ "an high priest of good things to come" (Heb. 9:11). (See also Heb. 7:22,26,27.) The priestly attire covered the body except for the feet.

I believe that God desired to leave one part of man uncovered, open and exposed to Himself. Priests could not cover their entire body under their priestly attire just as we cannot cover up the areas where we miss the mark. If we try to mask them with our calling, anointing, office in the Body of Christ, or ministry, we cannot disguise them forever.

We are faced with opportunities to miss the mark every day. I believe that God gave instructions for the priests' feet to remain uncovered so that they could feel the dirt of society between their toes. The priest had to clean off the daily dirt of the world in order to go into the presence of Christ.

God expects us to gain control over our life and victory over our issues to be confronted while living and interacting in a world of sin. He desires for the epistles of our life, representing Christ (see 2 Cor. 3:2,3), to free and provide an escape for a world that is entrapped by sin. The way of escape in a world that is plagued with sin is living a life for Christ Jesus.

Through the disclosure of sin in David's life we today have an example to follow. What David tried to conceal, God openly revealed. David found his pilgrimage back into the presence of God by working through the process of restoration. This process comes into fruition as we learn to forgive ourselves, renew our minds, and change our direction and habitual ways. If our minds are not restored and renewed, we will find ourselves back on the roller coaster ride of life: up and down, in and out, never growing, never gaining ground.

Some of us don't know that God can change those challenging areas we feel powerless to change. Some of us do know but don't understand how to give them to God for Him in His strength to turn them into something strong. Those of us in either category may hide behind our frustrations, as discussed earlier. However, some of us may try to fool ourselves and those around us about our issues needing to be confronted. We may disguise them, or mask them in some other way, to make the unconfronted issues we don't know how to strengthen or don't want to improve sound spiritual by calling them "a thorn in my flesh," or some other term. There are even national conferences, presented in such a way to magnify our shortcomings, setting us up to be more and more conscious of sin and less and less conscious of our righteous good works. This will lead us deeper into our frustrations rather than into freedom from them.

After our growth issues have been exposed, God wants us to allow Him to work with us in healing us, turning the undeveloped areas into strengths or removing them, or growing us up in them. If instead we choose to continue to lick our exposed wounds, nurture our naughtiness, or excuse our errors—in other words, stay stuck in the Peter Pan Syndrome—we will inhibit our progress toward fulfilling our destiny and make life difficult for ourselves and those around us as a by-product!

Just as God wanted the priests of the Old Covenant to feel "the dirt of society between their toes," God desires for us, as priests of the New Covenant, to stay mindful that we are *in* the world but not *of* the world, by feeling the dirt of society and our frailties "between our toes."

No longer are priests required to be of a certain lineage, to dress in certain attire of detailed symbolic significance, and to perform specific duties in certain ways "lest they die" in order to relate to God on behalf of the people. No longer do they need to follow specific cleansing preliminaries before presenting sacrifices to God or approaching His presence on behalf of others. In the New Covenant, Jesus made all of us (who accept Him) priests with immediate access to God's powerful presence.

First Peter 2:5 (NKJV) says:

> *you also, as living stones, are being built up a spiritual house, a holy priesthood, to offer up spiritual sacrifices acceptable to God through Jesus Christ.*

We are under construction. We are in a building process and part of a construction project. The head architect and master builder is God. He is building us into a spiritual house and holy priesthood. The purpose and role of the priesthood is to worship God in and through making sacrifices that are holy and acceptable to Him and to represent Him to others. We are to be ambassadors for Christ to implore others to be reconciled to God. (See 2 Cor. 5:20 NKJV.)

The prerequisite for obtaining an acceptable sacrifice that is holy and gratifying to God is to acknowledge our areas where we have missed the mark when we approach Him in desperate need of restoration. We must look closely and examine who we really are and rehearse the choices that we have made that placed us in our present situations. As the priests of old were to cleanse themselves before offering sacrifices as priests on behalf of the children of Israel, or to approach God's presence in the tabernacle of meeting, we too are in need of the purging power of God in our life.

All that the Father desires of us is that we live our life broken (in the sense of ready to admit our mistakes and shortcomings to Him for Him to help us), open, and honest before Him. The High and Lofty God chooses to live in a broken, godly sorrowful, penitent, repentant, and remorseful vessel, bringing that vessel into His high and holy dwelling. He uses the attribute of His goodness to draw us back to Himself so that we can repent, and He can quickly restore us into fellowship again.

To expect godly results in life we must purpose to do things God's way. God's way yields God's results, and if we build upon any other foundation than that which is laid and ordered by God, we will labor in vain. If the foundation is faulty, what shall the righteous do? In 2 Corinthians 4:7, we read that God promised to place the excellency of His power in our earthen vessel.

> *But we have this treasure in earthen vessels, that the excellency of the power may be of God, and not of us.*

If we will give Him our shortcomings, the excellency of His power will shine through us as He becomes strong in our areas of disappointment.

God not only tabernacles *among* men, He has now, in the New Covenant, come to make His abode *in* men. By dwelling in man, He has made His power available to restore the divine order He originally intended for man.

God intends for our spirit to dominate our mind and body. He also intends for us to have dominion and authority over the physical realm by operating from our spirit in accordance with the governing spiritual principles God set in motion at Creation—as it is in heaven, so shall it be in the earth, and to His Kingdom there shall be no end.

As Acts 17:24, 27-28 (NKJV) tells us, "God, who made the world and everything in it...does not dwell in temples made with hands. ...He is not far from each one of us; for in Him we live and move and have our being...."

The structure that exists on the earth with the capacity to house God's presence and glory is man. God, the greatest force in the universe, will dwell in those who choose to receive the High Priest Jesus of the New Covenant, who died and rose from the dead to restore us to the dominion and authority God originally created for us.

CHAPTER 11

WORSHIP BRINGS SIMPLICITY

Remember how life was before things became so demanding and complicated? God wants us to go back to a place of simplicity in our walk with Him. He wants us to lead an uncomplicated life by following His appropriately simple method of listening to what He tells us, then doing it. This is easy when we know how to worship Him in spirit and truth.

God does not require us to follow a sequence of rituals to enter His presence. Of course, we are to assemble ourselves together and let all things be done decently and in order, as Hebrews 10:25 and 1 Corinthians 14:40 tell us. As long as traditions and rituals in a service invite God's presence, they fulfill the purpose for which they were established. But He does not require a song or a hymn, or a ceremonial offering for us to enter His presence. As we have seen, all that He requires is for us to worship Him in spirit and truth by coming clean before Him and allowing Him to wash us with the water from the laver of His Word.

As we saw before, God is interested in our heart. For God to be able to do everything He wants to do for us and through us, we must have our heart completely open to Him. When our confidence and trust are in Him and we keep ourselves open to Him by admitting any shortcomings that we need His help in handling instead of trying to hide them, we are positioned to hear from Him and obey. A lifestyle of hearing and obeying God simplifies life.

Satan tries to complicate our life as much as possible to keep us out of close fellowship with God. When we aren't in close fellowship with God, we don't hear the instructions He is trying to give us, and we do things according to the way we think they should be done. When we follow our way, often different from the direction God is trying to give us, we complicate our life even more by adding more things to do to the things He intended.

PERPETUAL PRAISE

Perpetual praise is a term I use which denotes a consistent lifestyle of unbroken fellowship with God. Our vertical relationship of unbroken fellowship with God should also be exemplified in our horizontal relationship with each other as believers according to 1 John 1:7, which states:

> *But if we walk in the light, as he is in the light, we have fellowship one with another, and the blood of Jesus Christ his Son cleanseth us from all sin.*

We can conclude from this scripture that if we walk in the light as He is in the light, *then* and only *then* will we experience true fellowship with each other. However, when we hide or refuse to walk in the forensic clarity of the illuminating life of God, our fellowship is at risk.

One extremely vital way to assure that we walk in a state of perpetual praise is for those of us who are leaders to not only study when we are preparing to teach a message but to abide in a mode of continual study and meditation, keeping ourselves filled with the knowledge and truth of God. When we develop this attribute as a lifestyle, we will cross over into what I call a "state of overflow." God desires to bring us to a seasoned place of operating from the overflow in our life. When we run to study or pray only when it is time for us to teach at a major meeting, we begin to see our privileged opportunity of communion and fellowship as an obligation and duty.

Once we develop a lifestyle of perpetual praise and fellowship, we begin to become sensitive to the Lord's continual leading and guiding as we see in Isaiah 58:11:

> *And the LORD shall guide thee continually, and satisfy thy soul in drought, and make fat thy bones: and thou shalt be like a watered garden, and like a spring of water, whose waters fail not.*

God desires people who are willing to allow themselves to live and move and have their being in Him alone! He does not want hired saints who rush in to get their time in His presence as a necessary deposit to function momentarily.

Perpetual praise and communion simplifies our life and promotes a healthy lifestyle of walking intimately with our God. He longs for this attribute to be developed in our life. A married couple would never want their spouse to perform pleasures simply from a perspective of obligation and duty! The true romance begins at the start of the day—at least for the woman! Everything else in the day is an extension of, "Good morning, honey. I love you."

Certainly no one wants a loved one who has to rush to get everything together to prove that they really do love you and are willing to fulfill their necessary duties. *No,* you want their love for you to come from the heart. This is the same way our Father feels when we rush around to "prove" we love Him as part of our preparation to minister for Him. Our love for Him is apparent when we make a point of consistently doing what we know to do to keep ourselves in a place of wanting to be in His presence as much as possible because we enjoy learning from and spending time with Him. When passion and the simplicity of worship proceed from the heart, we pant for the unbroken fellowship through perpetual praise. Psalm 42:1 (NASB) tells us:

> *As the deer pants for the water brooks, so my soul pants for Thee, O God.*

HONORING GOD IN OUR HEART

In an earlier chapter, we read Jesus' graphic expression of the things that defile our heart. From this and other scriptures, we know how to guard our heart to keep it undefiled in order to stay in close fellowship with God. Because the mouth speaks out of the abundance of the heart, we need to renew our mind to the Word of God and put the Word into our heart, so that we can speak it back out from our heart.

> *But those things which proceed out of the mouth come forth from the heart; and they defile the man.*
>
> Matthew 15:18

In this scripture, Jesus shows the eternal connection between the mouth and the heart. We already saw how important it is for the heart and mouth to agree, and Jesus made very strong statements concerning this connection during worship. From reading His statement in Matthew 15:7-9 (NKJV) we can see that true worship supersedes oratorical lip service. Even the prophets of old warned of this.

> *"Hypocrites! Well did Isaiah prophesy about you, saying: 'These people draw near to Me with their mouth, and honor Me with their lips, but their heart is far from Me. And in vain they worship Me, teaching as doctrines the commandments of men.'"*

Jesus viewed hypocritical worship as proclaiming worship with our mouth while housing a different attitude within our heart.

Because we draw near to God with our mouth does not mean that we honor Him in our heart. If our voices do not reflect our daily choices, God considers that to be vain worship, which is useless, senseless, and definitely unacceptable to Him.

Some of us think of "worship" as the activities in the worship service we attend on Sunday and, for some of us, on Wednesday evening. We may think of worship as the slow songs we sing to usher us into the Lord's presence or the preliminaries before the delivery of the message of God's Word. To us, worship may be singing the songs projected on a screen or the traditional songs, so poetically proclaiming God's glory and might, printed in hymnbooks. We may think of worship as such supernatural manifestations in a service as a "glory cloud" rolling in, the gifts of the Spirit in operation, people falling under the power of God, intensely dancing in the Spirit as David did, or waiting in silence before the Lord.

TO OBEY IS BETTER THAN SACRIFICE

Whether these activities are actually acts of worship is determined by our heart attitude—whether we are worshipping God in truth in the midst of them. If we are only sacrificing our time and energy to be present and participate physically in the activities while our heart is far from God, we are in the same category as King Saul. The prophet Samuel told Saul that to obey is better than sacrifice because Saul's life exemplified the opposite.

The prophet Samuel said to Saul:

> *..."Has the LORD as great delight in burnt offerings and sacrifices, as in obeying the voice of the LORD? Behold, to obey is better than sacrifice, and to heed than the fat of rams."*
>
> 1 Samuel 15:22 NKJV

Saul offered sacrifices to God in the very act of disobeying God's directions to him. Saul offered as a sacrifice to the Lord sheep and oxen from the very spoil he had taken instead of utterly destroying it as God had told him to do! (1 Sam. 15:3,8,9,15,21.)

Saul's kind of sacrifice does not fit in the category of presenting our bodies as "a living sacrifice, holy, acceptable to God"! As discussed before, a sacrifice is something that you allow *God* to place on the altar that costs you something and means a great deal to you. We know that God viewed an obedient lifestyle as being far more acceptable than a sacrificial temple offering. In examining ourselves in the light of the true meaning of worship, we may find that, like Saul, we are also offering sacrifices, and ones of our own design, to the Lord rather than obeying Him.

David knew how to offer a proper sacrifice to the Lord. As a servant of God, he knew about giving costly sacrifices without holding back. He never wanted to give the Lord anything that didn't cost him something. In saying to God, "You do not desire sacrifice, or else I would give it..." (Ps. 51:16 NKJV), David wasn't trying to flatter God, he had the capabilities to lavishly sacrifice to the Lord. We read in 1 Chronicles 21:24 (NKJV) that David said:

> *"...I will surely buy it for the full price, for I will not take what is yours for the LORD, nor offer burnt offerings with that which costs me nothing."*

And again David states in 1 Chronicles 29:3 (NKJV):

> *"Moreover, because I have set my affection on the house of my God, I have given to the house of my God, over and above all that I have prepared for the holy house, my own special treasure of gold and silver."*

David made this sacrifice not only out of national treasure, but also out of his personal bank account. (See 1 Chron. 29:3,4.) Based on an average current price of gold and silver per ounce at the time of this writing, the value of one talent of gold and silver, and the value of David's special treasure of gold and silver (v. 4), the current equivalent of David's sacrifice follows.

GOLD	SILVER
\$325.00/oz. X 16 = \$5,200/lb.	\$4.45/oz. X 16 = \$71.20/lb.
\$5,200 X 82 lb. = \$426,400/talent	\$71.20 X 94lb. = \$6,692.80/talent
\$426,400 X 3,000 = \$1,279,200,000	\$6,692.80 X 7,000 = \$46,849,600
Total Value in U.S.\$ for Gold	**Total Value in U.S.\$ for Silver**
\$1,279,200,000	**\$46,849,600**

Grand total for present value of King David's offering is:

\$1,326,049,600

(One billion, three hundred twenty-six million, forty-nine thousand, six hundred dollars)

Even though David did know how to sacrifice appropriately by giving out of his heart to God, as represented by the best he could give according to Old Testament sacrifices, we discover, through reading in the Bible about David's life and reading the psalms he wrote, that the way to God is not through altar sacrifices, but through a broken spirit and a contrite heart. As David wrote in Psalm 51:17 (NKJV): "The sacrifices of God are a broken spirit, a broken and a contrite heart—these, O God, You will not despise."

We must come back to the very essence of sacrificial worship. Jesus was our sacrifice for sin. Today our sacrifice in worship is to approach God with a contrite heart to give Him all our areas in which we need to develop.

Another aspect of laying down our life before God in true worship is maintaining a heart attitude of willingness and readiness to obey Him. Many churches insert the following statement in their bulletin: *"Enter to worship...depart to serve."* Some people interpret this to mean that serving is displaying Christian bumper stickers on their cars, singing Christian songs on their jobs, or preaching at the workplace when they are being paid to work!

A Christian bumper sticker on a car is fine, again, as a reflection of a heart given totally to God and someone who worships Him in truth. Obeying what the Bible tells us to do is the part of worship that serves: telling a lost person without hope about Jesus, feeding the poor, laying hands on the sick, taking care of the shut-in, homeless, widow, and orphan.

SEEKING MAN'S APPROVAL COMPLICATES LIFE

God wants to search beneath the surface into the depths of your heart—much deeper into the real you. He is not impressed with the way things appear to be to the naked eye.

In Luke 16:15 (NKJV) Jesus speaks of the Pharisees who justified themselves before men instead of God.

> *And He said to them, "You are those who justify yourselves before men, but God knows your hearts. For what is highly esteemed among men is an abomination in the sight of God."*

Many times in life we seek the approval of men and women who have rejected God. If there are places in your life where you have departed from your first love (Jesus) and exchanged activity in front of people for true worship and duty for true sacrifice, please acknowledge this to God and ask for His forgiveness. He wants you to grow closer to Him and hear His voice, so that you can move steadily forward on the path He has for you rather than making choices on your own that complicate your life and sidetrack you from completing your destiny.

As we come almost to the close of this chapter, put the book aside, if possible, and apologize to the Lord for how complicated you have allowed your life to become. Tell Him how sorry you are for being more focused on external, nominal things than on internal, spiritual things. Allow your heart to be remorseful of the areas of your life where you have sought the approval of man more than the approval of God and repent of this.

Search and examine yourself to find out what areas in your life you have allowed to derail pertaining to your purpose, passion, and calling. Rehearse the times you have been regretful when you momentarily took your eyes off the Lord. It really is all about Him at the end of the day! That's all He wants—your fervent commitment to Him. He desires to be Lord again over the areas of your life in which you have slipped into an unconscious, self-willed lifestyle.

In every area of our life in which we lack accountability, we also have fear and pride. God wants access to any area like that so that His headship can reign and He can be glorified in your life. Whatever shortcoming you keep to yourself is an open door for self-destruction. Give God your all so that He can make His total abode in you.

The enemy attempts to deceive us into believing that we have everything under control. Only with the help of the Father are things really under control. There is nothing too hard for Him in the appointed time. Things that are impossible with men are possible with God. With Him all things are possible. (See Matt. 19:26.)

God is waiting for your reckless abandonment toward Him in the area of worship. Worship is a place of absolute surrender. The Father is waiting in that place to restore to you the joy of your salvation and remove the stressful chaos in your life. The majority of the things that we give our attention do not amount to anything in eternity. The opinions of men, possessions, accolades of life, reputations, ministry budgets, or event calendars will not matter in eternity.

As He opens the eyes of our understanding to see life for what it really is, we will eventually lessen our "things to do list," and He will teach us how to trust Him for the things we are endeavoring to do in our own strength. We will learn the art of true delegation as we trust Him in the lives of the people we lead. To simplify our life and progress directly on the path He has for us to fulfill our destiny, it is time to discover what the Lord requires of us, and not man, by speaking in line with what God has for us and walking closer and closer with Him through true and divine worship.

PART 4

MATURE YOUR SOUL: THE VISIBLE GLORY

CHAPTER 12

RESTORED TO POWER

Just as God desires to abide in us, He desires that we abide in Him. By abiding in us, God makes His power available to us. He has delegated to us, earthen vessels, the excellency of His power and His authority. God will release His glory through us when we abide in Him. As we yield more of ourselves to Him, He will be able to manifest His glory in greater measure through us. This is part of His plan for us.

From the time of Adam to the New Covenant, God revealed a different facet of Himself to different individuals to prepare man for restoration. God was preparing man to be restored to the dominion and authority as in the Garden of Eden before the fall. From the fall of man until now, God has been in the business of restoring.

RESTORATION OF MAN'S DOMINION

God created man, Adam, in His own image, on a level to fellowship and commune with Him, placing the quintessence of all that makes Him God into man. Adam lived in the glory of God; his very nature was the nature of God. He walked with God and had an insatiable appetite for Him. Adam never knew life separated from God before the treason, when man disobeyed God in the Garden and sin separated man from fellowship with God.

Before man fell, Creation could not distinguish the difference between Adam and God. God's essence was also Adam's essence because God truly created Adam in His image and likeness. From the beginning, it was *El Elyon's* original mandate to house the very nature of Himself inside man. In delegating to man His power and authority, He made Adam privy to the same creative ability He has. Adam was to rule and reign on the earth as his Father did in heaven.

Adam knew no limitations, intimidations, fear, ego complexes, or insecurities. None of these existed in the Garden. Leadership in its highest level was operative and in full manifestation in the Garden with the only leadership characteristic that existed, dominion and authority. This act of ruling and reigning over God's earth is supernatural leadership at its climax.

Adam received direct instructions express from heaven, and as long as he followed these directives of God, he was guaranteed success in life. Adam never had to question God's intent because the Almighty made His will crystal clear. However, when Adam forfeited his leadership role and allowed what was supposed to be a gift to him, Eve, to challenge his authority, he compromised his supernatural leadership position. Genesis 3:13 (NKJV) tells us that Eve was deceived:

> *"And the LORD God said to the woman, 'What is this you have done?' The woman said, 'The serpent deceived me, and I ate.'"*

Eve never received direct instructions from the Almighty. Nonetheless, Adam knew exactly what God had instructed him to do but allowed the enemy to tempt and draw him into disobedience with the deception that Satan would give Adam something that would make him like God. (Gen. 3:5.) Adam allowed Satan to deceive him into thinking that he should try to obtain something he already had! Adam had already inherited from his Father the image and likeness of God. Through the serpent Satan said:

"For God knows that in the day you eat of it your eyes will be opened, and you will be like God, knowing good and evil."

Genesis 3:5 NKJV

Adam was already like God indeed. He already possessed authority over the serpent, and all he needed to do was operate in his divine leadership capacity to rebuke the serpent.

COMPROMISE BRINGS LOSS

Adam's actions caused the divine order of leadership to become perverted. When Adam compromised the glory of God, he ended up losing. In life, whatever we compromise to get we will *always* ultimately lose! It may, at the time, appear that we are on the winning end of the stick, but it's only a matter of time before that which is hidden will be revealed.

There is no provision and accommodation for sin in God's presence. Sin always separates us from the presence, plan, provision, and peace of God. The luxury of sin is costly in our life. Sin has wages, and it always demands death. When we sin, something always dies. That is the price that sin requires. Our dreams die, the anointing dies, the peace dies, the confidence in the indwelling presence of God dies. God does not leave us, but our awareness and consciousness of His presence dies. Condemnation and guilt enter, and subconsciously we stray away from God. But thanks be to God, who always causes us to triumph in Christ Jesus! (See 2 Cor. 2:14.) The moment we invoke 1 John 1:9, we are immediately restored into proper relationship with our Heavenly Father:

If we confess our sins, he is faithful and just to forgive us our sins, and to cleanse us from all unrighteousness.

He is such a perfect Father. He has experienced the separation from His Creation and longs to guard that communion that has taken Him 6,000 years to restore.

The glory of God is the manifested presence of God. It is the tangible manifestation of God's character. In the New Covenant, God placed the excellency of His power in an earthen vessel. (See 2 Cor. 4:7; John 17:22.) If we weigh the temptation that Adam faced with the glory manifested within us, we can clearly see that there is no comparison. Paul said that even the afflictions in life, which he labeled as light, were not to be compared with the eternal weight of glory. (See 2 Cor. 4:17.) In other words, nothing compares to the glory of God.

GOD'S REVELATION OF HIMSELF TO MAN THROUGHOUT TIME

As we view God's dealings with man from Adam to the present, we can see a loving Father craving the restoration of His intimate relationship with man. Below, we look at two of the people of the Old Covenant to whom God revealed different aspects of Himself, Abraham and Moses.

ABRAHAM

God approaches Abraham as a friend and reveals His covenant nature to him. God teaches Abraham, as the chief custodian to the nations, a higher level of dominion and authority, of leadership. God makes him the financial steward over the nations and calls him away from his cultural upbringing into his awaiting inheritance. We read in Genesis 12:1-3 NKJV:

> *Now the LORD had said to Abram: "Get out of your country, from your family and from your father's house, to a land that I will show you. I will make you a great nation; I will bless you and make your name great; and you shall be a blessing. I will bless those who bless you, and I will curse him who curses you; and in you all the families of the earth shall be blessed."*

God positions Abraham as a leader and gives him a divine inheritance that establishes God's covenant throughout the earth, making a nation out of one man, a nation in which all mankind will have the opportunity to establish citizenship. He births inside Abraham (formerly "Abram," whose name God changes to "Abraham," meaning, "a father of many nations," Gen. 17:5) the sheer definition of faith, and Abraham becomes the founding father of it. Abraham lays the foundation of faith and the covenant promises of God that will transcend his generation. He becomes a link between God and man pertaining to our covenant rights because we are now Abraham's seed and heirs according to the promise.

> *Christ has redeemed us from the curse of the law, having become a curse for us (for it is written, "Cursed is everyone who hangs on a tree"), that the blessing of Abraham might come upon the Gentiles in Christ Jesus, that we might receive the promise of the Spirit through faith.*
>
> Galatians 3:13,14 NKJV

How profound it was of our Heavenly Father, in spite of the deadness of Sarah's womb, to give a promise of a seed. This anticipation eventually becomes anxiety for both Sarah and Abraham, who compromise to obtain what they ultimately lose. As a result, they have to go back to the original blueprint and intent of God.

God uses the waiting process to teach Abraham faith and patience, one of God's methods that each subsequent generation will need to learn in order to obtain the results of that promise.

MOSES

Through Moses, God continues to reveal different aspects of His character as He progressively prepares man to know how, in the New Covenant, to live in restored dominion and authority. Moses' example of obedience, the opposite of the example we saw in King Saul's life, again divulges that a guaranteed key for favor and success with God is obedience. Moses, who learns God's ways and operates in an intimate place with God, exemplifies the words the prophet Samuel spoke much later to King Saul, "...to obey is better than sacrifice..." (1 Sam. 15:22).

God also teaches us about His glory, its purpose, and how to partake of it through the example of Moses' life. God is preparing us to be the type of New Covenant believers and leaders who will be strong enough to house Him, in all His Shekinah glory, and allow that glory to manifest into the earth.

This Shekinah, "the visible majesty of the Divine Presence,"[1] is the same Divine Presence that was in the thick cloud and fire under which Mount Sinai quaked. (Exod. 19:16-18.) It is the same Divine Presence that was in the cloud that rested on the tabernacle of meeting when the glory then filled the Tabernacle—the sanctuary God told Moses to build for Him to dwell among His people (see Exod. 40:34 NKJV; 25:8). It is the Tabernacle accessible only through following God's explicit instructions "lest they" (the priests ministering to God on behalf of men) "die," as we examined previously. This is the same Divine Presence that went before the children of Israel in the wilderness to lead the way by day in a pillar of a cloud and by night to give them light in a pillar of fire. (See Exod. 13:18-22.)

Not only throughout the history of the Old Covenant is God preparing us as New Covenant believers to house and allow to manifest through us the same Shekinah, He is preparing us to house an even greater manifestation of His glory! God promises us that the glory of the "latter house shall be greater than of the former" (Hag. 2:9).

A common mistake among some believers today is assuming that we can partake of the glory without aligning ourselves with the proper order of God. Partaking of the glory for us today is possible because the New Covenant believer's accessibility to the glory is the very restoration of God's original, prescribed order for man in the Garden before the fall—that of operating in dominion and authority in life! We can see that for God's glory to manifest through us as believers today, we must align with God's prescribed order, His distinct way of doing things that He designed for us to follow. To enter into His realm and way of living, we are to live by the principle He lives by, His Word.

God has always wanted order in His house, His purpose being to release His glory without measure. Just as Adam had an insatiable appetite for God and lived in God's glory before the fall, Moses developed an insatiable appetite for God's presence, especially for experiencing God's glory. Moses was able to partake of God's glory because he aligned himself in obedience with God's methods of operation. Unlike King Saul, Moses desired to obey and put his trust in God to use him in spite of the limitations Moses saw in himself.

PLEASURE VERSUS PURPOSE

God called both Abraham and Moses out of a life of convenience, temporal luxury, and securities to obey His plan for them. The plan God had for each of them was not only for their lives but for the lives of the people of their generation and generations to come. We can see from reading about the lives of both men that what we do as believers, especially those of us in leadership, affects the lives of others. The key ingredient for guaranteed favor and success with God is obedience. To obey God is better than any sacrifice that we might offer to try to earn God's favor or His approval of something we did in disobedience as did King Saul. We cannot earn God's approval or love. We already have it. If we disobey, rather than trying to appease God into accepting what we did by offering a sacrifice or penance, we need to repent by coming clean before Him, accepting His forgiveness, and moving on with Him.

God wants obedience from us. He wants us to obey Him in order to play our part with other believers in the Body of Christ as He orchestrates our individual destinies to perform His will that transcends generations. For example, God's deliverance of the Israelites from slavery in Egypt was a part of His purpose that transcends all generations.

Fulfilling our purpose in life often means forsaking activities that we would rather be doing. To maintain our closeness with God, we will need to make choices to obey Him rather than pursue our own pleasures. As we grow in our relationship with God, we mature to a level in which nothing else satisfies us but the presence of the Almighty.

GOD CALLS MOSES TO DELIVER EGYPT

Moses' first encounter with God is through an angel of the Lord appearing to him in a flame out of the midst of a bush. Unlike Adam, Moses doesn't know how to relate to God at all when he first encounters Him; therefore, God relates to Moses patiently and tenderly as the loving Father He is.

Moses sees the bush burning, yet it is not being consumed. He turns aside to see this sight, to see why the bush is not being consumed, something he has never witnessed before. And when he does, he encounters something else he has never experienced before—the power and glory of God! God speaks to Moses out of the bush, instructing him to take off his shoes because the place where he stands is holy ground. (See Exod. 3:2-5.) It is at this time that God gives Moses the assignment to bring the Israelites out of Egypt.

> *And the LORD said: "I have surely seen the oppression of My people who are in Egypt, and have heard their cry because of their taskmasters, for I know their sorrows.*
>
> *"Come now, therefore, and I will send you to Pharaoh that you may bring My people, the children of Israel, out of Egypt."*
>
> Exodus 3:7,10 NKJV

Moses is a man who operates in a high level of leadership in Pharaoh's house. Nothing is off limits to him as he lives a life of luxury, authority, and pleasure. But what Moses is about to embark upon in this new level of leadership will be a great paradigm shift. He doesn't fully understand that he is about to exchange pleasure for purpose. He does have an indication from hearing God's directions that this type of leadership will be quite different from the type he knows, in which he feels self-confident and in control.

When Moses protests that the people won't believe him or listen, God gives him the ability to display supernatural power so that the people will believe their God appeared to him. (Exod. 4:1-9.) When Moses presents to God his limitation of being slow in speech and tongue as a reason he is not a good candidate for leading the people out of Egypt, God responds that He will be with Moses' mouth and teach him what he should say. (Exod. 4:10-12.) In other words, through God's relationship with Moses, we see an example of another aspect of God's character (as Paul refers to later in 2 Cor. 12:9): God's strength is made perfect in Moses' weakness!

The price of pleasure versus purpose is a revelation that every one of us believers, every leader, must one day come to reckon with in order to fulfill the purpose of God in each of our lives.

The first stage of Moses' metamorphosis begins as described in Exodus 2:11-12. God infuses His sovereign mandate into Moses, and Moses responds as if it has been physically injected. When Moses sees an Egyptian beating an Israelite, he becomes enraged at how his people are being treated.

> *Now it came to pass in those days, when Moses was grown, that he went out to his brethren and looked at their burdens. And he saw an Egyptian beating a Hebrew, one of his brethren. So he looked this way and that way, and when he saw no one, he killed the Egyptian and hid him in the sand.*
>
> Exodus 2:11,12 NKJV

Moses senses a type of indignation that he has never experienced before while consumed with the pleasures of the palace. The turmoil inside him toiling between two natures lands him in a situation with an Egyptian soldier. Without a thought, Moses responds to the defense of his Hebrew brother and ends up with a murder charge! Now a fugitive, who was once a prince, Moses has an encounter with God through a bush conversation. God begins to reveal not only His glory to Moses but the very purpose of the glory. God is in the process of making Moses a leader who will be able to organize the people for the great exodus and develop a people who will truly worship their God.

As an awesome leader, Moses leads the children of Israel out of Egyptian captivity, but unfortunately the children of Israel are not fully aware of why they were liberated. They think that God is delivering them so that they no longer will have to make bricks, wake up early, and be accountable to Pharaoh—no more submission, no more answering to the hierarchy.

God is delivering them from the bondage of their taskmasters because He heard their cry out of their oppression. Little do the Israelites know that He is also delivering them for His express purpose. He delivers them for Himself, to house His presence. He wants His presence to surround them so that the nations of the earth will know that they are His chosen, peculiar people, a holy nation to Himself who are called to and translated into His miraculous will.

In Exodus 19:1-7 (NKJV) we can see this clearly revealed.

> *In the third month after the children of Israel had gone out of the land of Egypt, on the same day, they came to the Wilderness of Sinai.*
>
> *For they had departed from Rephidim, had come to the Wilderness of Sinai, and camped in the wilderness. So Israel camped there before the mountain.*
>
> *And Moses went up to God, and the Lord called to him from the mountain, saying, "Thus you shall say to the house of Jacob, and tell the children of Israel:*
>
> *'You have seen what I did to the Egyptians, and how I bore you on eagles' wings and brought you to Myself.*
>
> *'Now therefore, if you will indeed obey My voice and keep My covenant, then you shall be a special treasure to Me above all people; for all the earth is Mine.*

'And you shall be to Me a kingdom of priests and a holy nation.' These are the words which you shall speak to the children of Israel."

So Moses came and called for the elders of the people, and laid before them all these words which the LORD commanded him.

God states that He brought them out of Egypt for Himself that they may be a special treasure to Him above all people. In life, we must come to understand that God's deliverance in our life is not only about us; it's about God's sovereign will in the earth for all humanity. In other words, it's all about God's plan for humanity, not just about us!

God is preparing ex-slaves to be leaders and examples to the nations. He is preparing a people to walk with Him and experience His glory, and with the manifestation of His glory comes provision and protection. He provides a pillar of fire by night to warm them from the chilling winds of the desert and a pillar of cloud by day to protect them from the scorching desert sun. Through the presence of His glory, He provides quail and bread from heaven. In the presence of His glory, the Israelites' shoes and clothes do not wear out during the entire forty years! All the surrounding nations are able to view this.

MOSES ENCOUNTERS THE GLORY OF GOD

Before Moses can encounter the glory, he first has to be consecrated. In a previous chapter, we looked in detail at the Old Testament example and shadow of heavenly things to come with the New Covenant. Moses' consecration before encountering the glory is an example and shadow to us of the need to come clean before God in order to experience the fullness of His power and fellowship in life.

In his new level of godly leadership, Moses has to learn to be a servant to the people and an intercessor for them. Moses' consecration allows him to hear from God for the people. He cannot require consecration from the people without requiring it of himself. That would not be proper leadership. Moses cannot demand a standard of holiness for the people and not maintain it in his own life. Frankly put, he has to live what he is preaching as a leader. This is the place that our power to lead becomes manifest.

Under the leadership of Pharaoh, Moses is not accountable to the children of Israel at all. They are the slaves and servants to the regime in which he lives. Moses benefits from their labor that provides a luxurious lifestyle for all who are living in the palace. The national economy is at the expense of the labor of the children of Israel.

In following God's leadership, Moses finds himself under a totally different priestly order that is poles apart in mindset. He must now be a shepherd to the people instead of a taskmaster and also be the mediator between God and the people. Because Moses has the responsibility of being the mediator between God and man, God requires more of Moses than He does of the children of Israel. Moses has to sanctify himself and adopt a lifestyle of fasting and prayer. He also occasionally separates from his wife and family so that the family pressure they inflict upon him cannot influence him.

Moses has to develop the fruit of patience in his life, an attribute God also emphasized with Abraham and Sarah, because he sacrifices his life for the children of Israel, carnal, whining babies who are never satisfied. Moses possibly thinks to himself sometimes, *Is this all worth it?*

The children of Israel want only the provision and protection of God, but Moses desires to know the ways of the God of provision. Therefore, God demonstrates to the children of Israel His capabilities, His power, and His provision, but to Moses He shows His ways because Moses operates in a more intimate relationship with God.

Intimacy with God is a must for believers, and especially leaders, in this century. Listening to teaching tapes, watching Christian television, and going to the latest conferences are helpful in learning about God, but we don't grow into an intimate relationship with God through these activities. We must come away with God as Moses did and wait in His presence until He reveals His glory.

We believers, and especially leaders, must remain diligent to stay on track with God and hungry for His presence by examining ourselves for limitations we need to present to God, guarding our heart against ingratitude or pride that might creep in and compromise our devotion to God, and guarding our tongue to keep speaking in line with God's Word and our destiny. We need to grow into and stay in that mature place where nothing else satisfies us like His presence. A consecrated life is exemplary. Just as God's glory shone from Moses' face after Moses had been in His presence, God's presence will also engulf us and enable us to do the work of the ministry in this perplexed century, and reap the harvest as great numbers of unbelievers come to Jesus.

Prophetic promises are coming to pass, and we will witness more prophecy fulfilled in our time than in the past centuries combined. We are closest to the consummation of the church age than we have ever been before, and are also living in the greatest age of the harvest. Daniel 12:3 NKJV states:

> *Those who are wise shall shine like the brightness of the firmament, and those who turn many to righteousness like the stars forever and ever.*

Previously, we noted other prophets who foretold the great harvest.

> *"And it shall come to pass afterward that I will pour out My Spirit on all flesh; your sons and your daughters shall prophesy, your old men shall dream dreams, your young men shall see visions. And also on My menservants and on My maidservants I will pour out My Spirit in those days."*
>
> Joel 2:28,29 NKJV

Now it shall come to pass in the latter days that the mountain of the LORD's house shall be established on the top of the mountains, and shall be exalted above the hills; and all nations shall flow to it.

Isaiah 2:2 NKJV

Many nations shall come and say, "Come, and let us go up to the mountain of the LORD, to the house of the God of Jacob; he will teach us His ways, and we shall walk in His paths." For out of Zion the law shall go forth, and the word of the LORD from Jerusalem.

Micah 4:2 NKJV

Those of us in leadership must hear directly from God on behalf of the people we lead, and all of us as believers, through our lifestyle example, must usher the people we lead or to whom we minister individually into a place of intimate lifestyle worship, a surrendered lifestyle to God. We cannot afford to miss the hour of our visitation and outpouring due to a lack of consecration. Remember, God promises us that the glory of the latter house, or temple (NKJV), will be greater than that of the former.

"'The glory of this latter temple shall be greater than the former,' says the LORD of hosts. 'And in this place I will give peace,' says the LORD of hosts."

Haggai 2:9 NKJV

The Shekinah glory of the Lord in our times will be greater in us, we who "are the temple of God," in whom "the Spirit of God dwells" (1 Cor. 3:16 NKJV), than it was in the previous Old Covenant temple or Tabernacle in which it rested! If the level of the glory is greater in this time in history than it was in any other, then the level of consecration must be greater. God is demanding godly leadership and for all believers to prepare to operate according to God's divine order, His methods and in His dominion and authority, to handle the level of glory He will pour out to meet the needs in these times.

As described in detail previously, the manner in which God's presence appeared and affected Mt. Sinai was so terrifying to the Israelites in the camp that they all trembled. (Exod. 19:16.) Many Bible scholars believe that the passage in Hebrews 12:21 describes the encounter with God's presence described in Exodus 19:9-25 and Moses' reaction to it: "so terrifying was the sight that Moses said, 'I am exceedingly afraid and trembling'" (NKJV).

Moses, although amazed at the magnitude of the manifestation of God's presence in this experience, is not surprised by the nature of the method God uses. Moses is already familiar with some of God's methods, having already experienced this one on a much smaller scale when Moses first experienced the Lord's presence as a fire in the bush that burned without being consumed. Because of the relationship he is forming with God, even though Moses' flesh reacts in fear to the physical sight, Moses is not afraid of God's intent and is able to carry on in obedience to the Lord's instructions.

Moses is hungry and thirsty for God's presence. What the children of Israel fear to experience and draw near to, Moses walks in the midst of and remains there forty days and forty nights. Exodus 24:12-18 (NKJV) tells us:

> *Then the LORD said to Moses, "Come up to Me on the mountain and be there; and I will give you tablets of stone, and the law and commandments which I have written, that you may teach them."*
>
> *So Moses arose with his assistant Joshua, and Moses went up to the mountain of God.*
>
> *And he said to the elders, "Wait here for us until we come back to you. Indeed Aaron and Hur are with you. If any man has a difficulty, let him go to them."*
>
> *Then Moses went up into the mountain, and a cloud covered the mountain.*
>
> *Now the glory of the LORD rested on Mount Sinai, and the cloud covered it six days. And on the seventh day He called to Moses out of the midst of the cloud.*

The sight of the glory of the L*ORD* *was like a consuming fire on the top of the mountain in the eyes of the children of Israel.*

So Moses went into the midst of the cloud and went up into the mountain. And Moses was on the mountain forty days and forty nights.

The experience that Moses has in meeting with God results in Moses' obtaining detailed instructions for the blueprint of the Tabernacle. This pattern has to be a replica of that which is in heaven for God to obligate Himself to occupy it with the glory of His presence.

The insatiable appetite Moses develops for the presence of God is so great that more of God is never enough, especially when it comes to the glory of God. Moses' hunger and thirst for God's glory positions him to be selected by God as the chief builder of the Tabernacle, the first dwelling place on the earth among men God chooses to occupy since the time of Adam.

CHAPTER 13

ABIDING IN HIM

Just as Moses ushered in the presence of God living *among* men, John the Baptist ushered in the presence of God dwelling *inside* men. John comes on the scene in the New Covenant revealing to us the purpose of God's indwelling presence. *We* would now be the tabernacles to house God's glory.

Just as God gave Moses requirements of consecration, He also set John apart. John came on the scene with a voice like a trumpet, crying out in the wilderness, "Prepare ye the way of the Lord, make his paths straight" (Matt. 3:3). In other words, "Get your house in order because the Messiah is coming!"

His message spoken to the people of his time to prepare for the coming of the Messiah speaks to us. His message is one of repentance, instructing us to change our way of living, thinking, leading, and consequently, the example we set for others. John warns us to line up our life according to the will of the Father. John came on the scene operating in the spirit of Elijah to turn the heart of the Father back to the children, the disobedient to the wisdom of the just, and to make ready a people who would be prepared for the Lord.

This is exactly our state as believers today! There is great pressure upon believers and leaders in this century to yield to the pleasures of a self-willed life. But we read that Jesus said in John 4:34 (NKJV):

"...My food is to do the will of Him who sent Me, and to finish His work."

We will never be able to finish the work that has been mandated to us until we surrender our will, agenda, and ambitions to the will of the Father. If those of us who are leaders are going to lead effectively, we must first surrender our *will;* and as we learn from John 3:30, Jesus must increase in our life and we must decrease. We are reminded in John 15:16 (NKJV) that we didn't choose Jesus; He chose us and appointed us to bear fruit that would remain.

"You did not choose Me, but I chose you and appointed you that you should go and bear fruit, and that your fruit should remain, that whatever you ask the Father in My name He may give you."

Galatians 5:22-23 (NKJV) lists the fruit of the Spirit:

But the fruit of the Spirit is love, joy, peace, longsuffering, kindness, goodness, faithfulness, gentleness, self-control. Against such there is no law.

This is effective ministry and leadership: bearing fruit that remains and transcends to successive generations. True and efficient ministry and leadership are accurately judged after we have passed on. No one is a success without a successor. It is imperative to note that the Scripture passages in John do not talk to us at all about *how* to bear the fruit that is identified in Galatians. In John 15:4 (NKJV) the Bible says:

"Abide in Me, and I in you. As the branch cannot bear fruit of itself, unless it abides in the vine, neither can you, unless you abide in Me."

Could it be perhaps that the reason we are not experiencing lasting fruit is because we, as leaders, are not abiding in Jesus? "How do we bear fruit?" By abiding in the Vine! We cannot bear fruit without the Vine, Jesus. John 15:5 (NKJV) states:

"I am the vine, you are the branches. He who abides in Me, and I in him, bears much fruit; for without Me you can do nothing."

In this verse John emphasizes much fruit! We should be able to judge effective leadership by the fruit that is borne, and all believers by their fruit. "Every tree is known by its own fruit…" (Luke 5:44 NKJV). If we are not bearing fruit, we are merely caught up in duties that are under the disguise of ministry.

It is the indwelling presence and glory of God that does the work according to John 14:10-11 (NKJV):

"Do you not believe that I am in the Father, and the Father in Me? The words that I speak to you I do not speak on My own authority; but the Father who dwells in Me does the works.

"Believe Me that I am in the Father and the Father in Me, or else believe Me for the sake of the works themselves."

Repeatedly, we can see the indwelling presence of God coupled with bearing fruit and doing the work. Just when you thought it couldn't get any better, John 17:4-10 (NKJV) reveals that the same glory that Jesus shared with the Father has been given to us:

"I have glorified You on the earth. I have finished the work which You have given Me to do.

"And now, O Father, glorify Me together with Yourself, with the glory which I had with You before the world was.

"I have manifested Your name to the men whom You have given Me out of the world. They were Yours, You gave them to Me, and they have kept Your word.

"Now they have known that all things which You have given Me are from You.

"For I have given to them the words which You have given Me; and they have received them, and have known surely that I came forth from You; and they have believed that You sent Me.

"I pray for them. I do not pray for the world but for those whom You have given Me, for they are Yours.

"And all Mine are Yours, and Yours are Mine, and I am glorified in them."

We see again in this text of Scripture that the glory is connected to the finishing work. Jesus Himself is glorified in us and the purpose of the glory is not to display our gifts *one to another!* His presence indwells us for the *work of the ministry!* John 17:18 (NKJV) states:

"As You sent Me into the world, I also have sent them into the world."

We are sent on His behalf to demonstrate the glory of God to the lost throughout the world. Jesus prays for all believers in John 17:20-23 (NKJV):

"I do not pray for these alone, but also for those who will believe in Me through their word;

"that they all may be one, as You, Father, are in Me, and I in You; that they also may be one in Us, that the world may believe that You sent Me.

"And the glory which You gave Me I have given them, that they may be one just as We are one:

"I in them, and You in Me; that they may be made perfect in one, and that the world may know that You have sent Me, and have loved them as You have loved Me."

Jesus prayed that the glory given to us would be a witness to the world. We were ordained by God to be carriers of this glory to the world; we have a promise that we would do greater works. There are 6.5 billion people on the face of the earth waiting for a manifestation of the glory of God. Romans 8:19-21 (NKJV) tells us:

For the earnest expectation of the creation eagerly waits for the revealing of the sons of God. For the creation was subjected to futility, not willingly, but because of Him who subjected it in hope; because the creation itself also will be delivered from the bondage of corruption into the glorious liberty of the children of God.

All of creation is groaning in anticipation of the glorious liberty of the children of God!

Whatever temporal pleasure we deny ourselves is not worthy to be compared to the glory revealed within us. Nothing that we are struggling with is worth the anointing! The enemy is after our glory because he lost his, and he despises anyone who is anointed and doing the work of the ministry. Our lifestyle of intimacy with God reminds him of his eternal failure and dethroned position.

The secret to a consecrated, set-apart life is intimacy with the Father. We should take time with Him and remove anything from our life that is causing a hindrance to the glory manifesting in our life. We are God's elect chosen before the foundations of the world, chosen to do good works that were established in Him. He longs for us to be in perpetual union with Him and desires to see us walk in our glorious liberty. There is a level of power and anointing waiting to be released in us as we yield to His presence. This will produce effective ministry and lasting fruit that will transcend to successive generations. Paul ended his struggle by saying in Galatians 2:20 (NKJV):

> *"I have been crucified with Christ; it is no longer I who live, but Christ lives in me; and the life which I now live in the flesh I live by faith in the Son of God, who loved me and gave Himself for me."*

If we are dead to sin, our struggle is over because we will have entered into another life.

Allow the light and the glory of God to envelop you as you are reading this, and let His glory draw you into Himself. Magnify the Lord daily and exalt His name in every area of your life. Give thanks to Him in all things. If you can't give thanks for something, you don't need it in your life! You will soon awaken, and the things of this world will become strangely dim in the light of His glory and grace. Just continue to look to Jesus, seek His face and worship Him. As you practice this as a way of life, a metamorphosis will take place.

Before you know it, you will find yourself eager to bear fruit for Him and to finish the work!

CHAPTER 14

REFLECTING GOD'S NATURE

God's principles reflect His nature, the fruit of His Spirit. As we abide in Jesus and allow the fruit of the Spirit to manifest in us to bear fruit on the earth that remains, we are manifesting God's nature. Previously we saw the importance of building godly character to maintain the ground we take for the Kingdom. We develop and maintain godly character by building upon God's principles, through consistently making choices that line up with them.

One of the most vital components for a believer's lifestyle in representing Jesus is maintaining godly character, and this is especially vital for effective leadership. Building and maintaining good leadership characteristics as well as godly character traits result from intentional effort. A principle is a "basic truth, law, or assumption...," a "rule or standard," a "fixed or predetermined policy or mode of action...."[1] When we live according to principles, we develop an unwavering lifestyle of good character, building a sphere of self-accountability around us. Self-accountability means that we develop a lifestyle of being accountable to ourselves by taking self-inventory!

We must be true to who we are and how we see ourselves as leaders. Sometimes one of the hardest tasks to perform is to take inventory and observe our character as leaders in the Kingdom. The way that we are when no one is around is who we really are. It can sometimes be painful to be truthful with ourselves, especially when we become accustomed to the applause of men.

Living by principles provides an automatic self-check for us as leaders. God Himself is bound by controlling principles. When He uttered out His Word, His original council, thought, and nature were given voice. His uttered words later became flesh. God's inner voice and nature are expressions of His inward character. God's character, which no man could see, became flesh through God's utterance, and mirrored and reflected in totality His inward character through Jesus. In other words, God did not speak out false intentions. The words that He spoke reflected the same intent He housed inside of Him—His intent and His sovereign will are the same.

God orchestrated His principles to reflect His nature; He then bound Himself to these controlling principles through His own Word. When we, who are created in His image and likeness, align ourselves with the way God operates, we will receive the same results.

God operates only through His principles and laws. As we govern and live our life by His principles, we are guaranteed to obtain corresponding results. If we do things God's way, we will get God's results. As we practice this as a way of life, we will develop the type of character that will supersede nominal habitual practices. When we refuse to participate in situations that are against the principles of God, we will produce a most valuable and vital ingredient in the building blocks of our character called *integrity.* The Bible says that integrity will preserve us and keep us alive according to Proverbs 11:3 (NKJV):

> *The integrity of the upright will guide them, but the perversity of the unfaithful will destroy them.*

DEVELOPING CHARACTER IS WORK

We did not earn our gifts and callings; they are sovereignly given to us through the grace of God without repentance at His discretion.

However, character is an ongoing conscious effort of daily maintenance. Paul tells us in 1 Corinthians 15:31 (NKJV):

> *I affirm, by the boasting in you which I have in Christ Jesus our Lord,* ***I die daily.***

Paul was transparent when he described his internal struggle prolifically in Romans 7:14-25 (NKJV):

> *For we know that the law is spiritual, but I am carnal, sold under sin.*
>
> *For what I am doing, I do not understand. For what I will to do, that I do not practice; but what I hate, that I do.*
>
> *If, then, I do what I will not to do, I agree with the law that it is good.*
>
> *But now, it is no longer I who do it, but sin that dwells in me.*
>
> *For I know that in me (that is, in my flesh) nothing good dwells; for to will is present with me, but how to perform what is good I do not find.*
>
> *For the good that I will to do, I do not do; but the evil I will not to do, that I practice.*
>
> *Now if I do what I will not to do, it is no longer I who do it, but sin that dwells in me.*
>
> *I find then a law, that evil is present with me, the one who wills to do good.*
>
> *For I delight in the law of God according to the inward man.*
>
> *But I see another law in my members, warring against the law of my mind, and bringing me into captivity to the law of sin which is in my members.*
>
> *O wretched man that I am! Who will deliver me from this body of death?*
>
> *I thank God—through Jesus Christ our Lord! So then, with the mind I myself serve the law of God, but with the flesh the law of sin.*

God always gives us a way out of any entrapment. Paul gives us a declaration of hope as he ends the diabolical dispute with this statement in verses 24-25 (NKJV):

O wretched man that I am! Who will deliver me from this body of death?

I thank God—through Jesus Christ our Lord! So then, with the mind I myself serve the law of God, but with the flesh the law of sin.

We can see that building character takes work and a conscientious daily walk with the Holy Spirit. We are further instructed by Paul to work out our own soul salvation with fear and trembling in Philippians 2:12 (NKJV):

Therefore, my beloved, as you have always obeyed, not as in my presence only, but now much more in my absence, work out your own salvation with fear and trembling.

Notice that this text is not speaking of the salvation of our *spirit man* but rather our *soul,* which makes up our mind, will, and intellect. "Salvation" in this context is taken from the Greek word *soteria* meaning "rescue or safety (physically or morally)"; it also means to "deliver, health, salvation, save, saving."[2] Its meaning is similar to that of another Greek term, *sozo,* meaning "to save," that is, to "deliver or protect," "heal, preserve, save (self), do well, be (make) whole."[3]

Both of these terms speak of much more than our traditional view of salvation that includes the present-day forgiveness from sin and possession of eternal life in heaven following the coming of Christ. In this context salvation is used more descriptively to define the process of spiritual maturation each believer embarks upon when he or she accepts Jesus Christ as Lord and Savior. This process of spiritual development and maturation focuses on the soul: the renewing of our mind, and the submission of our will and intellect to the will and purpose of God.

This is the *real* war zone and battlefield where discipline is the primary base substance. I firmly believe that in the area of salvation concerning the soul, men are separated from the boys and the women from the girls. It is the place in which we become disciplined. This is not a position we possess through birthright; it is a place that we possess with constant effort and work.

CHARISMA VERSUS CHARACTER

The easiest escape for us, as leaders, is to rely heavily upon our charisma gifting instead of building our ministry upon character. If we are honest, we can boldly say that modern-day ministry places more emphasis on the delivery of the message than on a demonstration of character and power in the Holy Spirit. The most classic example of this principle is found in 1 Thessalonians 1:5-7 (NKJV):

> *For our gospel did not come to you in word only, but also in power, and in the Holy Spirit and in much assurance, as you know what kind of men we were among you for your sake. And you became followers of us and of the Lord, having received the word in much affliction, with joy of the Holy Spirit, so that you became examples to all in Macedonia and Achaia who believe.*

It is important to observe that Paul clearly stated that the Gospel did not come to them "in word only," but in "*power,*" "the *Holy Spirit* and in much *assurance.*" He tells the people of Thessalonica that the delivery of the Word alone wasn't enough to be fully effective, but the delivery of the Word being coupled with the power of God would produce fruit that would remain.

Again, the latter portion of verse 5 states:

> *...as you know what kind of men we were among you for your sake.*

What a statement of character. We are instructed by God to know those who labor among us. The apostle made sure that character was displayed during his short time of apostolic ministry impartation. His moral integrity was not only for his own sake but also for the sake of those to whom he was ministering. We can see from this one passage that the lack of moral integrity and character affects the lives of those to whom we are assigned. Verse 6 (NKJV) further demonstrates this:

And you became followers of us and of the Lord, having received the word in much affliction, with joy of the Holy Spirit.

They first become followers of *him* and then of the *Lord.* Our life must reflect the character of God so that men can imitate our lifestyle. The imitation of our lifestyle happens before those who follow us or those to whom we minister ever come into the fullness of their walk with the Lord. This is why the Word of God declares that we are epistles read of men according to 2 Corinthians 3:1-2 (NKJV):

Do we begin again to commend ourselves? Or do we need, as some others, epistles of commendation to you or letters of commendation from you? You are our epistle written in our hearts, known and read by all men.

Every day our life is making a declaration that is recorded in the archives of heaven. What will history record of your life? What statement are you making to those around you daily? The things that we do, the things that we say, and the very way that we live our life each day are the things that make the greatest impact. The way we live our life makes the greatest impression and provides the greatest witness.

First Thessalonians 2:8 states (NKJV):

So, affectionately longing for you, we were well pleased to impart to you not only the gospel of God, but also our own lives, because you had become dear to us.

Paul's impartation was his very life and not just the Gospel in Word only. Yet it is common among some, in today's ethics of ministry, to invite ministers who can draw a big crowd, with the priority, the greatest thrust and focus, on the delivery of the message as opposed to the character of the messenger. But in Paul's letter to the church at Thessalonica, we see more emphasis given to the character of the messenger and the impartation that was deposited. Paul only had three Sabbaths with the infant church in Thessalonica and yet a deposit that produced fruit that remained was made. We can get a different panoramic view from Acts 17:1-4 (NKJV):

Now when they had passed through Amphipolis and Apollonia, they came to Thessalonica, where there was a synagogue of the Jews. Then Paul, as his custom was, went in to them, and for three Sabbaths reasoned with them from the Scriptures, explaining and demonstrating that the Christ had to suffer and rise again from the dead, and saying, "This Jesus whom I preach to you is the Christ." And some of them were persuaded; and a great multitude of the devout Greeks, and not a few of the leading women, joined Paul and Silas.

Timothy returned with a letter to Paul giving an account of the condition of the church in 1 Thessalonians 1:9-10 (NKJV):

For they themselves declare concerning us what manner of entry we had to you, and how you turned to God from idols to serve the living and true God, and to wait for His Son from heaven, whom He raised from the dead, even Jesus who delivers us from the wrath to come.

Paul is very encouraged as Timothy brings him the wonderful victory report that the leadership left behind was operating in the true apostolic order of succession. They were implementing the things that they had seen and heard of Paul in that short time and were passing on those truths to the regions beyond.

We can see in 1 Thessalonians 3:6 (NKJV) Paul's great admiration and fulfillment as Timothy continues his report:

But now that Timothy has come to us from you, and brought us good news of your faith and love, and that you always have good remembrance of us, greatly desiring to see us, as we also to see you—.

We can see how Paul had great concerns for them in this chapter and why he commissioned Timothy to check on them. He wanted to be assured that the labor of his impartation wasn't in vain, knowing that his time had been so short with them. First Thessalonians 3:1-5 (NKJV) says:

> *Therefore, when we could no longer endure it, we thought it good to be left in Athens alone, and sent Timothy, our brother and minister of God, and our fellow laborer in the gospel of Christ, to establish you and encourage you concerning your faith, that no one should be shaken by these afflictions; for you yourselves know that we are appointed to this.*
>
> *For, in fact, we told you before when we were with you that we would suffer tribulation, just as it happened, and you know. For this reason, when I could no longer endure it, I sent to know your faith, lest by some means the tempter had tempted you, and our labor might be in vain.*

Paul continued to remind the church of Thessalonica that his impartation and ministry to them was not in the delivery of the Word only, but in the power of the Holy Spirit coupled with the character of his life.

It is important in this crucial hour of the consummation of the church age that we do not compromise godly character for good preaching. We should examine whether the preaching that brings the crowd to an ecstatic climax brings the type of results we see manifested in the lives of the believers in Thessalonica. Paul made an emphasis on imparting his life into the believers in Thessalonica, and he was constantly aware that his conduct and character were equally as important as his manner of delivery.

Some leaders today are more concerned about the great preaching ability of some ministers, who are able to influence the crowd for the conference budget to be met, than they are with the character of the ministers. As long as leaders hosting meetings consider the measure of success to be the numbers of people in attendance, those leaders may avert their eyes from the areas where the visiting ministers lack character.

When the success of a meeting is determined by whether a portion of the crowd has been redirected into overflow rooms, the charisma of the speaker is more important than the character of the speaker. "They really wrecked the house!" is a term some ministers are using today to mean a meeting was a success when the visiting minister came in with great preaching charisma and roused the crowd into a big frenzy. However, the question that should be asked following ministry is, "Was there fruit after the meeting?" Paul sent Timothy to inspect his *fruit* and to inspect what he was expecting.

While we continue to organize conference after conference, we must be reminded that 500,000 people die daily without ever hearing the name of Jesus mentioned. We don't want to habitually find ourselves in the cycle of living for great preaching, continually taking water to the ocean, without thinking about and directing our efforts toward the many who have never heard the Gospel once. I am in no way insinuating that we should not continue to strengthen and encourage the believers—the need for equipping the saints is imperative! We can see this in Ephesians 4:11 (NKJV):

> *And He Himself gave some to be apostles, some prophets, some evangelists, and some pastors and teachers.*

However, the purpose of these ministry gifts is to equip the saints for the work of the ministry so that the Body of Christ can be edified. Verses 12 and 13 (NKJV) continue:

> *For the equipping of the saints for the work of ministry, for the edifying of the body of Christ, till we all come to the unity of the faith and of the knowledge of the Son of God, to a perfect man, to the measure of the stature of the fullness of Christ.*

The end result of great preaching should motivate the saints to do the work of the ministry, lest we find ourselves camped out at "great preaching" for the sake of blessing and encouraging only ourselves.

The most densely populated parts of the world today are the least evangelized, preached to, or equipped. Could they not use some great preaching also? At what point do we take that which has been preached to us and impart it into the lives of others.

Paul, in the final stages of his life and ministry, wrote a letter from his prison cell, recorded in 2 Timothy 2:1-2 (NKJV), that contained valuable truths to be imparted into his spiritual son, Timothy. He urges him to pass it on to others who will implement what they have heard, lest they become hearers only.

> *You therefore, my son, be strong in the grace that is in Christ Jesus. And the things that you have heard from me among many witnesses, commit these to faithful men who will be able to teach others also.*

In the priestly order written in Leviticus 8:24 (NKJV) the tip of the priests' right ear, the thumb of the right hand, and the toe of the right foot were anointed with blood.

> *Then he brought Aaron's sons. And Moses put some of the blood on the tips of their right ears, on the thumbs of their right hands, and on the big toes of their right feet. And Moses sprinkled the blood all around on the altar.*

This was done before the priests ever said anything because the priests themselves had to be consecrated and cleansed, as we saw previously. The ears represented the things they would hear, which would affect the things they would do. The thumb represented the things they would touch and the cleansing of their hands. (David in Psalm 24:4 speaks of having "clean hands, and a pure heart.") And lastly, the big toe of the right foot represented their paths—where they would allow their presence to go, where they would allow their bodies, and their actions and accountabilities, to go.

We go in life where our feet take us. This is why God desires our feet to be shod with the preparation of the Gospel of peace. The Word of God is to be light to our path. It appears that the consecration of these bodily parts is more important than what comes from our lips as indication that it is possible to love the Lord with our lips, actions, deeds, and life situations and still be totally detached from His presence.

For leaders, there must be strong accountability and self-inventory of our character. We must purpose to reflect the same lifestyle as our words.

CHAPTER 15

THE UNDERESTIMATED FORCE OF HUMILITY

Within the Kingdom of God lies a concept that is easily overlooked yet is so profound. When this concept is the missing ingredient in the life of the believer, or the fabric of a ministry, the shallow fruit produced will never remain. Even more importantly, a level of intimacy and trust with God will never be achieved.

A characteristic we must strongly guard against allowing to enter our heart, as discussed previously, is pride. The people who have begun allowing charisma to carry them, rather than continuing to build their character and minister from a relationship of dependence on direction from God, have allowed pride to enter their heart.

Created in the image and the likeness of God, we resemble and vividly reflect Him. The word *image* means a representation of the form and features of someone or something, to make a likeness of, or to reflect or depict vividly. The word *likeness* means a resemblance or copy. This is the place the divine exchange was made through redemption's purchase. We gave up our selfish, self-willed nature in exchange for the life and nature of Christ Jesus. Second Corinthians 5:17 (NKJV) tells us:

Therefore, if anyone is in Christ, he is a new creation [or *creature*, KJV]; *old things have passed away; behold, all things have become new.*

The Greek word for *creature* is *ktisis*,[1] which means "original formation." A creature that has never existed before, a creature that doesn't even resemble any that existed before. This first manifestation of this divine exchange is that old things—former things—habitual things—and our old-natured things are passed away. We then behold, observe, and gaze upon something that has become new. The redemptive reality of the divine exchange is beyond human comprehension. Sometimes we find ourselves endeavoring to obtain what has already been purchased and given freely to us. Salvation is a free gift and the greatest act of love towards humanity.

The simplicities of God escape us and leave us profoundly speechless, yet in His manifold wisdom God unfolds His mysteries to anyone who is hungry and passionate enough to search them out. The wisdom of God is found buried deep within the Scriptures, hidden like buried treasure. Diamonds are found in the depths of the earth surrounded by dirt and rocks. Oil and gold are also mined from the depths of the earth. Almost all natural resources and rare minerals are mined from the lower parts of the earth where there is very little beauty. Finding these treasures and prized possessions requires a great amount of risk and hard labor coupled with consistency. The wealth and visibility of these resources are not a surface value nor are they observed on the surface. They all require searching, and a shallow-minded, inconsistent person will never obtain their worth and valued possession.

The wisdom of God, Kingdom concepts, and methodology are the very same way. God Himself will take risk to bring us to a place of seeking and thirsting for Him. The carnal-minded person will miss finding God's wisdom because the things of the Spirit cannot be carnally discerned. First Corinthians 2:14 (NKJV) declares that the carnal mind will never comprehend spiritual matters:

> *But the natural man does not receive the things of the Spirit of God, for they are foolishness to him; nor can he know them, because they are spiritually discerned.*

One of the most treasured Kingdom concepts is found in Matthew 25:40 (NKJV):

> *"And the king will answer and say to them, 'Assuredly, I say to you, inasmuch as you did it to one of the least of these My brethren, you did it to Me.'"*

This series of parables begins with Jesus revealing what the Kingdom of heaven is likened unto. Most of the people to whom Jesus was extending this revelation were carnally minded. In Matthew 25:1-13, Jesus methodically lays out the concept of God's Kingdom by using the parable of the wise and foolish virgins. Through this parable, He was conveying to us the importance of staying keen and always maintaining a mindset of readiness; guarding against procrastination, lethargy, and slumbering sleep. The parable also symbolically challenges us to stay filled with the Holy Spirit. The parable wraps up by charging us to be watchful, vigilant, alert, and ready because we do not know the day or the hour that the Son of man is coming.

After leaving us with this thought, Jesus gives us the parable of the talents in Matthew 25:14-30. Here we are given a proverbial lesson on stewardship and accountability in which we learn how heaven monitors our every action concerning what we do with what is distributed to us. We also learn that God will take from the one who does nothing with the little that he has been given and redistribute it into the stewardship of the one who uses his resources most profitably.

We are allowed the privilege of gazing into God's counsel—how He thinks and why He does what He does—as He reveals Kingdom concepts to us through this parable. We have seen how important and beneficial it is in our life as believers to understand His ways.

Remember, once we gain insight into the way of the Lord, we are able to make decisions in life based upon His unwavering principles. He staunchly proves to be the same yesterday, today, and forever. Heaven and earth will pass away, but His Word and His counsel will stand forever. His eternal words are forever stable according to Psalm 119:152 (NKJV):

> *Concerning Your testimonies, I have known of old that You have founded them forever.*

When we live by the testimonies, word, counsel, and way of God, we are able to gain understanding. David said in Psalm 119:130 (NKJV):

> *The entrance of Your words gives light; it gives understanding to the simple.*

God is so amazing—the very entrance of His Word gives light and understanding even to the simple. He doesn't ever withhold wisdom from the ignorant. This gives all of us hope.

Our Father openly reveals His heart on matters of Kingdom resources. If only every believer and leader could gain this understanding: God monitors everything! Our God expects us to be faithful stewards over what He has entrusted in our proprietorship. In the parable of the talents, the wicked servant was full of fear and excuses, and his lack of trusting God stopped the production of Kingdom results; therefore, the Master calls him a lethargic, wicked, and lazy servant.

We cannot conclude that this servant was unable to produce because Matthew 25:15 tells us that the talents were distributed according to each man's *own* abilities. I love God for this attribute and character trait! He never expects us to do what He has given someone else to do. This is the thought He expresses in 2 Corinthians 10:12 (NKJV):

For we dare not class ourselves or compare ourselves with those who commend themselves. But they, measuring themselves by themselves, and comparing themselves among themselves, are not wise.

Our Heavenly Father already has deposited eternal purposes and abilities within us. These abilities were predetermined and established before time began; however, we are obligated to cultivate them. In this will lie our responsibility for what we will have done with what God has given us. This will be judged, and there will be no excuse. I fear for the non-active Christian on the day of the judgment seat of Christ! I am fearful not that they will be damned to hell (because salvation is not based on works but is a gift received from God), but because of their absence of rewards that will result from not rendering the Lord the return for His investment in their life on the earth. We must be conscious in our everyday life of the accountability that we will face on that great day.

As we practice this awareness, we become eternity-conscious so that we will not allow the cares of this life to choke and smother the life of God and His eternal plan for us. When we begin to reprioritize, we will awaken to an inner drive that sets its affections on things above rather than being so attached to the entrapments of this world. Our desire will be to do the will of Him who sent us. We will begin to take full advantage of every skill, talent, experience, and resource for the advancement of the Kingdom. What a reproach to God it is not to take full advantage of what cost the Father the blood of Jesus!

To not live this life in its totality is a disgrace to Calvary's cross. Perhaps the greatest awakening will be when we see individually what we could have done for God; and more importantly, the minute things we allowed to distract and detour us off course.

OUR LIFE ISN'T ONLY ABOUT US!

One of our greatest challenges in the Body of Christ is walking in humility. True humility is a virtue and an attribute that the Father adores. He seeks and prefers the humble instead of the proud. God is not proud; He has no need to be proud because no one precedes Him according to Job 41:11 (NKJV):

> *Who has preceded Me, that I should pay him? Everything under heaven is Mine.*

From the beginning of His ministry on the earth until His crucifixion, Jesus acted, even when displaying the glory of His power, in humility. His everyday actions and His miraculous demonstration of power were public for the benefit of the people living then, but also recorded for us today to follow His example in our daily living. We are to be imitators of Christ.

When the woman was caught in adultery, the Bible, in the John 8:3-11 (NKJV) account, says the scribes and the Pharisees asked Jesus a question to try to find something in His answer with which to accuse Him. When they said to Him, "Now Moses, in the law, commanded us that such should be stoned. But what do You say?" (v. 5), Jesus stooped down and began to write in the sand. Ready to stone her, they kept asking Him. When they continued, "...He raised Himself up and said to them, 'He who is without sin among you, let him throw a stone at her first'" (v. 7). One by one, the people who had planned to stone her departed. Perhaps Jesus began to write their names in the sand as He questioned them.

Jesus came from heaven to earth, pitching His tent among us, to demonstrate the way of God to us. He demonstrated the lifestyle of the Almighty, and as we follow Jesus' pattern, we are presented with opportunities to develop humility. However, the most important aspect of humility is the acknowledgment that life is really not all about us. We can never demonstrate and glorify the way of the Father by exalting ourselves. Concerning Himself, Jesus said, *"And I, if I am lifted up from the earth, will draw all peoples to Myself"* (John 12:32 NKJV).

Very few men ever reach the plateau of humility. If there were an attribute that best describes the Messiah, it would be humility.

Matthew 20:20-23 (NKJV) tells us of a concerned mother who went to Jesus on behalf of her two sons:

> *Then the mother of Zebedee's sons came to Him with her sons, kneeling down and asking something from Him.*
>
> *And He said to her, "What do you wish?" She said to Him, "Grant that these two sons of mine may sit, one on Your right hand and the other on the left, in Your kingdom."*
>
> *But Jesus answered and said, "You do not know what you ask. Are you able to drink the cup that I am about to drink, and be baptized with the baptism that I am baptized with?" They said to Him, "We are able."*
>
> *So He said to them, "You will indeed drink My cup, and be baptized with the baptism that I am baptized with; but to sit on My right hand and on My left is not Mine to give, but it is for those for whom it is prepared by My Father."*

From this account we read that Jesus says He does only what His Father says He can do, and says what His Father says. Humility is powerful yet generally unseen. If we practice Jesus' example as a way of life, we will be guaranteed to walk in true humility.

CHAPTER 16

PREPARED FOR ANYTHING

Writing from his cold, damp, and mildewed prison cell, Paul takes a mind journey through the stages of his life, reflecting on the hard times he endured during his ministry. He then writes a profound letter to Timothy. With unmitigated stubbornness and tenacious stamina, Paul kept on keepin' on!

How can a person develop thick skin, stick-to-itiveness, fortitude, and determination? How is it that one person will cave in at the drop of a hat while another will get up after defeat and return to the heat of the battle? Why does the very essence of a challenge motivate one person and discourage another? Is it a gifting, or can the most nonchalant, noncommittal person transform their persona into a vessel of honor?

It appears that Timothy had a few challenges in being confident of his ability to carry out the assignment given to him. Timothy was very young and was taking the place of a very outspoken man, Apostle Paul, a veteran who had experienced the harsh cruelties of man. Paul was a champion in articulating his heavenly calling before doubting authorities. Through them, he learned to bury his past and press toward his future.

If there was a golden nugget or pearl of wisdom that Paul deemed necessary to leave with his spiritual son, Timothy, it would be found in the letters of his final words. In them, Paul encourages, strengthens, and instructs Timothy to become bold. Paul was aged and feeble when he wrote Timothy, yet he took the time to express his feelings and his expectations of Timothy to him. If anyone understood the burden of the leadership that was being placed on Timothy, it was definitely Paul, his spiritual father. Timothy's mandate was to establish mature leadership in the midst of erroneous doctrines, persecutions, and apostasy that had crept into Ephesus.

Paul, who once referred to himself as "an insolent man" (1 Tim. 1:13 NKJV), admitted that only God could cause a metamorphosis in his extreme arrogant demeanor. Paul's transformation came into fruition because of his willingness to yield to the Holy Spirit, but the mechanism that seasoned and matured him was the experience of suffering for the sake of the Gospel.

> *For this reason I also suffer these things; nevertheless I am not ashamed, for I know whom I have believed and am persuaded that He is able to keep what I have committed to Him until that Day.*
>
> 2 Timothy 1:12 NKJV

The "reason" Paul refers to is Jesus, "who abolished death and brought life and immortality to light through the gospel" (v. 10 NKJV). The types of "these things" Paul refers to are those cited in cross references such as "persecutions" and "afflictions," which came to him "at Antioch, at Iconium, at Lystra" (2 Tim. 3:11).

The Word of God tells us that Jesus learned obedience in Hebrews 5:8:

> *Though he were a Son, yet learned he obedience by the things which he suffered.*

The words "suffer" in 2 Timothy 1:12 and "suffered" in Hebrews 5:8 are translated from the Greek word "*pascho*,"[1] meaning "To suffer, to be affected by something from without, to be acted upon, to undergo an experience.... (II) Used of evil, meaning to suffer, to be objected to evil."[2] In other words, the meaning is to experience hardship through circumstances.

Paul experienced suffering, and there was no doubt that Timothy would have to endure suffering also. Paul's aim in writing Timothy was to prepare him for the future consequences of being a leader.

Is it the will of God for us to suffer? Do we have to suffer? What is the purpose of suffering? Didn't God send His Son to deliver us from all forms and attempts of opposition and suffering? Aren't we free in life never to have to experience afflictions?

There was once a very popular teaching circulating throughout the Body of Christ that placed great emphasis on the problems, calamities, and opposition believers face. We must understand that even though God continues to work in us every day because we will never reach perfection on the earth, this does not mean that we are bound to live under the grip of the enemy without any way of escape or deliverance. Absolutely not!

Despite the many attempts of the enemy, we are always more than conquerors and always triumph in Christ Jesus. These types of gray areas are what create denominational divides. One camp believes that it is impossible to mature in Christ without suffering, and the other camp believes that God never wants us to suffer at all! On both sides of the spectrum we have extremes and leaders who represent the extremes.

If we go through life thinking that we will never face hard times, how will we ever be able to train leadership to endure? On the other hand, if we believe that in order to mature in Christ and glorify God we must suffer through everything, we could easily become nonresistant in areas of our life in which the enemy is trying to defeat us. In other words, we would be allowing the enemy to run havoc in our life by thinking the suffering is drawing us nearer to God!

Out of all the church ages, the church of the twenty-first century must be equipped to confront opposition—if you indeed believe that we are living in the last days. Whether you believe in pre-Tribulation, mid-Tribulation, or post-Tribulation Rapture (of the church who "shall be caught up together with them in the clouds, to meet the Lord in the air" according to 1 Thess. 4:17), you are still going to face some form of opposition. Jesus Himself predicts the signs of the times and the end of the age, as we read in the book of Matthew. Jesus' disciples, after coming to Him privately, asked Him to give them the inside edition—they wanted to know when the signs of the end would be and what would be the sign of His coming. Matthew 24:4-14 states:

> *And Jesus answered and said unto them, Take heed that no man deceive you. For many shall come in my name, saying, I am Christ; and shall deceive many. And ye shall hear of wars and rumours of wars: see that ye be not troubled: for all these things must come to pass, but the end is not yet. For nation shall rise against nation, and kingdom against kingdom: and there shall be famines, and pestilences, and earthquakes, in divers places. All these are the beginning of sorrows.*
>
> *Then shall they deliver you up to be afflicted, and shall kill you: and ye shall be hated of all nations for my name's sake. And then shall many be offended, and shall betray one another, and shall hate one another. And many false prophets shall rise, and shall deceive many.*
>
> *And because iniquity shall abound, the love of many shall wax cold. But he that shall endure unto the end, the same shall be saved. And this gospel of the kingdom shall be preached in all the world for a witness unto all nations; and then shall the end come.*

Now again, this is not a discussion of whether the Rapture of the church will be pre-, post-, or mid-Tribulation; we are addressing the importance of enduring hardship as a leader. In verses 6-7 Jesus states:

> *And ye shall hear of wars and rumours of wars: see that ye be not troubled: for all these things must come to pass, but the end is not yet. For nation shall rise against nation, and kingdom against kingdom: and there shall be famines, and pestilences, and earthquakes, in divers places.*

When Jesus says that these things *must* come to pass, then they *must* come to pass! He also said in verse 13 (NKJV):

> *"But he who* ***endures*** *to the end shall be saved."*

Endure means "to continue": "persist, remain, last," "sustain"; "To sustain adversity": "suffer, tolerate, bear," "undergo," "experience."[3] We are living in a time in society when people are not willing to endure. Many of those who are not willing are in leadership. The enemy is not going to roll over and play dead to allow us to finish the work without opposing us. Also in this same text of Scripture, Jesus addresses our covenant assignment of preaching the Gospel in all the world "and then shall the end come" (v. 13). Spineless leaders who are not able to endure hardness cannot expect to accomplish this assignment!

Today we see believers, including leaders, who are not willing to endure tough marriages. I have seen statistics that reveal the divorce rate is higher among believers than unbelievers! This ought not to be so! Today, we see some leaders who do not want to endure correction, accountability, or submission. This is not an observation of a trend that is beginning or a negative confession; it is a statement of truth.

Hard times are coming as we can already see in the instability of our economy. We hear of wars and rumors of wars and are seeing the events Jesus described in Matthew 24 coming to pass. Only in the Western world have there been some leaders who have been able to get away with preaching a soft type of Gospel without any sense of conviction. In Sudan, over hundreds of thousands have been slaughtered due to their teachings, and countless hundreds have also been killed in China, Indonesia, and North Korea.

To keep my statements balanced, I reiterate that we do have power over the enemy, but we cannot stop him from attempting to attack us. We can take authority over him and rebuke him in the name of Jesus. But to think that he will never attack or that there is no possibility of opposition would be like the United States Army going into battle believing that their opponent will never retaliate.

Some of our leaders preaching a soft Gospel almost give the impression that God gave us armor for the purpose of wearing it in a parade! God gave us armor, spiritual weapons (see Eph. 6:10-17; 2 Cor. 10:4,5), and methods to learn and use in order for us to be prepared to know how to endure hardness.

We have armor to protect us in battle against an enemy who hates our very existence. Paul told Timothy *"endure hardness as a good soldier of Jesus Christ"* (2 Tim. 2:3)! How? We can learn to endure hardness through developing spiritually; otherwise, how can those of us who cave in at the least opposition be used of God? A good soldier does not cave in at the face of adversity. If we do not spiritually develop to endure and train up other believers in how to clothe ourselves in the armor of God, the spiritual weapons of warfare available to us and how to use them, and developing godly character, we will develop cowards instead of valiant leaders.

Paul tells Timothy in 2 Timothy 2:4 (NKJV):

> *No one engaged in warfare entangles himself with the affairs of this life, that he may please him who enlisted him as a soldier.*

What does it mean to be entangled in the affairs of this life? Does this denote that we should not pay our mortgages, further our education, or commit to the responsibilities of the household? Of course not. Paul is challenging Timothy to stay focused in the midst of it all and to set his greatest affection on the things above, continually seeking to please the recruiter who enlisted him. In Timothy's case, as well as our own, we were enlisted by the Almighty and our aim should be to please Him and Him alone.

We have the privileged assignment of developing leadership that will endure the perils of the times. Second Timothy 2:10 tells us:

> *"Therefore I endure all things for the sake of the elect, that they also may obtain the salvation which is in Christ Jesus with eternal glory."*

CHAPTER 17

PRESSING THROUGH

Our endurance is not only for our own sake, but also for the sake of those in the faith. Paul continues to write to his spiritual son, Timothy, and consistently alerts him of the hard times that await him. The early church faced harsh persecution; because of the liberty that we have in our country today, it is hard to imagine ministering under such restrictions.

In 2 Timothy chapter 2, Paul teaches the young minister about perilous days and also assures him that these days *will* come. He then methodically defines to his prodigy what will be the signs to observe during these perilous times. The word *peril* is defined as "exposure to the risk of harm or loss: danger"; "something that endangers: hazard"[1]; in other words, imminent danger. In such hostile times, mankind will become lovers of themselves and money. A great emphasis will be placed on money; there is a vast difference between a lover of money and a responsible steward who has been proven to handle high finances. It is the *love* of money that is the root of all evil, not money itself. (See 1 Tim. 6:10.) A responsible steward knows that the purpose of prosperity is to seek and to save the lost.

Let's examine Paul's warnings. Second Timothy 3:1-5 (NKJV) tells us:

But know this, that in the last days perilous times will come: For men will be lovers of themselves, lovers of money, boasters, proud, blasphemers, disobedient to parents, unthankful, unholy, unloving, unforgiving, slanderers, without self-control, brutal, despisers of good, traitors, headstrong, haughty, lovers of pleasure rather than lovers of God, having a form of godliness but denying its power. And from such people turn away!

It is very important that we examine the fourth verse very carefully. Paul said that men would be "...headstrong, haughty, lovers of pleasure rather than lovers of God"; men would choose pleasure over purpose. During the pressure of hard times, whatever is in you will come out of you. Sometimes we don't know what is in there until we are faced with pressure. When you apply pressure to an orange, apple juice doesn't come out. What comes out is the substance of whatever is contained in the fruit. If there has ever been a time that the church must prepare for operating under pressure so that God's character comes out when squeezed (for us to come through successfully), it is now. Some believers seem to be in a trance, thinking that things will always be the same, but the closer we approach the consummation of the church age, the more the enemy applies pressure, persecutions, and temptations. His aim is to stagnate the believer.

Thanks to God, we have authority over the enemy, but that is not the case we are addressing. It is one thing to have authority over him, but it is another thing to have authority over him but not practice it. It is important to become accustomed to exercising that authority. A soldier never goes to the front lines of war without having ever practiced his artillery skills during boot camp. The soldier prepares ahead of time; he conditions his body through discipline before he goes into the heat of the battle. As a matter of fact, I've learned that the U.S. Special Forces train in more harsh conditions than they will face in the actual war so that in the eye of adversity they won't yield to pressure! We need believers and leadership who are trained to endure hardship in order to come out successfully on the other side of the situation. Remember, it isn't just about us; it's about the Body of Christ and God's plan for man!

Just when we think that Paul is finished instructing Timothy concerning endurance, we find him once again addressing the issue later in 2 Timothy 3:10-12 (NKJV):

> *But you have carefully followed my doctrine, manner of life, purpose, faith, longsuffering, love, perseverance, persecutions, afflictions, which happened to me at Antioch, at Iconium, at Lystra—what persecutions I endured. And out of them all the Lord delivered me. Yes, and all who desire to live godly in Christ Jesus will suffer persecution.*

The beauty of the Lord's ways is that He always leads us to the path of victory. He never said we would never pass through difficult situations, but we know that through it all we can still come out of the situations victorious. Why? Because He will never leave us or abandon us in battle; He is the One who is our very present help in times of trouble. God never promised us a trouble-free life, and it is erroneous to think that we will live one, but He did promise to be our deliverer.

Timothy saw doctrine, purpose, faith, longsuffering, and perseverance modeled in the life of Paul; he carefully observed these character attributes that Paul had developed through enduring the hard times he had experienced. We must not carry our sorrows and disappointments always with us; we must go through them and move on. These are the times stamina and fortitude are matured in our life as we go through divers challenges.

As Timothy observed Paul in his persecutions and afflictions, he learned that the Lord is always present to deliver in a time of need. There are some trails that we go down from which the Lord doesn't instantly deliver us. We cannot cave in when we are faced with adversity if God doesn't deliver us in twenty seconds or less. We must endure confidently knowing that the matter is not *if* God will deliver, but *when* God will deliver. The battle that we endure between the attack and the victory is where endurance plays a major role.

Leadership must possess this because it is where we either win or lose the battle.

After Paul comforts young and tender Timothy, like a father he delivers the powerful words of God in 2 Timothy 3:12 (NKJV), bringing him into perspective by saying:

> *Yes, and all who desire to live godly in Christ Jesus will suffer persecution.*

Paul said that "all," "all" meaning no one is exempt, will suffer some form of persecution if we desire to live godly in Jesus. Not even Paul, the man of faith himself, was exempt! How can our faith ever be developed if we never experience anything to put it to the test? Why would God make faith available to us if we would never need to use it? He has given us all things that pertain to life and godliness. Because we live godly, we will need faith and endurance to pass through the consequences of the persecutions that this godliness brings.

Paul's final words to Timothy pertaining to this subject are found in 2 Timothy 4:1-4 (NKJV) where Paul begins to speak even stronger to his "son":

> *I charge you therefore before God and the Lord Jesus Christ, who will judge the living and the dead at His appearing and His kingdom: Preach the word! Be ready in season and out of season. Convince, rebuke, exhort, with all longsuffering and teaching. For the time will come when they will not endure sound doctrine, but according to their own desires, because they have itching ears, they will heap up for themselves teachers; and they will turn their ears away from the truth, and be turned aside to fables.*

The easiest thing for Timothy to do in the midst of the battle was to speak the language of the flesh or speak what he saw and experienced. When facing spiritual warfare, we must speak and say what God is saying about the situation. When Jesus was in warfare and being tempted, He spoke only the written word! If this was the requirement for Jesus in defeating the enemy, then surely it must be a requirement for us because we are to be imitators of Him.

In 2 Timothy 4:2-5, Paul uses the word *endure* twice. First he instructs Timothy to endure sound doctrine; secondly, he tells him to endure afflictions. We must first endure sound doctrine before we can ever endure afflictions. This has been a great challenge of today's leadership in the church. Paul tells us that mankind will not want to hear truth or sound doctrine because the pallet of their appetite would be to hear words that itch their ears.

Paul also says that they will heap for themselves teachers. In other words, they would employ for themselves a hireling who will come and preach to them what they want to hear. They will turn their ears away from the truth and desire fables instead of the true and living Word of God. It is amazing that believers could come to a place in their hearts where they desire to hear a fable, which is a falsehood or a lie, rather than the truth!

This was the last warning that Paul gave to Timothy before he said these words found in 2 Timothy 4:6-8 (NKJV):

> *For I am already being poured out as a drink offering, and the time of my departure is at hand.*
>
> *I have fought the good fight, I have finished the race, I have kept the faith. Finally, there is laid up for me the crown of righteousness, which the Lord, the righteous Judge, will give to me on that Day, and not to me only but also to all who have loved His appearing.*

These were Paul's departing words to his endearing son. Within these final words, I could imagine Paul saying, "Timothy, my son, you will go through things when I am gone, but just as you have seen and observed of me, pass this same exemplary attribute on to those that you are assigned to raise up. Teach them that they must endure hardship." Jesus had similar departing words to His disciples just before He was about to be offered up in Matthew 24:9-13 (NKJV):

"Then they will deliver you up to tribulation and kill you, and you will be hated by all nations for My name's sake.

"And then many will be offended, will betray one another, and will hate one another.

"Then many false prophets will rise up and deceive many.

"And because lawlessness will abound, the love of many will grow cold.

"But he who endures to the end shall be saved."

One of the greatest prayers that we can pray is: "Father, give me the power to become a disciple and endure hardships as a good soldier of Jesus Christ." This attribute can come into maturation by preparation, by growing closer to the Father and through the practice of living our life according to His way of doing things. Only by facing the challenges that confront us in our life and choosing not to take the path of least resistance, speaking the Word and remaining steadfast and unmovable, will we be prepared for enduring through any circumstance, any hardship, to come through victoriously—to be prepared to handle any circumstance that comes our way.

We know that path we are enduring is working in us the attributes of patience, endurance, and longsuffering on our behalf. As a believer, the fruit of longsuffering is given to us by God to help us endure to the successful conclusion. The conclusion may or may not be one we anticipate, but we do know that even though "many are the afflictions of the righteous," "the LORD delivers him out of them all" (Ps. 34:19 NKJV) and "thanks be to God who always leads us in triumph in Christ..." (2 Cor. 2:14 NKJV)!

Remember, God does everything in seed form, which means that the fruit will need time to grow and mature. There is nothing mystical or magical that will happen to produce spiritual fruit in our life—it all happens supernaturally. God will practically place *"super"* on our *"natural"* effort and crown us with success as we endure.

CHAPTER 18

RELEASING GOD'S GLORY

God will release the power of His Shekinah glory, the greatest force in the universe, on the earth in a greater measure than He ever has before, as we saw in Haggai 2:9 (NKJV): "'The glory of this latter temple shall be greater than the former...'" (Hag. 2:9 NKJV). He will release this power through His New Covenant temples—we believers in whom He dwells!

God is able to release this power in great measure through those of us who have developed His character—those of us it squeezes out of under pressure! We develop God's character by developing the fruit of the Spirit, God's character traits. By abiding in Him and yielding more of ourselves to Him, we develop His fruit, His character.

Each fruit of the Spirit is planted in us the moment we are born again, but it is up to us to cultivate each one into maturation in our life. Some of us have developed patience but not love. Some of us may have cultivated and developed self-control but not peace—we do not have the fruit of peace working in our life. However, we must not be too hard on ourselves because growth is a process.

Everything God does in the life of the believer is in seed form. It takes time for seeds to grow up to the point of producing their own kind. But we can rest assured that as long as we are consistent, the fruit maturity will come.

In the last decade, we saw several men of God fall who, although used by God to manifest His power through them to minister to others, failed to develop godly character. These leaders were extremely developed in ministering God's power through the gifts of the Spirit but had not developed God's character, the fruit of the Spirit. Simply because some believers operate in the gifts, they are not justified or excused from developing the fruit of the Spirit in their life. The eyes of the public are on the demonstration of God's power through us and the way we use our gifts, but are equally upon our life. Therefore we should give great effort to developing the fruit as well as the gifts of the Spirit in order to give the world an accurate impression of what God is like. God is love (1 John 4:16), and the other fruit of the Spirit and the gifts in operation issue out from His love to draw people to Him, to help and restore them to the way He originally created man to be and function before the fall, to empower them.

If ever there has been a time when we in the church must develop God's character so that it, rather than our human nature, will emerge when we are under pressure, the time is now; because if ever there has been a time in the history of the church when the Shekinah glory of God should be released into the earth to manifest on behalf of mankind, it is also now!

The fruit of the Spirit will keep us where the gifts of the Spirit take us. The fruit guarantees longevity in ministry. The gifts will operate even when the believer isn't spiritually mature, as we have seen. God will use an immature believer to minister to seasoned saints because the gifts and the callings are without repentance.

Mankind needs supernatural ministry now! God's Shekinah glory is more powerful than the multi-faceted demonic forces which have been launched against the church. Mankind needs supernatural demonstration of the most powerful force in the universe in the perplexity of this rapidly changing world.

God hid within Himself the mystery that was concealed throughout the ages; this mystery was later to be unfolded in us as

Christ in us, the hope of glory! (See Col. 1:27.) Believers who have fallen into mediocrity and apathy must stop and consider, then rally to the thought that the living God never intended for His church to operate that way!

Down through the years, traditions of orthodox religions and denominational barriers have minimized the power of God and the gifts of the Spirit in the church. The infilling of the Holy Spirit and the functioning of the fivefold ministry gifting have been explained away. Erroneously, the apostolic and prophetic gifts have been taken from the forefront of the church of today. Self-proclaimed theologians who authorized themselves above the active ability of the Scriptures, openly declared tongues, prophets, and the working of miracles to be no longer operative.

The arguments they devised as their apologetics explain that the gifts of the Spirit were needed during biblical times to confirm the Word of God as true and Christ really to be the Son of God, but state that the era has passed. The same arguments are equally disputable today. If there ever has been a time in which we need a manifestation and demonstration to validate the infallibility of the divine truths of God, *it is now!*

I have read statistics stating there are over 1.2 billion radical Muslims in the world. These Muslims cannot be convinced to convert to Christianity by philosophical reasoning or by describing endless genealogies. The Hindus of India are persecuting Christian believers and martyring pastors daily. Over 2 million believers in Sudan have given their lives boldly standing for their faith in the twenty years the fighting has been going on, according to information I obtained from The Voice of the Martyrs. Nothing short of a demonstration of the power of God will win Muslims to Christianity. We have a black book with ink-filled white pages by which we live and so do the Muslims. The only way for them to determine the truth is not by *explanation,* but through powerful *demonstration!*

The church needs everything that heaven has made available to us to empower and equip us for the opposition we will encounter. It is easy for those who support the line of reasoning that the gifts are non-operable and no longer needed today to make such statements from the nonconfrontational and nonhostile environments in which they live. But those whose lives are threatened daily in an environment hostile to them because of the choice they have made for their faith gladly welcome the operation of every gift God has made available to help protect their lives! They do not spend their time arguing the miniscule issues of theological ideologies when their focus is to survive to evangelize!

OPERATING IN THE GIFTS OF THE SPIRIT

Three of the spiritual gifts[1] through which God manifests His power are: the "working of miracles," the "gifts of healing," and the gift of "faith." (1 Cor. 12:9,10.) These three gifts demonstrate the power of God. These action gifts are lethal weapons against the strongholds of the enemy. Our people are constantly plagued and tormented in their personal lives and come to church in hope of finding some type of deliverance. In many cases, instead of godly counsel based on the Word, we offer a philosophical explanation or a counseling session to work the person through some sort of a process that does not deal with the actual cause.

Often what the person actually needs instead is to be taught (or reminded) how to begin walking on God's path for them by being taught how to operate according to God's ways. The person may not know, or has lost sight of, how to locate the scriptures that apply to their situation, how to renew their mind with those scriptures, and how to train their tongue to speak in line with them. They need to know that the Truth in those scriptures will set them free, sometimes instantly, but oftentimes through a transformation process over time.

We follow the leading of the Spirit to know what type of ministry people need, of course. In some cases, the solution after dealing with emergencies is giving the person godly instruction while treating the person with love, kindness, or other appropriate fruit of the Spirit we have cultivated.

In other cases, handling the situation by giving instruction, or especially, trying to bring resolution by holding a three-hour counseling session, is actually trying to reason with the devil! We need to know how to operate like the early church and know when to cast the devil out of the person! In the meeting God used to launch me into ministry in Kenya, the appropriate ministry to the madman, the man who daily stormed around the streets, naked with matted hair, living by eating food from rubbish bins, was to cast the devil out of him!

When in the country of Gadarenes, Jesus encountered the madman who lived in the mountains and tombs and cried out night and day, cutting himself with stones, who pulled apart chains and broke shackles in pieces when people tried to bind him. Jesus cast the devil out of the madman, completely delivering the man. (Mark 5:1-20.) We do not find an account in the Bible of the man coming back to the same place annually for the renewal of his deliverance.

The supernatural gifts and power of God are intended to be the empowerment and lifestyle of the New Covenant believer and were never intended to be optional equipment or an alternative process. People are hungry for a demonstration of the power of God. We will never completely meet the needs of people by depending only on programs, good but not-directed-by-God ideas, or fads and gimmicks to draw large crowds.

We must manifest the supernatural power of God while giving people godly counsel and allow the gifts to operate and flow freely. Recently a pastor I know in Winston-Salem, North Carolina, gave two accounts of the operation of the "word of wisdom" (1 Cor. 12:8), one of the revelation gifts, in giving godly counsel to people who had come to him for help.

One account was of a young man who had to go to court. As the gentleman was leaving, the gifts began to operate through the pastor. The pastor told the young man that supernaturally he saw that the person prosecuting the young man would never show up in court.

The young man left with an assurance that he had the word of the Lord from the man of God operating in the supernatural. Just as the pastor had decreed, the prosecuting candidates never appeared in court. The case was thrown out. This is God's glory released in supernatural ministry!

The other account the pastor shared with me was about a member of his church who was falsely accused. If the Lord had not intervened on the person's behalf, their name and character could have been publicly defamed and their reputation destroyed. The Lord showed this same pastor that the member could be at ease because nothing detrimental would become of the attack against them. The following day, just as the pastor had seen through the revelation gifts, the would-be onslaught of the enemy was aborted, dismantled, and the member walked away with his reputation intact. Again this is supernatural ministry, allowing the gifts of the Spirit to operate.

The revelation gifts unfold the magnitude of God's plan. The counsel of God is hidden and revealed only to those who diligently seek and search for it as if searching for treasures. The mysteries are not hidden *from* us—they are hidden *for* us. The Spirit distributes these gifts individually as He wills to meet the particular needs. Each revelation gift does just as it proclaims. It reveals something unknown or hidden. The "word of wisdom" reveals things to come; the "word of knowledge" reveals the past and present; and last but certainly not least, the "discerning of spirits," discernment (1 Cor. 12:8,10), reveals that which is not obvious or usual. Revelation is needed in our times today as never before because we are living in prophetic times: We are living in the times when prophecies God foretold through the Old Covenant prophets and in the New Testament are coming to pass.

The mechanism and structure of the revelation gifts work cooperatively to reveal the will of God. Revelation is the conduit, the very channel that God uses to flow into His vessels and bring to earth that which He established in Himself before time began. Second Timothy 1:9 (NKJV) tells us:

> *Who has saved us and called us with a holy calling, not according to our works, but according to His own purpose and grace which was given to us in Christ Jesus before time began.*

He is working in us both to will and do His good pleasure and uses the revelation gifts. Revelation reveals to us what already is and things to come. God has an insatiable appetite to bring clarity and understanding to His people. Therefore, He employed the agency of the Holy Spirit to distribute gifts to the Body to assist and empower us for supernatural ministry.

I believe that the enemy fights so hard to hold the believer captive in the bondage of impotent traditions to achieve his aim of disengaging the church of its power. Our covenant rights as believers and our entitlement guarantee us access to the power gifts. We have a right to never be denied the benefit of these gifts. We have a right to belong to a church that operates in these power gifts.

Our Heavenly Father did not leave us powerless. God does not have a scarcity mentality. He always thinks along the lines of more than enough. God's very nature is abundance. To those of us who receive His Son, God has sent the Spirit of His Son into our hearts (Gal. 4:6); we have received "...the Spirit of adoption by whom we cry out, 'Abba, Father'" (Rom. 8:15 NKJV). Many scriptures refer to the provision of our Heavenly Father for us. Our Father always thinks of providing for us what we need to efficiently complete His work, and He abundantly supplies His mysteries to His people by His Spirit.

Another function of the gifts, the verbal gifts, is to proclaim the hidden counsel of God, "...Him who works all things according to the counsel of His will" (Eph. 1:11 NKJV). We need these gifts operating in the church today. As T.L. and Daisy Osborn taught me, and as I saw when God launched me into ministry in Kenya, the dinner bell for the unbeliever is a demonstration of God's power, His miracles. Each gift in demonstration draws the lost to the Source of sustenance they need and is an empowerment weapon for the believer.

There is no substitute for these gifts. God equipped the church with everything we need to overcome the wiles of the enemy. Denying that the gifts are in operation today limits us from using the power God has made available for us to accomplish His work. There is no reason for the church to be weakened in any arena.

Can you imagine that God would start the early church out strong, operating effectively in the gifts of the Spirit, only to remove the availability of His power through the gifts so that the end-times church would finish weak? As Christians, we need to operate in what has been provided for us. Romans 8:32 (NKJV) tells us:

> *He who did not spare His own Son, but delivered Him up for us all, how shall He not with Him also freely give us all things?*

If God was not willing to hold back His most precious possession, His Son, why would He not freely provide for us everything that we need for effective ministry today? Second Peter 1:3 (NKJV) states:

> *As His divine power has given to us all things that pertain to life and godliness, through the knowledge of Him who called us by glory and virtue.*

Sometimes we may have a child who begins hanging around with the wrong crowd but tries to deceive us into thinking that their friends aren't so bad. When we parents are operating in the gifts, we hear what the child is saying, but the working of discernment in us reveals that the child is indeed hanging around with bad company. First Corinthians 15:33 (NASB) tells us, "Do not be deceived: 'Bad company corrupts good morals.'" Other versions word this statement as "...evil communications corrupt good manners" (KJV) and "'Evil company corrupts good habits'" (NKJV).

We who are mothers who also operate in the word of knowledge may hear our children say one thing with their mouth, but if it isn't true, our spirit sees exactly what actually happened. We can see that we parents who allow God to operate these gifts through us can save our children's lives and also allow them to experience the power of God at a young age.

God intends for the gifts to operate in all arenas: The gifts operate to minister to others and also operate on our behalf. For example, in business a believer operating in the gifts may be about to enter into a deal that looks completely safe from visual and legal perspectives, yet the word of wisdom begins to operate in the believer revealing otherwise. They see futuristically that not only is something shady going on that will come out, but they also see that the company will fold in six months and leave them bankrupt!

An unbeliever who has never heard of Jesus or one who has heard but is closed to hearing more may respond and receive Him after seeing or experiencing a miracle, the source of T.L. and Daisy Osborn's statement: Miracles are the dinner bell for salvation. An extremely vital benefit to the believer (through whom the gifts operate) and unbeliever occurs in a situation such as the one below.

For years a believer has been extending an invitation to an unbelieving coworker to visit church. The unbelieving coworker finally accepts the invitation after the traumas of receiving a doctor's report of terminal illness and exhausting all remaining insurance coverage.

The coworker comes to church every service with a doubtful, almost judgmental, attitude. Then one service the pastor, operating in the word of knowledge and the word of wisdom, calls out certain illnesses inflicting people in the congregation. He informs the congregation that that he envisions spiritually a certain woman who is extremely frustrated. She has been given a doctor's report of terminal illness and has just exhausted her insurance coverage. He then invites whoever the woman is who the Lord is describing to him to come forward. He says, "The Lord is going to heal her today!"

By then, the coworker has dropped every defense. Every wall she ever erected against the church has crumbed like the Jericho walls, and she goes forward to receive her healing. The gift of healing, and in this case, faith, are operating in the pastor. The woman receives the manifestation of her healing and gives her life to the Lord—all because of a church allowing the Lord to operate as His Spirit wills through His gifts to reach and meet the needs of the individual in each situation.

God is the just and ultimate equalizer. John 1:12 states, "But as many as received him, to them gave he *power* to become the sons of God, even to them that believe on his name." As many as receive Jesus, to them Jesus gives the power to become sons of God who are born of God. (vv. 11-13.) In this hour, there is a releasing of the spiritual gifts. The next move of God will be corporate and will involve the entire Body. No one particular denomination will monopolize this move of God—no one group will have a corner on this move!

God is sovereign and has promised to pour out His Spirit on all flesh with the result being a demonstration of His Spirit: "...your sons and your daughters shall prophesy, your old men shall dream dreams, your young men shall see visions. And also on My menservants and on My maidservants I will pour out My Spirit in those days" (Joel 2:28,29 NKJV). As long as we have flesh on our bodies we are candidates for this move of God. It will be more than a move—it will be a renewal and refreshing of God's people and a time of restoring all that God intended the church to have and be from the beginning. It will be a restoration of the church back into her place of empowerment. This move will cause a struggle between the ideas of human reasoning and tradition and the realities of the Lord's supernatural realm.

If I were the person reading this book, I would throw my hands above my head in praise and begin to thank the Lord for allowing me to be a part of what He is doing in this hour. I would purpose not to miss my hour of visitation and the great outpouring from the Holy Spirit.

CHAPTER 19

SUPERNATURAL MINISTRY

By the divine design of our wise Heavenly Father, there are nine gifts of the Spirit and also nine fruit of the Spirit. God orchestrated the fruit and gifts to balance each other and flow in harmonious precision for proper administration. Because the fruit are needed to operate in the supernatural ministry as much as are the gifts, attempting to operate effectively in the power of the gifts without coupling them with the godly character traits of the fruit will profit us very little.

The purpose of the fruit differs from the purpose of the spiritual gifts. Whereas the Holy Spirit distributes the gifts individually as He wills to minister to particular needs, but also for the profit of all (see 1 Cor. 12:7,10 NKJV), each believer has the responsibility to cultivate and mature the fruit, the seed planted in them when they were born again. The gifts manifest through us believers as the Spirit wills and as we are open to Him operating through us; the fruit manifests through us as a result of our actively cultivating it, allowing it to mature, and consciously displaying it. The fruit does not operate through us or develop in us automatically.

DEVELOPING THE FRUIT OF THE SPIRIT

Godly character is the end result of developing the fruit in our life. God wants us to reflect His character and His nature. God desires for the believer to walk in holiness. In fact, He commands us to be holy as He is holy.

> *As obedient children...like the Holy One who called you, be holy yourselves also in all your behavior; because it is written, "You shall be holy, for I am holy."*
>
> 1 Peter 1:14-16 NASB

We are able to be holy as God is holy—to walk in holiness—as a result of two different spiritual works: sanctification and holiness.

SET APART BY GOD

"Sanctification" means "separation, a setting apart," in the New Testament from the Greek word *hagiasmos*. "Sanctify" in the Old Testament, from the Hebrew term *qodesh,* carries a similar meaning.[1] God is the One who sanctifies us. God separates man from sin to Himself as His own work.[2] Jesus, through sacrificing Himself and shedding His blood, sanctified the church by setting it apart for God.[3] (See Heb. 10:10; 13:12.) "The Holy Spirit is the Agent in sanctification."[4] (See 2 Thess. 2:13; 1 Peter 1:2.) In other words, sanctification is a sovereign work of God; it is not a task that we can accomplish on our own.

We see an example in the Old Testament account of God setting apart Jeremiah for service. There was nothing Jeremiah did to sanctify himself because God sanctified him even before he was conceived!

> *"Before I formed you in the womb I knew you; before you were born I sanctified you; I ordained you a prophet to the nations."*
>
> Jeremiah 1:5 NKJV

Believers are called and sanctified by God the Father, and this sanctification preserves us in Christ Jesus, as we see in Jude verse 1 (NKJV):

> *Jude, a bondservant of Jesus Christ, and brother of James,*
> *To those who are called, sanctified by God the Father, and preserved in Jesus Christ.*

BEING HOLY AS GOD IS HOLY

Sanctification is the inward work of the outer manifestation of holiness. Sanctification is a work accomplished by God, but holiness requires the absolute participation of the believer. It is the believer's responsibility to walk in holiness.

God's instruction, "…'Be holy, for I am holy,'"(1 Peter 1:16 NKJV), places the responsibility on the believer. The word "holy" in this verse is from the Greek word "*hagios.*" "Its fundamental idea is separation, consecration, devotion to the service of Deity, sharing in God's purity and abstaining from the earth's defilement."[5] The use of "holy" in verse 16 is specifically described: "Metaphorically it means morally pure, upright, blameless in heart and life, virtuous, holy."[6] "…the quality, as attributed to God, is often presented in a way which involves divine demands upon the conduct of believers…." in "…cleansing themselves from all defilement, forsaking sin, living a 'holy' manner of life…."[7]

The *Jamieson, Fausset, and Brown Commentary* entry for 1 Peter 1:16 gives a good representation of the way sanctification by the Spirit and the believer's responsibility to choose to walk in holiness and draw on God's power to act on the decision, work together. "The creature is holy only in so far as it is sanctified by God. God, in giving the command, is willing to give also the power to obey, through the sanctifying Spirit."[8]

Holiness exemplifies the character and nature of God and reveals the way of God. Holiness involves the conduct of the believer's moral excellence and integrity and should be displayed in our lifestyle. It should not be something that we seclude to religious activity.

Holiness is attainable because God expects it of us. But holiness is not a working of the flesh; it is a yielding to the way of God. The fruit of the Spirit are the instruments that God has ordained to help us obtain holiness. The more we develop fruit in a particular area of our life, the more we will manifest the essence and virtue of holiness.

As we believers continue to yield to the working of the Holy Spirit in our life, spiritual maturity and wholeness will come. It is the great confidence we have with which Paul comforts us in Philippians 1:6 (NKJV):

> *Being confident of this very thing, that He who has begun a good work in you will complete it until the day of Jesus Christ.*

It is scriptural to pray for the Holy Spirit to teach us and comfort us as we endeavor to progress in this ongoing process. We will be a vessel of honor to God and most definitely meat for the Master's use.

> *But in a great house there are not only vessels of gold and silver, but also of wood and clay, some for honor and some for dishonor.*
>
> *Therefore if anyone cleanses himself from the latter, he will be a vessel for honor, sanctified and useful for the Master, prepared for every good work.*
>
> 2 Timothy 2:20,21 NKJV

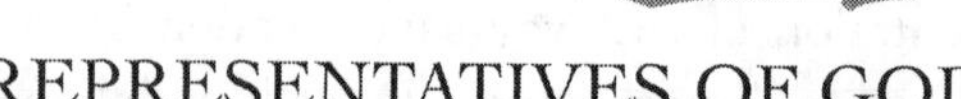

REPRESENTATIVES OF GOD'S POWER AND HIS NATURE

From shedding more light on the gifts as they coincide with the fruit, we see how important it is to maintain a balanced perspective. In operating in the gifts, allowing the Spirit to operate them through us as He wills, we must give equal attention to continue cultivating the fruit and walking in holiness as a lifestyle.

Maintaining this balanced perspective will help us walk in humility rather than allowing haughtiness to begin leading us. Because the gifts release God's power, it is easy for believers who operate in the gifts, but who have not developed the fruit, to abuse the purpose of the gifts. This is where great manipulation creeps in. These believers begin to think that they possess the gifts, that they have ownership of them. Remember, the gifts are the gifts of the *Spirit,* not of ourselves, lest some of us become lifted up in pride and boast.

People who are ministering the gifts of the Spirit in a haughty way are not accurately representing who God is to people. People who minister the gifts while exhibiting the fruit of humility are not only ministering God's loving nature to people, but are also giving all the glory to Him, rather than trying to take some of it for themselves.

SANCTIFIED TO WALK IN HOLINESS

Through Jesus, we are sanctified and cleansed with the washing of water by the Word. (Eph. 5:26.) "If we confess our sins, he is faithful and just to forgive us our sins, and to cleanse us from all unrighteousness" (1 John 1:9).

Jesus said, "Let your light so shine before men, that they may see your good works and glorify your Father in heaven" (Matt. 5:16 NKJV). We can let our light shine by developing and walking in the fruit of the Spirit, "love, joy, peace, longsuffering, kindness, goodness, faithfulness, gentleness, self-control" (Gal. 5:22,23 NKJV). As we abide in the Vine, Jesus, and He in us, we will bear much fruit. (John 15:5.) We read in verse 8 (NKJV) that Jesus states, "'By this My Father is glorified, that you bear much fruit; so you will be My disciples.'"

The Father is glorified by letting our light shine before men, that they may see our good works and glorify Him, and by our bearing much fruit. Operating in the gifts of the Spirit releases the power of

God's Shekinah glory into the earth, and developing the fruit and walking in it, bearing much fruit, results in the Father being glorified.

Unfortunately, until we develop in certain areas, we may go around and around in endless cycles until we decide to grow up into maturity and allow these fruits to be evident in our life. There is no way around it; there are no shortcuts. But once the effort is made, the Holy Spirit will be there as our enabler, teacher, and guide. It must become a conscious effort daily. Believe me, we will have enough opportunities in the course of an average day to develop great fruit. Likewise, daily we will have opportunities to operate in the spiritual gifts.

God has already equipped us with everything needed to experience life in its totality, a life that is not just length of days but is victorious and overcoming in Christ Jesus. This is why He always causes us to triumph in Christ Jesus, not in ourselves, but in Christ Jesus. Not only will this be a benefit in our life, but also it will draw men to the Father as we demonstrate the character, nature, and power of God to the lost of the world. This is how God intended our life to be; this is what cost Him the blood of Jesus—for us to live this life in its fullness without any limitations. Our Heavenly Father is just waiting for us to walk in and develop what He has already provided.

UNDERSTANDING WHAT WE ALREADY POSSESS

Many believers use much of their energy and time trying to obtain what they already have. Instead, we need to understand what God has given us and how to function accordingly, in the ways God designed for us to function.

What we already have been supplied by God are simple truths, but we must remind ourselves of the profoundness of the simplicity. Oftentimes it is the simplicity of God that escapes men. The terms "sanctification," "consecration," "justification," and "righteousness" are sometimes mistakenly used interchangeably to mean "holiness." The English terms are translated from several different Greek words in different contexts with different shades of meaning. The workings of the five terms are interrelated, sometimes giving the impression from the use in a particular verse that the meaning is the same. For example, "holiness" may be translated as "sanctification" from certain Greek words in some instances in some Bible versions. As we saw in a definition of the Greek word for "holy" in 1 Peter 1:16, "consecration" is used as part of the definition. But the meaning of each of the five terms describes a completely separate work.

We have already looked at "sanctification" and "holiness." We are sanctified by a work of God. As a result of God's work of sanctification, we are able to walk in holiness as He instructs and enables us to do. Our responsibility is to obey by using the means He has made available to us. For example, we have seen the importance of bridling our tongue and diligently guarding our heart, because if our heart is not dedicated to the things of God, the things that we speak out of the abundance of our heart will defile us. The Word teaches us to walk in the Spirit, the fruit of the Spirit, so that we won't walk according to the flesh. The Word tells us how to abide in Jesus, the Vine, to bear much fruit and do good works, fruit that remains, that will bring glory to God.

THE FREE GIFT OF JUSTIFICATION

Our good works are a result of our relationship with God, through the redemption Jesus provided for us, not a means to salvation. We are justified as a free gift from God. We receive this "justification" by faith; there is nothing we can do to earn it. Justification means to be cleaned and to have a clean slate, to be sentenced and found guilty yet receive a pardon. In other words, to have the appearance of innocence, just as if you had never sinned. To have your sins remitted or erased, not atoned. We can clearly see the meaning in Romans 4:1-5 (NKJV):

> *What then shall we say that Abraham our father has found according to the flesh? For if Abraham was justified by works, he has*

something to boast about, but not before God. For what does the Scripture say? "Abraham believed God, and it was accounted to him for righteousness." Now to him who works, the wages are not counted as grace but as debt. But to him who does not work but believes on Him who justifies the ungodly, his faith is accounted for righteousness.

IN RIGHT STANDING WITH GOD

"Righteousness" is our position in Christ Jesus. Jesus obtained righteousness for us. It is also a benefit of redemption. Paul's letter to the church at Philippi spreads a table for us to clearly examine the meaning of "righteousness."

> *Yet indeed I also count all things loss for the excellence of the knowledge of Christ Jesus my Lord, for whom I have suffered the loss of all things, and count them as rubbish, that I may gain Christ and be found in Him, not having my own righteousness, which is from the law, but that which is through faith in Christ, the righteousness which is from God by faith.*
>
> Philippians 3:8,9 NKJV

Our own righteousness is as a filthy rag. The reason is that we cannot present ourselves righteous. The position of righteousness is a result of Jesus' crucifixion and resurrection. We could not go to the cross to restore our relationship with God for ourselves. This is the reason that no matter how we try to come to God in our own self–righteousness, we don't impress God because we all need a Savior. We must all obtain true righteousness by the way of the Cross. This could not be better articulated than the way Paul reveals it to the church of Galatia:

> *"I do not set aside the grace of God; for if righteousness comes through the law, then Christ died in vain."*
>
> Galatians 2:21 NKJV

CALLED INTO OUR PLACE IN GOD

Some believers think "consecration" is the same as sanctification. Consecration is a totally different act. Once we are born again, we are sanctified. The next act, which many believers miss, is placement, inaugurating or dedicating us, into service for God's use.

Just as sanctification calls us *out* of something, as Jesus through His sacrifice set the church apart from sin for God, "consecration" places us into something. Jesus as High Priest "is consecrated for evermore" (Heb. 7:28 KJV). He has made us, those who believe in Him, priests, giving us the ability "to enter the Holiest" "by a new and living way which He consecrated for us..." through His sacrifice. (Heb. 10:19,20 NKJV.) In this verse, "consecrated" means "not as though already existing, but has inaugurated as a new thing"[9]; or dedicated.[10]

Jesus called the church as "a royal priesthood" "out of darkness," which would be the act of sanctification, "into His marvelous light," which would be the consecration.

> *But you are a chosen generation, a royal priesthood, a holy nation, His own special people, that you may proclaim the praises of Him who called you out of darkness into His marvelous light.*
>
> 1 Peter 2:9 NKJV

God takes the believer through a process in Romans 8:29-30 (NKJV):

> *For whom He foreknew, He also predestined to be conformed to the image of His Son, that He might be the firstborn among many brethren.*
>
> *Moreover whom He predestined, these He also called; whom He called, these He also justified; and whom He justified, these He also glorified.*

I find it so awesome that God, in His infinite foreknowledge, predestined the believer, called him, justified him, and brought him to the crowning honor of glorifying him—the ultimate end. Our challenge in life is not defining who we are, what we can do, or what we can have, but understanding what we already possess.

PART 5

COMPLETE YOUR CALL

CHAPTER 20

THE PERSONAL TOUCH

God can never be separated from His people. Our Heavenly Father never abandons His children. As we delve into the heart of God concerning His people, we find that God unconditionally loves His own. He may strongly disapprove of some of our behavioral practices, yet He never forfeits His love for us, and He never will forfeit it. Nothing will separate us from the Father's love or stop Him from loving us. (Rom. 8:38,39.) However, and allow me to make this fact crystal clear: God, in His love, grants us the free will to choose to obey or to disobey Him.

He always wanted to establish His family. Before the church institution, church governments, doctrinal decrees, the Ten Commandments, and the Levitical order of the Law, He established His family and made a way of reconciliation for us. His laws are forever established. When establishing His laws He made provisions through grace and faith in the person of His Son, our Redeemer, Christ Jesus, to reconcile us back to Him.

For thousands of years, God's number one priority in heaven has been man. The Bible describes a specific time when there is joy in the presence of the angels of God: when one man repents. (See Luke 15:10.) How valuable, precious, and priceless is His redeeming love for mankind. The psalmist David expresses to us so poetically in Psalm 8:4-8 (NKJV):

What is man that You are mindful of him, and the son of man that You visit him? For You have made him a little lower than the angels, and You have crowned him with glory and honor. You have made him to have dominion over the works of Your hands; you have put all things under his feet, all sheep and oxen—even the beasts of the field, the birds of the air, and the fish of the sea that pass through the paths of the seas.

GOING AGAINST THE WAY OF GOD IS A HARD WAY TO GO

At times some believers seem to forget that being created in God's image and likeness, with the same innate instinct and nature to reign with Him, was not man's idea! Mankind could never achieve this heavenly status on our own. We are seated with Him in heavenly places only because He ordained it to be so. Remember, the only way that we can produce fruit is if we remain connected to the Vine. This is not a cause for haughtiness but rather for humility. It is hard to go against the way of God, but even those who know Him as Father, after receiving and becoming joint heirs with His Son Jesus, still sometimes, even often, choose to disobey Him.

On the road to Damascus, when Jesus confronts Saul, who becomes the Apostle Paul, He is actually telling Paul that it is hard to go against the way of God. And through the life of Paul the Apostle during this experience, God reveals His redemptive plan for us.

This encounter takes place long before Paul comprehends the mysteries of God, long before he suffers persecution for the sake of the Kingdom, and long before he becomes a great church planter. During this time the church is valiant, yet still young, tender, and very dear to God. This zealous persecutor polices the adolescent church in a venomous rage. But in Acts 9:4-5 (NKJV), notice how God deals with Paul concerning God's people.

GOD CANNOT BE SEPARATED FROM HIS PEOPLE

Then he fell to the ground, and heard a voice saying to him, "Saul, Saul, why are you persecuting Me?"

And he said, "Who are You, Lord?" And the Lord said, "I am Jesus, whom you are persecuting. It is hard for you to kick against the goads."

The Lord displays Himself as attached to His people! In this passage of Scripture we do not see a God who is aloof and distant; neither do we see a God who averts His eyes from the persecution of His people. Paul as Saul is making havoc of the church (See Acts 8:3), but the Lord says Paul is persecuting *Him.* We see a characteristic of God that shows us He is a God who cannot be separated from His people. This is a mystery of God revealed—Christ in us the hope of Glory (Col. 1:27), God in man.

Paul must glimpse this revelation because he responds by saying, "Who are You, Lord?" The Lord answers Paul, revealing again that He is a God who cannot be detached from His people. The Lord tells Paul who He is and states, "It is hard for you to kick against the goads." He is telling Paul that it is hard to go against the way of God.

During this era of time, a goad was used on an animal to bring it into submission and to train it to go the way of his master by following instructions and directions. The animal in rebelling against the way of his master, or kicking against the goad, would hurt only itself, not the master. The goad was designed for the ultimate use of bringing the animal into a place of reckless abandonment, submission, and obedience to its master. The Lord is trying to tell Paul that Paul is only hurting himself to go against the Lord and His will. It is harmful to go against the will of God and to oppose His people.

God actually, in a humorous way, sends the persecutor to deliver the persecuted! Then God chisels away at the pride of Paul, stone by stone and brick by brick, by sending him to sit at the feet of those whom he once sought to kill. The person who once murdered now becomes the mercenary to the people he persecuted. Before God can use Paul, He has to first break through to him physically, spiritually, emotionally, and socially. God breaks through to Paul when Paul, blind for three days following the encounter, has to depend on someone else to lead him around!

> *So he, trembling and astonished, said, "Lord, what do You want me to do?" And the Lord said to him, "Arise and go into the city, and you will be told what you must do."*
>
> *And the men who journeyed with him stood speechless, hearing a voice but seeing no one.*
>
> *Then Saul arose from the ground, and when his eyes were opened he saw no one. But they led him by the hand and brought him into Damascus.*
>
> *And he was three days without sight, and neither ate nor drank.*
>
> Acts 9:6-9 (NKJV)

Paul, the man who was once confident, has to rely on someone else. Paul has to first be dethroned before he will be open to hearing God instruct him. After Paul is brought down from his exalted position, the first words he hears are words of deliverance for God's people, the same people he dislikes and had persecuted with vigor!

Let's observe one more factor concerning the union of God and His people found in Acts 5:1-4 (NKJV):

> *But a certain man named Ananias, with Sapphira his wife, sold a possession. And he kept back part of the proceeds, his wife also being aware of it, and brought a certain part and laid it at the apostles' feet.*
>
> *But Peter said, "Ananias, why has Satan filled your heart to lie to the Holy Spirit and keep back part of the price of the land for yourself?*
>
> *"While it remained, was it not your own? And after it was sold, was it not in your own control? Why have you conceived this thing in your heart? You have not lied to men but to God."*

Ananias thought that the idea of sharing all things was the apostle's idea alone, but the apostles were full of the presence of God. God was living in and through them, manifesting His presence as they made themselves conduits of the true and living God. The matter was judged and Ananias dropped dead, and his wife, Sapphira, who was privy to what her husband had done, received the same judgment. She died three hours later when she came to act out her part in the conspiracy.

We have looked in detail at the history of God's intent to cohabitate with man, to become one with His people, beginning in the Garden of Eden with Adam, whom God created to live in His glory and manifested presence. God revealed Himself to individuals throughout the Old Testament in order to prepare man to receive Him through Jesus' sacrifice, into the ultimate abode He desires, people themselves. For those who choose to receive Him, He makes His abode in them, becoming inseparable with them.

In understanding the extent to which God goes in order to restore man to relationship with Him, we are able to grasp the concept that because God and His people are one and inseparable, the things done to His people are actually done to Him. This shines a new light on the subject, doesn't it? Let's get down to where the rubber meets the road.

As you read the remainder of this chapter, please clear your mind and get alone in a quiet room because I am believing that the *logos* Word of God is about to become *rhema* to you as you read. May you become empowered with full understanding of the meaning behind these words and God's ability to carry out His number one priority through you. I am trusting that these words will seemingly lift off the pages as understanding fills your heart about this subject that has been overlooked at a great price.

If we purpose in our heart to allow God to bring revelation of this golden Kingdom concept, it will change the entire way we view our brothers and sisters in the Body. This revelation will also change the way we relate; and it will demand justice and equity, and elevate us to an integral position with one another. We will be forced to continually examine our deeds, motives, intents, and purposes.

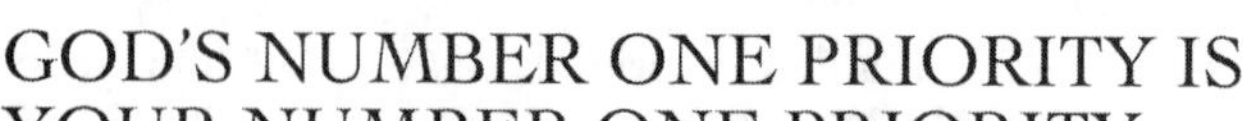

GOD'S NUMBER ONE PRIORITY IS YOUR NUMBER ONE PRIORITY

If we will always remember that God and His people are one, the priorities we place on the important things in life will shift from merely obtaining victories, to *how* we obtain the victories and at what price. Always live according to the principle that whatever we compromise to get, we ultimately will lose. We will begin to weigh matters from a broader perspective as we grasp that God and His people are one. We will need to reexamine the principles we operate by in life, in handling business deals, and in the way we treat each other. This is perhaps what has delayed Spirit-led revivals in our generations and previous ones. God examines with equal importance our behavioral practices with one another as much as He examines our "sacrifices," in the sense of the right kind of God-directed sacrifices. Let's look at Matthew 5:23-24 (NKJV):

> *"Therefore if you bring your gift to the altar, and there remember that your brother has something against you,*
>
> *"leave your gift there before the altar, and go your way. First be reconciled to your brother, and then come and offer your gift."*

The beatitudes are God's Kingdom concepts for relating correctly with one another. This foundational truth, that the beatitudes tell us how to function with each other, is so important yet easily overlooked. The guidelines in Matthew 5:1-48 clearly state how God expects His creation, man, to operate in the earth. In Matthew 5:23-24 God literally means to leave our gift or sacrifice at the altar and go deal properly with our fellowman before He will be able to accept our gifts and sacrifices. We can be assured that in the long run we will find greater pleasure in obedience rather than sacrifice. God explains in detail how we are to handle and relate to each other. How conscious are we of the manner in which we relate to others every day? How much do we value people and our relationship with them?

THE KINGDOM IS NOT SELFISH

The way of God is diametrically opposed to the way of society. This is why He prayed that the will of the Father in heaven be established on earth. We are the couriers of His truth, His will, and His ways. We are the demonstrators of Kingdom living. Kingdom living is God's way of thinking, living, and operating. His way is not selfish because He is love. Love can never be selfish. Selfishness cannot cohabit with a heart housed with the love of the Father because love continually seeks for avenues and opportunities to give—love always gives. When we are unsure of love issues in any area of our life, we must ask ourselves, "Does this act of love give?" If giving is not displayed, it is not true love. The Scriptures tell us in John 3:16:

> *For God so loved the world, that he gave his only begotten Son, that whosoever believeth in him should not perish, but have everlasting life.*

For God so loved the world that He gave. His love plan for humankind placed a demand on Himself to give. And He didn't only give something that was good, He gave the very best that heaven had to offer—His blameless, perfect, and sinless holy Lamb. Jesus was slain, given, and predestined as a sacrifice for our sin. God gave His Son because love seeks the opportunity to give before the need arises. God gave His Son before the foundations of the world.

Love is not selfish or does not have to have its own way. Love does not need to be right; it does not need to be in control or concealed. Love is transparent and makes itself vulnerable and an open target. The reason love has no fear in being transparent is because love knows that it cannot fail. God is Love. Every area that we don't want revealed, where we want to keep people out, is an area where love is lacking.

Adam hid and covered himself when he violated the love plan. When he walked in accordance with the love plan he was naked, open, unashamed, and unafraid. It was the love of God's glory that encompassed and protected him. There was no fear in the love plan. Fear invaded only where love exited his life because perfected love casts out fear. Every hidden struggle is an area of fear, lack of faith, and lack of love. This is why faith works by love.

Often we have to love by faith, especially when the person is unlovely to us. We please the Father when we walk the love walk. The husband who demands his secluded life, the teen who rebels for his privacy, and the wife who feels neglected: All must walk the love walk by faith. With God the way up is down—it's the paradox to life. A paradox is an enigma, something that appears to be one way but is another, and appears to be a contradiction. With God, to keep our life we must lose it, by being open to obey Him and being used by Him, and to be great we must serve. To be first, we must be willing to be last, and to be exalted, we must humble ourselves.

The process of practicing this challenging, disciplined, and selfless way of living will breed spiritual maturity and the confident character of God. It develops a foundation inside of us that can weather life's storms, the perplexities of life, and the diversity of the cantankerous personalities of people.

WINNERS

Daily we face the choice to be a giver or a receiver. A subtle teaching today is a misconception concerning winning. Yes, God has made us to be winners, but the manifestation of winning is not always in material gain. Winning is most often intangible and unseen. Winning doesn't always appear as openly being positioned on top, having the last word, or winning the debate in an argument. Most often winning is yielding first and trusting God to defend us. The Bible tells us in Psalm 5:11:

But let all those rejoice who put their trust in You; let them ever shout for joy, because You defend them; let those also who love Your name be joyful in You.

We can shout for joy because when the Lord defends us, it is a perpetual defense. Of course, when we are confronted with the opportunity, our carnal instinct will be self-preservation. The mindset of our Lord is to lay down His life. He said no man took His life but He laid it down. (See John 10:18.) Through this He taught us that it is better to give than to receive. The reason He could say this was that He Himself was given as the Savior to all humanity. His very existence on the earth was the embodiment of God's gift given to man for redemption.

Jesus taught us to live to give, not to give to live! God sends us opportunities and sometimes challenges into our life as a life lesson in giving. As we purpose to live to give, rather than giving just to survive and live selfishly, we will develop a different mindset for life. The giving way of life always positions us in a better posture. Jesus said it is more blessed to give than to receive. What did He mean by saying blessed? Blessed means empowered to prosper, empowered to overcome. So as we make investments into the lives of others, we are immediately positioned to be empowered to prosper. This is the way of the Father. It is joyful to be on the receiving end, but the greatest joy is to be the giver. Our Lord was the ultimate giver. Not only was it His nature to give; it was His very persona. He was the gift given.

Until we learn to be sensitive in how we treat one another and position ourselves as the giver in our relationships, we will continue missing an ingredient in life that will rob us of developing the fruit and releasing God's nature to the available extent. Paul said that he made himself a servant to all, that he might win more people to the Gospel of the Lord. (See 1 Cor. 9:19.)

Just as Christ loved the church and gave Himself for her, husbands are to love their wives. (Eph. 5:25.) Just as the church is subject to Christ, wives are to be to their own husbands. (Eph. 5:24.) The wife in serving her husband and family is the one who is commanded to adapt and give up her time, her love, and her privacy the most. But she doesn't lose if she allows her mind to be renewed to God's way of doing things. She will never go neglected or unrewarded before God. Wives, learn to seek your reward from the Father; continue to store up treasures in heaven and invest in your family. The master will reward your investments. Keep your eyes on the master. I dare you to look to Him to reward you; allow Him to esteem you. He will reward you like no man could ever!

The selfish person is the one in bondage; the person who gives is the free one. There is no yoke big enough to bind the giver. The mature person is always the first to repent, give, and serve. The strong bear the fragility of the underdeveloped. We must allow our love and maturity to undergird the weakness of others' selfishness until our love melts away their lack of sensitivity. The area we resist or refuse to grow up in is the area of greatest interest to God. Mark 10:17-22 (NKJV) tells us of a man that came to Jesus by night:

> *Now as He was going out on the road, one came running, knelt before Him, and asked Him, "Good Teacher, what shall I do that I may inherit eternal life?"*
>
> *So Jesus said to him, "Why do you call Me good? No one is good but One, that is, God.*
>
> *"You know the commandments: 'Do not commit adultery,' 'Do not murder,' 'Do not steal,' 'Do not bear false witness,' 'Do not defraud,' 'Honor your father and your mother.'"*
>
> *And he answered and said to Him, "Teacher, all these I have observed from my youth."*
>
> *Then Jesus, looking at him, loved him, and said to him, "One thing you lack: Go your way, sell whatever you have and give to the poor, and you will have treasure in heaven; and come, take up the cross, and follow Me."*
>
> *But he was sad at this word, and went away sorrowful.*

Did he have the wealth or did the wealth have him? The free person is always the one seeking the opportunity to give. They always have giving on their mind. The giver is generous in attitude: They esteem their brother higher than themselves and, in the fruit of love, seek not their own. (See Rom. 12:10; 1 Cor. 13:5.) This approach doesn't come effortlessly, but God promises us that He will crown our effort with success. Whatever measure we give shall surely be measured back to us. I have found ceaseless fulfillment in giving to those who have nothing to offer me materially. This way of living pleases our Father because this is how He operates.

The Bible tells us that in life we could easily be entertaining angels unaware. I have experienced this firsthand on the mission field. I was stranded with a team in the middle of the bush in Africa when our vehicle broke down. All of sudden, two men at least seven feet tall appeared before us. They frightened us because they seemingly came out of nowhere. The first thing they said to the team was, "Be not afraid, for we have been sent to comfort a woman who has lost her son, and we have been sent to help you also." We never recounted what they said until they were gone. They repaired the vehicle within seconds without tools, and as we shouted for joy, I remembered that we hadn't thanked them, but they were gone. A chill came over us as we realized that we had entertained angels unaware. We must be mindful of the people God sends across our path.

God microscopically monitors the way we treat the people He sends us as a gift. He can never be separated from His people, so whatever we do to them, we do to Him. According to Matthew 25:40 (NKJV):

> *"And the King will answer and say to them, 'Assuredly, I say to you, inasmuch as you did it to one of the least of these My brethren, you did it to Me.'"*

I was once in a situation where I was falsely accused, and I had all the evidence I needed to defend my case. But my Father said, "Don't you open your mouth. Let Me defend you." The hardest thing to do in the midst of accusation is to hold our tongue and allow the Lord to fight our battle!

Instead of defending myself, I worshipped the Lord daily. God sent me a man of God with wisdom to pray with me and encourage me daily through it all. Needless to say the Lord did just as He promised. He exalted me above my enemies, and He is still exalting me above them because integrity preserves us. (Ps. 25:21.)

If we ask the Lord to make us conscious on a daily basis of how we treat people, we will likely be amazed that we do not act as great respecters of others around us. James 2:1-5 (NKJV) tells us:

> *My brethren, do not hold the faith of our Lord Jesus Christ, the Lord of glory, with partiality.*
>
> *For if there should come into your assembly a man with gold rings, in fine apparel, and there should also come in a poor man in filthy clothes, and you pay attention to the one wearing the fine clothes and say to him, "You sit here in a good place," and say to the poor man, "You stand there," or, "Sit here at my footstool," have you not shown partiality among yourselves, and become judges with evil thoughts?*
>
> *Listen, my beloved brethren: Has God not chosen the poor of this world to be rich in faith and heirs of the kingdom which He promised to those who love Him?*

The Good Samaritan in the Luke 10:30-35 account was willing to help the man who was walked over by everybody else. With God, man's rejected becomes God's elected! The stone that the builders rejected, Jesus, became the chief cornerstone. (Acts 4:10,11.)

By grasping this concept alone, we could handle rejection in life much better. There is One who will never reject us; the rejection of man is temporary. The 3,000 people described in Acts 2:36-47 who repented, were baptized, and praised Jesus were among those who had previously shouted in favor of His crucifixion.

CHAPTER 21

PASSION FOR EVERY PERSON

The Bible gives account after account of Jesus' willingness to go out of His way for *the one person.* Although He was thronged with people, the size of crowds and ministry we would term today "massive crusades," He always made time in His schedule to minister to *the one.* The Savior of the entire world is as accessible today and relates as personably as He did then so that each person He ministers to feels as though He is centering His attention to help that person alone. The Bible contains many scenarios of a Messiah who can be touched and is personal, sensitive, and understanding. Examples are flooding my mind as I attempt to select those most apropos to reflect this attribute of Jesus of ministering to *the one.*

Should I start with the woman with the issue of blood who, in the midst of the crowd, manages to touch the hem of His garment? Out of all the people around Him, He distinctively differentiates the touches of *want* from the touch of *desperation* and notices that virtue has gone out of His body. I am thankful that we have a Redeemer who is sensitive enough to acknowledge a desperate need in the midst of a multitude.

Or shall I recall the woman at the well who was drawing water at a time of day when women should not be at the well? The desperate need of the woman at the well magnetically drew Jesus to Samaria. John 4:3-5 states:

> *He left Judaea, and departed again into Galilee. And he must needs go through Samaria. Then cometh he to a city of Samaria, which is called Sychar, near to the parcel of ground that Jacob gave to his son Joseph.*

The need of the woman draws Him to a *certain* city in Samaria called Sychar, to a *certain* plot of land, to a *certain* well at a *certain* time to meet a *certain* woman. The pain of the woman blocks her discernment of the Christ standing before her, yet Jesus is so patient with her and ministers to her in the area of her pain. Jesus takes an interest in her failure, and He doesn't rush her through a counseling session.

As He methodically and skillfully peels off every layer of defense mechanisms that the hardships and disappointments of life have built around her heart, Jesus is not concerned about what people would think about Him being a Rabbi and talking to a woman. She is not just any woman; she is a woman with a past that the whole town of Sychar knows about. He doesn't use her emotional state to manipulate her into giving an offering; rather, He empowers her to rise up and motivates her to leave the types of relationships that she has used in the past to try to satisfy a thirst that she has never been able to quench. After her experience with Jesus, she runs into the city no longer thirsty but fulfilled, and immediately begins an evangelistic ministry to the very men she once tried to please.

Do you remember a man named Zacchaeus? Jesus singles him out when He sees him in a sycamore tree. Jesus calls him by name and invites Himself to dinner at Zacchaeus's home. He is a man short in stature compared to other men and yet Jesus elevates him to a stature that cannot be measured in cubic inches.

Do you recall the woman who had a spirit of infirmity eighteen years, who was bent over and couldn't raise herself up? Jesus, who was teaching in one of the synagogues on the Sabbath, called her to Him and healed her. The ruler of the synagogue then spoke in indignation to the crowd that they should come to be healed on one of the six days on which men ought to work, not on the Sabbath day. Jesus called him a hypocrite because each one of the people in the synagogue would lead their ox or donkey from the stall to water it on the Sabbath—ought not this daughter of Abraham whom Satan had bound for eighteen years be loosed on the Sabbath? (See Luke 13:10-16 NKJV.) He zeroed in on *the one,* the one woman, to heal her.

During Jesus' ministry on earth, He is so sensitive and focused on the needs of others that He does not complain about His own needs. We see that He never worries about the financial budget of His ministry or any other type of provision He would need. We read the account of one financial need when He orders one of the disciples to open the mouth of a fish and pull money from the fish's mouth sufficient to pay the necessary taxes!

When Jesus is concerned about the massive crowd following Him, He multiplies five loaves of bread and two fish, and feeds the masses until they are satisfied. The Bible always depicts Jesus as a servant to the people. The people knew that He genuinely loved them, and they loved Him.

Jesus even defends *the one* who was caught in the act of adultery. In John 8:10-11 we see Him using His wisdom and influence to make a way of escape for her and leaves her with a prophetic promise.

> *When Jesus had lifted up himself, and saw none but the woman, he said unto her, Woman, where are those thine accusers? hath no man condemned thee? She said, No man, Lord. And Jesus said unto her, Neither do I condemn thee; go, and sin no more.*

She had been the object of men but had never had a man fight for her defense! She was sentenced to die according to the Law, but on that day Jesus gives her self-worth, esteem, protection, and purpose.

The passion of Jesus' heart toward *the one* is revealed in the parable of the lost coin in Luke 15:8-10.

Either what woman having ten pieces of silver, if she lose one piece, doth not light a candle, and sweep the house, and seek diligently till she find it? And when she hath found it, she calleth her friends and her neighbours together, saying, Rejoice with me: for I have found the piece, which I had lost. Likewise, I say unto you, there is joy in the presence of the angels of God over one sinner that repenteth.

Jesus gave these parables to the Pharisees and scribes so that they could hear and learn the importance of motivation and true ministry, not only to the masses but also to *the one.*

Another teaching Jesus used to illustrate this importance is the parable of the lost sheep found in Luke 15:1-7.

Then drew near unto him all the publicans and sinners for to hear him. And the Pharisees and scribes murmured, saying, This man receiveth sinners, and eateth with them.

And he spake this parable unto them, saying, What man of you, having an hundred sheep, if he lose one of them, doth not leave the ninety and nine in the wilderness, and go after that which is lost, until he find it? And when he hath found it, he layeth it on his shoulders, rejoicing. And when he cometh home, he calleth together his friends and neighbours, saying unto them, Rejoice with me; for I have found my sheep which was lost.

I say unto you, that likewise joy shall be in heaven over one sinner that repenteth, more than over ninety and nine just persons, which need no repentance.

The owner of the sheep leaves the ninety-nine and goes to search for *the one.* Once the sheep is found, he brings him home and calls all of his friends to rejoice with him. Can you image how this parable pierced the theology of the Pharisees and Sadducees?

Once on a mission assignment to a small village, Mutare in Zimbabwe, I experienced an encounter that has both molded and shaped the motivation of my ministry. It is so easy to be faithful when the Master "calls" you to the *masses;* however, He desires the same level of faithfulness as He assigns you to *the one.*

The mission assignment to Mutare was quite strenuous and had proven to be quite taxing, to say the least. Each day I was flown from one end of the country to the other. My average day consisted of twelve to sixteen hours of ministry. Each day I asked the Lord to strengthen me as my physical body was feeling the effects of the hectic ministry schedule.

The nation was in a political uproar; the economic status of the country was extremely unstable. The tension was mounting daily as the indigenous people of Zimbabwe protested against the Rhodesian paradigm. Amazingly, 80 percent of the wealth of Zimbabwe is controlled by 20 percent of the population, according to statistics I was given when I was in Zimbabwe. The fight over land and rights, deeds and titles, entitlement and inheritance continued daily. Farms were seized and homes were sabotaged as the pressure from the West was placed upon Zimbabwe President Robert Mugabe to bring an end to the chaos of his country. It clearly looked like a picture of injustice, a situation in which only the mind of God could bring equity and peace.

My agenda was not a political one, but rather I was on a mission with a love plan from on High. The Father's intuition and omniscient ability to telescopically zero in on one person has never ceased to amaze me. How is it that He rules over the universe, knows each star by name, yet knows my thought from afar? How is our Father able to attend to every detail of our life, perfecting those things which concern us? What component of His unconditional love causes Him to deal in the affairs of men: their thoughts, their needs, their fears, as well as their dreams and desires?

His passion for *the one* is an attribute that we must all request. His search and His conquest are for *the one.* Though He views us collectively, He watches and cares for us individually. His eyes are ever upon us, and it is with His eye that He guides us. (See Ps. 32:8.)

In the midst of all of the chaos and calamity, this Perfect Father of ours allowed me to hear His voice calling. He rolled back all the activity of my mind and settled me on the inside long enough to hear His voice with amplified clarity. My mission was clear.

I knew that He was sending me on an assignment to someone whose petition had weighed dearly upon His heart. What a privilege to be a courier of His love. As believers, we have been given the awesome assignment of delivering Living Bread to dying men. We possess the ability to impart the love of God into the lives of those whom oppression left neglected. As His ambassadors, we are given the honor of representing His passion and desire for *the one.*

My host had an agenda, and the Master had His own. We must daily commit our agenda and our ways to the Lord because He is able to establish our thoughts only as we commit our works to Him. (See Prov. 16:3.) The preparation of the heart belongs to man, because we are freewill agents, having free rein over our thoughts, intents, and choices. However, the counsel and the answers from the tongue are from the Lord.

> *The preparations of the heart belong to man, but the answer of the tongue is from the LORD.*
>
> *All the ways of a man are pure in his own eyes, but the LORD weighs the spirits.*
>
> Proverbs 16:1,2 NKJV

It is only the counsel of the Lord that will stand ultimately. (See Ps. 33:11.) God's agenda always supersedes the agenda of man. How does He balance His sovereignty with the will and choice of men? *El Elyon,* the *Most High God,* has the omnipotent ability to turn the hearts of men to the counsel of His own will, yet without ever overriding their will and entitlement to choice. He alone is God. He alone is sovereign. He alone is majestic. He is all loving, gentle, and kind. Our God is merciful and just.

"HE TOLD ME YOU WERE COMING!"

Our host scheduled me to meet and minister to the church leaders. What a privilege! But the woman to whom God was sending me, whom I was calling "Mama," was deep within my heart. I fulfilled proper ministry ethics and kept with the schedule that was prepared for me, but the moment we were given free time, I insisted that I travel into the rural regions outside of Mutare. The driver wanted to know, "How far do you want to go?" I instructed him to just drive—that I would know when we reached her.

We traveled through several villages; however, my spirit didn't bear witness at all. After riding for quite some time, I saw a little church alongside the road. We were on the high road and the villages were in the valley. I saw a group of young girls and boys walking along the side of the road. I told the driver to slow down a bit, and I asked the children to come over to the car.

One of the girls stood out to me like a picture from a classic *National Geographic* magazine. This would have been an award-winning shot! She was the most beautiful, flawless, ebony little girl; she had the highest cheekbones that seemed to be sculpted into her delicate face. Her eyes were like almonds. If I could have, I would have packed her inside my suitcase and brought her home with me! She was the picture of the little girl I had always desired. When she smiled, her teeth were as white as the driven snow. She had a baby on her back who belonged to her sister. She was so young yet so mature and responsible.

I asked her if there was an elderly lady who lived in the village and matched the description I gave her. As I began to describe the picture of the woman I had seen in my spirit, the girl said, "That is my grandma; she's the oldest woman in the village." I then inquired about her residence, and the girl pointed a few yards down the road. I offered her a ride in the van while others chose to run alongside as we slowly pulled off and coasted down into the village.

A member of my team who travels and ministers with me, Yolanda, had her camera out to make sure that she would capture the memories. Our guide indicated that this was where her grandmother lived. Now remember, we were up on a high road and the village was down in a valley. Therefore, we all had to unload and walk down the winding path into the village. My driver looked at me inquisitively but nevertheless joined me in the journey to meet "Mama."

The village consisted of thatched-roof huts; it was the typical scene I have seen in Africa in the more than two decades I have been traveling there. The neighbors began to come out of their huts because the word had gotten around there were visitors from America in the village! We later learned that the news of our coming traveled and reached the village even before our arrival. My tour guide was proud as a peacock; she made sure that all the neighbors knew that we were going to see her grandmother.

As we approached the grandmother's hut, I could hear someone shouting in the distance in their local vernacular. I asked the girl, "What is she shouting?" The girl said, "She is saying, 'I knew you were coming—He told me you were coming!'"

I looked at Yolanda. Her eyes were tearing up, and I was already overwhelmed myself. Mama's grandson ran into the house and changed clothes. After a few minutes he returned with Vaseline on his face and in trousers so short he must have outgrown them at least two seasons before. His white shirt had been washed so many times that it was shredding at the elbows. His arms above his hands were towering up to the cuffs, for the shirt and the cuffs nearly reached his elbows. This must have been his Sunday best; he was so proud of himself. I made sure that I noticed how nice he looked and encouraged him.

Mama finally reached us nearly out of breath after running at least a half mile to reach us from the farming fields. Her hut was located between the location where we had parked on the high road and the beautiful farming fields. She came running to me, gave me a big hug, and said, "My God told me that you were coming to see me!"

Mama left us for a few seconds and began to coo for the chickens to come to her. She cried, "Coo da coo da coo da coo!" I observed several come to her when she called, but there was only one particular chicken she was looking for. Before long a fat chicken finally wobbled its way to Mama. She quickly grabbed it up and wrapped strong string around its legs. Then she came to me and gave me the precious gift. This chicken was the best one she had to give. I found it so amazing that Mama was tapping into the grace of God upon my life and had never read a book or listened to a tape concerning this area in her life. To me she was so amazing. I watched her every move.

Mama continued to tell me through the translator, "I have given my life to the Lord in my late years, and now I have become a deacon in my church. My plans are now to have a revival meeting in the surrounding villages. With God's help, I have nearly converted every surrounding village." She then requested for me to pray that God would use her and send her help to reach the unreached remote villages in the area.

Mama was nearly eighty years of age, but there was nothing old about her attitude! Her perception was very clear both physically and spiritually. There was no doubt at all that she was hearing from God with accuracy, and her relationship with Him was personal and evident to everyone around her. I prayed for all her children and grandchildren. Then it was Mama's turn for prayer. In Eastern culture I have seen how hospitality is revered so much more than in the Western culture. It is interwoven into their culture and is literally second nature to them. The same concept is the way of life in Africa, Asia, and the Middle East. It seems to be a way of life everywhere else in the world except for the Western culture.

When we look at Hebrew customs and culture, we see how hospitality and serving, which are both forms of giving, open the door for the hand of God to move. When the widow woman of God in the Old Testament used her last handful of meal to make a little cake for the prophet to eat, ultimately all of her and her son's needs were satisfied.

"Mama Mutare" made sure that she was going to receive an impartation! I possessed something that she desired, and she was not going to allow me to leave her village without her portion. Therefore, I prayed for Mama and her granddaughter who was epileptic. Mama's desire for herself was to be used by God more and more. She had several meetings in the surrounding villages and desired for God to use her to bring in a great harvest of souls. She also wanted her grandchildren to be blessed and healed.

After I prayed for her and her entire family, we began to gather our things and walk towards the car. One of the grandchildren motioned to carry my bag, which was customary in Africa. But Mama was upset with her, took the bag from her, and gave it to one of the other grandchildren who had been sick because she was the one who needed to be healed. She told us through an interpreter that she was allowing the small girl to carry the bag so that she could tap into the power and gifts upon my life through serving and showing gratitude.

Remember, the Word of God tells us that it was the leper who returned to say "thank you" who was made completely whole. Mama was no Bible school graduate, but she believed that God could do anything. She lived for Him—she simply walked with Jesus. My host told me, "In our culture, when we serve the man or woman of God who carries power, anointing, and giftings, you must find a way to be a blessing to them so that the grace will fall upon you." Now, of course, we have seen the aspect of serving being exploited in the Western culture, but I had a chance to view it in its purest form.

The gift of the chicken and the little girl carrying my purse were more monumental to me than any honorarium I have received in the West. As long as I live, I will never forget the encounter that I had with Mama Mutare and her family. It has remained with me over the years because through it I learned how God can speak to His children, no matter where they reside, and give them the ability to hear His instructions. Through Isaiah 30:21, the prophet tells us that God Himself opens our ears to hear Him instruct us in the way to go. As we learned from the psalmist David, the Lord will guide us with His very own eyes and instruct us in the way that we should go. (Ps. 32:8.)

Mama Mutare was hearing God and being instructed by Him concerning the offering and the carrying of my purse by the grandchild. The Lord opened her ears and guided her with His very own eye. I would much rather have His eyes guiding me than my own. My visual perception is limited while His is able to look forward and backward, up and down, all at the same time. He is the God who sees all.[1] In the Yoruba culture, there is a name that is used to describe God as the One who has a multifaceted ear. Even if we fall into the deepest pit, He is able to hear our faintest cry, and His arms are long enough to pull us out, no matter how deep the pit.

Our Father meets us on the level that we are on and then pulls us up on His level. Perhaps Mama Mutare needed a little confirmation and confidence as she stepped into her new ministry and outreach, so God spoke to His daughter to go and find her. It didn't matter to God that I had come all the way from America. Distance means nothing to Him—it doesn't limit Him at all. *He* sent Jesus from heaven to earth just to show us the way to live this life in its totality. It is easy for me to remain faithful to the masses and the big crusades, but can God trust me to go the desert and minister to just one?

Philip the evangelist followed God's guidance and went to the Ethiopian eunuch, giving him the truth he had been seeking. The eunuch, believing in Jesus, asked Peter to baptize him. As Peter and the eunuch were coming up out of the water, Philip's assignment was complete, and the Spirit of the Lord caught Philip away and transplanted him! The Lord had sent Philip to the middle of the desert to minister to *the one person,* then whisked Philip away. (Acts 8:26–40.)

Jesus even broke the cultural tradition to minister to *the one* when He went to the well at a time that He knew was customary only for women to draw water. He broke the rules to minister to one woman. In these scenarios, the Ethiopian eunuch and the woman at the well become catalytic tools in the hand of God to spread the Good News of Jesus Christ to their regions. Both were considered outcasts and were outside the house of Israel, yet our Savior was obedient to minister to the one.

Today, as ministry is evolving into a mass enterprise of marketing and advertising, let us not lose the quality and attribute of serving and giving in the midst of our attempt to do the work of the ministry. Mama Mutare taught me this valuable lesson in the most tangible way: *Ministry is serving people* and being willing to be obedient to serve *the one!*

CHAPTER 22

LIVING FROM THE INSIDE OUT

Because God deals and relates to man from the mindset and position of righteousness, He skillfully works with man on an individual basis. This working is ultimately for the express purpose of bringing men to the completion of Philippians 2:13, "For it is God which worketh in you both to will and to do of his good pleasure."

In so doing, He ministers through the power of the gifts of His Spirit for the overall profit of all of His children. What the Father is actually doing is orchestrating the destinies of individual people to flow in concert and harmony with His master plan for mankind. This is what makes Him so majestic yet so personal. Now we may not always understand the reason He is leading us in a particular way because we don't fully understand His overall plan. Our assignment is to simply remain open to His leading, walking in our sonship position with Him as our Father, trusting and knowing that He works all things together for those who are His own and for those who are called according to His purpose. (Rom. 8:28.)

We gain access to this privileged benefit of His guidance not because we earn it or deserve it. Neither are we excluded from this privileged benefit because we have been defiled or contaminated by the sin of our flesh. The cleansing power of His Word and the renewed mind of righteousness develop a new way of living and operating.

We now function from the inside out. We now allow the inward working of justification and righteousness to be seen and worked out in the committed act of sanctification and holiness. In other words, the visibility of the outward manifestation of holiness is a result of the inward work of righteousness imparted to us by redemption.

Once we operate in this new way of living, we can begin to understand why we may have an idea of what we think will meet a need, yet it may not be the best way to handle a situation. We see in the present; our Father sees into eternity, future, and past. He knows what we don't know, and He sees what we cannot see. This is why we must trust Him to guide us with His very own eye. In Psalm 32:8 He promises to instruct and teach us in the way in which we should go, and He will guide us with His eye. His eye has the ocular ability to see beyond our understanding.

In our redeemed place of righteousness, we are able to display God's fruit along with demonstrating His power, both of which are of equal importance to Him. Our Father knows exactly what fruit in combination with what type of gift or gifts a person needs to be open completely to receive all He wants to minister to them. Just as miracles are the dinner bell for the unbeliever, God's character, His fruit, His love, specifically in the form of the fruit of His goodness (as stated in Rom. 2:4), leads people to repentance.

God created our spirit to respond to Him. He never ordained feelings of intimidation, insecurities, and fear to reside in our life. He created our spirits to be free, pure, innocent, and undefiled. Guile and deceit are attributes that do not usher forth from the throne of God. God is holy and the life of God contains only the essence of Himself. The obscurities and struggles that we now face in life were never a part of God's original plan. He designed us to know His will and to be led inwardly by His Spirit—His Spirit communicating with our spirit in unbroken fellowship.

Thank God for the power of redemption! Just as Adam clearly knew and possessed the privilege of walking in the will of God, we also possess that same privilege. The will of God is not determined or charted by the external circumstances of our life; it existed before we were born. As this fact becomes more real to us, we will be able to stand as firm as the rock of Gibraltar regardless of the tumultuous storms of life. We must center ourselves on God and spend adequate time in His presence because everything we need is there. His presence is our umbilical cord.

> *God is the author of life, and we will never know how to live the life that He has purposed for us if we do not seek Him, the architect who knows the blueprint and the direction for our life.*

He purposed this within Himself; therefore, we can now understand why external perplexities can never alter our internal compass for life.

We have to learn to live from the inside out—not from the outside in. Living life from the inside does not resemble living in reaction to external circumstances at all. We must live according to purpose and not according to our reactions to what happens in our external life by succumbing to what our flesh dictates to us to do.

Living externally always creates a fleshly reaction instead of a sober and spiritual response from our spirit man. We should desire to come to a level of maturity in our life where we are Spirit led and decreeing daily that we will only pursue God's plan, purpose, and provisions for our life. If we, especially those of us who are leaders, vow to make this pursuit a way of life, we will be guaranteed success in every area of our life. Joshua 1:8 (NKJV) tells us:

> *"This Book of the Law shall not depart from your mouth, but you shall* ***meditate*** *in it day and night, that you may observe to do according to all that is written in it. For then you will make your way prosperous, and then you will have good success."*

MEDITATE THE WORD

God instructed Joshua how to live successfully through the observance of His plan for man according to His Word. The key is meditation. Revelation unfolds to us as we meditate; it is a missing component in leadership today because we are all too busy to be still and meditate upon the revelatory truths of God that we find in His Word. All believers, not just leaders, must set as a goal, meditation of the Word. Daily, God sends us messages and gives us direction, and we miss His instructions because our life is too cluttered with activity and deadlines. We give time and attention to everything but *God!*

It is important for those of us who are leaders to teach our people and families how to be led by the Spirit. Some believers have never been taught the basic characteristics of God pertaining to the leading of His people. If we do not understand God's mode of operation, how can we flow with Him as He endeavors to lead us? The following segments of teaching will emphasize the step-by-step, Spirit-led functions of God. I will prepare a table before you to ingest the variety of ways to follow His leadings that He has made available for us.

FOLLOW THE INWARD WITNESS

It is imperative to know that God's primary way of leading His people is through an inward witness. We have already established that the leading must line up with His teaching in the Word, but through the inward witness He gives us a peace when we are following His will. Some describe this inner peace as a velvety, warm, and secure feeling; for others this peace may feel like a sense of security or a sense that they know, that they know, that everything is all right. It is important not to try to have the same responsive feeling that others have.

Oftentimes it is hard to explain how we know what we know because we are trying to communicate a spiritual experience in terminology describing the physical world. For those who are trying to interpret from a carnal perspective, our description will sound like nonsense.

Remember, the Word of God warns us against this in 1 Corinthians 2:14 (NKJV):

> *But the natural man does not receive the things of the Spirit of God, for they are foolishness to him; nor can he know them, because they are spiritually discerned.*

CHAPTER 23

WISDOM THROUGH THE HOLY SPIRIT

Now let's take a look at James 3:13-17 (NKJV), which tells us about the two types of wisdom.

> *Who is wise and understanding among you? Let him show by good conduct that his works are done in the meekness of wisdom.*
>
> *But if you have bitter envy and self-seeking in your hearts, do not boast and lie against the truth. This wisdom does not descend from above, but is earthly, sensual, demonic. For where envy and self-seeking exist, confusion and every evil thing are there.*
>
> *But the wisdom that is from above is first pure, then peaceable, gentle, willing to yield, full of mercy and good fruits, without partiality and without hypocrisy.*

The wisdom that is birthed from self-seeking, bitterness, and envy is diabolical in contrast to spiritual wisdom from above. Godly wisdom exemplifies the fruit of the Spirit. God is so wise in His dealings with men—in this scripture He gave us a lucid blueprint to decipher between heavenly and earthly wisdom.

We can test this wisdom by asking ourselves the following questions: Is this wisdom peaceable, or does it leave us in turmoil? Is this wisdom pure and void of hypocrisy and partiality? Is this wisdom willing to yield and full of mercy?

When we are training our human spirit to be led by the Holy Spirit, we must never overlook our God-given indicators. We sometimes compromise these yellow and red lights in our life with excuses. We should separate our emotions from the indicators of God because He will not lead us by using our emotions. The number one way of frustrating our human spirit is involving and depending upon our emotions in deciding the actions we should take. Emotions are always temporary and subject to change.

Let's think of our emotions as whipped cream. When we begin to judge spiritual matters with our whipped cream-like emotions, temporary and changeable whipped cream will not be able to hold up against heat, wind, and pressure. It is only a surface topping to give an attractive appearance.

Paul taught the immature church in Corinth how to be led by the Spirit by first teaching them about spiritual wisdom in 1 Corinthians 2:6-7 (NKJV):

> *However, we speak wisdom among those who are mature, yet not the wisdom of this age, nor of the rulers of this age, who are coming to nothing. But we speak the wisdom of God in a mystery, the hidden wisdom which God ordained before the ages for our glory.*

We can glean from this scripture that the understanding of the difference between sensual and spiritual wisdom is very important. Paul shared with Corinth the formula for how spiritual wisdom operates. Spiritual wisdom comes to us in a mystery and is hidden. It is not hidden *from* us, but rather *for* us. Wisdom from heaven will not automatically make sense to our natural minds because a mystery has to be dissected and meditated upon, and then revelation and understanding will flow.

A mystery must be searched out. The Cross and plan of redemption were hidden from rulers of this age and from the benefactors of redemption—the church of the living God, the Body of Christ. Paul then proceeds in 1 Corinthians 2:9-10 (NKJV) to reveal infinite mysteries of how revelation is obtained:

> *But as it is written: "Eye has not seen, nor ear heard, nor have entered into the heart of man the things which God has prepared for those who love Him."*
>
> *But God has revealed them to us through His Spirit. For the Spirit searches all things, yes, the deep things of God.*

God reveals the mysteries through His Spirit. Why? Paul reveals that the Spirit is the entity of the Godhead that does the searching of the deep things of God—the hidden things of God! The Spirit searches the things that do not lie on the surface, the things that are not apparent. These things are important to learn in the formative stages of developing a Spirit-led life.

The things of the Spirit are not always as they appear to be. The Holy Spirit desires to work in conjunction with our human spirit to reveal the eternal purposes and mysteries of God. Romans 8:25-27 (NKJV) tells us:

> *But if we hope for what we do not see, we eagerly wait for it with perseverance. Likewise the Spirit also helps in our weaknesses. For we do not know what we should pray for as we ought, but the Spirit Himself makes intercession for us with groanings which cannot be uttered.*
>
> *Now He who searches the hearts knows what the mind of the Spirit is, because He makes intercession for the saints according to the will of God.*

The Holy Spirit is an employed agent of God. The workings and functions of the Holy Spirit are a part of God Himself that always existed in eternity to create, move, mobilize, and revive. The Holy Spirit is the action of God, the entity of the Godhead, whose purpose is to be a helper to us in life. He helps us understand and obtain the will of God for our life.

It is the Spirit of God who knows the mind of God; He is a part of God and has been a part of God from the beginning. The Spirit is the intimate foreknowledge of God and is also the revealer of ancient mysteries. The Holy Spirit is often overlooked because the character of His persona is different from that of the Father and the Son. The Spirit of God is not a *thing* or a power source only; *He is God!* He is equally as much a part of the trinity as the Father and the Son. He too can be grieved, quenched, and blasphemed.

The Spirit of God is our helper, intercessor, searcher, comforter, leader, speaker, and teacher. He searches the hearts of men, and He knows the mind of God. He works alongside the saints of God!

The Holy Spirit daily awaits our invitation for His help in our life. He will not override our will because He is a perfect gentleman, but will come in and forever take up residency within anyone who desires His presence according to Luke 11:13 (NKJV):

> *"If you then, being evil, know how to give good gifts to your children, how much more will your heavenly Father give the Holy Spirit to those who ask Him!"*

The Spirit is a gift of God to us and a promise from on high to always be with us and in us so that we are not left unaccompanied and uncared for as orphans. The Holy Spirit watches us bumping our heads against the wall as we reason away the counsel of God for our life, through human intellect. As we struggle to find the answers, the Holy Spirit eagerly waits for us to involve Him in our life so that He may reveal the purpose of God to us. This is why the enemy, in his cunning plan, seduced some of the religious institutions into thinking that the gifts of the Holy Spirit are no longer needed.

Many religions of men claim that the church today is exempt from the need for the move of the Holy Spirit through His gifts. They use exhaustive arguments and reasonings to attempt to rule out the reality of the availability of the Holy Spirit to move in His gifts through our life today. They have positioned their intellect above the wisdom of God. The Almighty Himself is the omniscient and all knowing God who gave us the Holy Spirit in full capacity as a helper here on earth.

The Holy Spirit retrieves the gracious design and divine blueprint for our life from the Father and holds it, waiting for us to give Him an invitation to come into our life to unfold the plan and help us achieve it. He knows exactly what God has planned for us. One of His many functions is to lead us into the perfect will of God.

We read in Romans 8:26, *...we do not know what we should pray for as we ought....* We believers do not know what we ought to pray. Why would the Word of God say this? I believe it is an indication that God intends for every believer to know the will of God for our life, which comes only from spending time in His presence: waiting, meditating, and developing the listening side of our prayer life. As we wait upon the Lord, He will show us, by His Spirit, what to do, where to go, and when to move.

Because God foreknew that many of us would find our life cluttered with chaotic activities, especially in church services disguised as service to God, He gave us a helper to intercede for us and be with us, a Helper to assist us in getting our life back in divine order. The "groanings" discussed in Romans 8:26 can only be uttered by the Spirit of God. This is the Holy Spirit doing the work of Romans 8:28 that states, *"And we know that all things work together for good to them that love God, to them who are the called according to his purpose." The Amplified Bible*'s rendering of this verse gives a more detailed picture of the way the Holy Spirit applies the finishing touches in our life as we allow Him to work:

> *We are assured and know that [God being a partner in their labor] all things work together and are [fitting into a plan] for good to and for those who love God and are called according to [His] design and purpose.*

God is at work in us to do His good will and pleasure. This process at work in us demands the orchestration of the Holy Spirit. Let's think for a moment about the areas in our life where we are yet to experience victory and clarity. These are the areas where we need the illumination of the revelation of God. This illumination is the job assignment of the Holy Spirit.

CHAPTER 24

STAYING SINGLE-MINDED

Struggling to try to gain understanding and make sense of something foreign to our human reasoning is what keeps us continually oscillating between two opinions. Trying to understand spiritual things with our human reasoning alone holds us hostage to double-mindedness. God desires for our human spirit to be in harmony and play in symphony with the Holy Spirit.

God desires for us to be led by the inward witness of the Holy Spirit. God's Spirit intercedes for us so that we do not have to fight alone; He stands in the gap for us on our behalf. This knowledge alone should calm our minds and prevent us from wavering—becoming double-minded. The Holy Spirit assists us in our weaknesses as we saw in Romans 8:26 (NKJV).

> *Likewise the Spirit also helps in our weaknesses. For we do not know what we should pray for as we ought, but the Spirit Himself makes intercession for us with groanings which cannot be uttered.*

Believers who are ignorant of the availability of the Holy Spirit, and the many benefits He has for us, are living in a self-inflicted prison. They are wearied in their soul—in their mind, will, and emotions. Human reasoning that is contrary to the Word of God, or that bases its conclusions solely upon the outward appearance of circumstances, battles the inward witness and godly wisdom in the mind.

If we never gain victory in our minds, we will live in a state of indecision, back and forth between following our human reasoning and opinions and following the leading of the Spirit. We will live in an ongoing quandary of: Is it yes or no? Do I go or stay? Do I give or do I take? Do I agree or disagree? Do I trust or refrain? Do I marry or remain single?

Allowing these questions of life to circle around in our mind makes our life difficult. God is consistent. The Bible says, "Jesus Christ is the same yesterday, today, and forever" (Heb. 13:8 NKJV). What God has spoken, He will make good, and what He has promised, He is well able to bring to pass.

When we don't see the full manifestation of what God promised right away, some of us begin vacillating, becoming double-minded. What does the Bible tell us about the lifestyle of a double-minded person? How effective can that person be in leadership, or how effective can any believer be in the course of life living this way? What type of spiritual fruit will that person produce, and will that person be able to hear and receive from God?

The Epistle of James answers all our questions about this poor person.

> *My brethren, count it all joy when you fall into various trials, knowing that the testing of your faith produces patience. But let patience have its perfect work, that you may be perfect and complete, lacking nothing.*
>
> James 1:2-4 NKJV

Within the context of this passage of Scripture, James is focusing on the trials and temptations of life, in other words: life, when it throws you a curveball! It is easy to see how the double-minded person reacts when pressures and tribulations come and hard times surface in life.

James tells us to anchor our souls when trials come. We do that by rejoicing and counting the tribulation as a joyous occasion. How can we count disaster as a joyous occasion? By focusing on the end result—what it will produce—and what good God is working in the midst of it, though initially unseen. By doing this we can see the light at the end of the tunnel.

The fruit of the Spirit that helps us get through all of this is patience. When patience is at a place of maturity in our life, we will be complete and whole, lacking nothing.

James 1:5 (NKJV) states:

> *If any of you lacks wisdom, let him ask of God, who gives to all liberally and without reproach, and it will be given to him.*

When we face situations in life in which we need wisdom, we learn from James that we have a covenant promise from God that we will receive it. If we ask the Lord for it, He will give it to us liberally and in surplus. But when we approach God to ask Him, we must ask in faith without any doubt. James, in verses 6-8 (NKJV), then begins to paint a clear picture of a person who doubts:

> *But let him ask in faith, with no doubting, for he who doubts is like a wave of the sea driven and tossed by the wind.*
>
> *For let not that man suppose that he will receive anything from the Lord; he is a double-minded man, unstable in all his ways.*

The doubting man resembles the waves of the sea that are recklessly driven and tossed by the wind. The waves of the sea present a perfect example of reacting rather than responding; the waves are reacting to the driving force of the wind rather than responding of their own will. The waves allow the wind, which cannot be seen by the human eye, to dictate their course. The waves are tossed back and forth by the wind for all eternity, never going on a chartered, purpose-driven course. The unseen realm randomly drives their course rather than purposefully guiding it.

The wind depicts our trials and tribulations in life. When we are driven solely by our trials, we will never receive anything from the Lord. We are not even allowed to *think* that we are going to receive anything from God. In today's hectic world, we will wear ourselves out contemplating the details of our trials; instead we should act in faith.

Double-mindedness stems from fear—being afraid of not making the *right* choice and being afraid of the consequences of making the *wrong* choice. The person who is double-minded is unstable in the midst of life's storms. The Word of God is the only remedy for double-mindedness. We must anchor our souls in the Word. According to Matthew 7:24-27, the man who builds his house upon the rock is able to stand against the winds, rains, and storms of life.

> *"Therefore whoever hears these sayings of Mine, and does them, I will liken him to a wise man who built his house on the rock:*
>
> *"and the rain descended, the floods came, and the winds blew and beat on that house; and it did not fall, for it was founded on the rock.*
>
> *"Now everyone who hears these sayings of Mine, and does not do them, will be like a foolish man who built his house on the sand:*
>
> *"and the rain descended, the floods came, and the winds blew and beat on that house; and it fell. And great was its fall."*

Reading the Word alone is not enough. We must renew our mind in the areas of our life where we are not stable. This is why God told Joshua to be of good courage and strong. He went on to instruct him in how to get the strength and courage: by not only reading the Word of God, but by meditating on it day and night, night and day. The engrafted Word of God is able to deliver our soul and mind from the bondage of being double-minded and operating in many fears. Fear is the opposite of faith.

Without faith it is impossible to please God and live a Spirit-led life. Oscillating between two opinions, human reasoning and God's leading, will eventually negatively affect the calm and peace in our life. The voice of reasoning that is contrary to the Word of God is the weapon that the enemy uses to cast doubt into our mind with the end result being to rob us of our blessing. When this type of reasoning becomes a way of life, we will frustrate our human spirit.

For those of us who are leaders, sometimes it is difficult for our people to have confidence in our words only. The Word of God tells us to swear to our own hurt and change not, as noted previously. Our people must know that we will follow through on our words. If we practice meditating on God's Word as a principle in life, we will eventually train our human spirit to hear from God and arrive on the winning end. The immature spirit will always speak first, then process what it has already proclaimed. Paul gives us an example of this in 1 Corinthians 13:11 (NKJV). A child speaks before making a complete analysis of his words.

> *When I was a child, I spoke as a child, I understood as a child, I thought as a child; but when I became a man, I put away childish things.*

DOING THINGS GOD'S WAY BRINGS GOD'S RESULTS

The purpose of the Spirit–led lifestyle is to walk in a place of confidence, peace, and accuracy. When we do things God's way, we will reap God's results. We have to learn how to trust in the Lord with all of our heart, not our head, and to lean not on our *own* understanding. (Prov. 3:5.) The verse states our own understanding. We can never rely on our own interpretations of the matters that occur in our life, but in all of our ways we are to acknowledge Him so that He can direct our paths. (Prov. 3:6.) We acknowledge Him by respecting Him and seeking Him to obtain advice, receiving and following His instructions, and becoming more acquainted with Him.

Our role in the Spirit-led life is minuscule! All we do is simply trust Him with our whole heart, regardless of the reasoning of our own head. We should never rely on our natural perception of a situation because we walk by *faith* and not by *sight,* not by our visual perception. In every single thing that we do, we must get acquainted with God's views concerning the matter and follow His instructions. Proverbs 3:5-6 (NKJV) tells us:

> *Trust in the LORD with all your heart, and lean not on your own understanding; in all your ways acknowledge Him, and He shall direct your paths.*

We have to become intimate with God in the decision-making process. God's role in our Spirit-led life is to direct our path. Notice He uses the word "shall," which is a word of absolute action that tells us there is no wavering or vacillating. God Himself takes it as His own responsibility to lead us on a straight path. We can look at this in another sense: He navigates us through life. This is important to meditate upon every morning—the navigation of the Spirit is guiding our life. We read in Psalm 32:8 (NKJV) that God said:

> *I will instruct you and teach you in the way you should go; I will guide you with My eye.*

His eyes can see what we cannot see, and His eyes see a panoramic view. His eyes see eternity future and eternity past simultaneously. We read in Isaiah 58:11 (NKJV):

> *The LORD will guide you continually, and satisfy your soul in drought, and strengthen your bones; you shall be like a watered garden, and like a spring of water, whose waters do not fail.*

Through this verse we can see that God does not take pleasure in obscurity.

Fasting also helps to hear clearly from God. It does not change God, but it does position us in a better place to hear from Him more clearly. Fasting removes the clutter from our life and the dimness from our view of spiritual things. It guarantees us more illumination than the noonday sun. God always gives clarity to His people.

We learned earlier how futile and immature it is to walk in a state of double-mindedness. It is our covenant right, as believers, to know the will of God for our life; we do not have to be pilgrims stumbling around in the dark when light has come to us through the person of the Holy Spirit. He is our inward witness and the number one way, along with His Word, that God leads His people.

It is also important to know that fear and doubt can rob us of our peace in many areas of our life. In other words, someone could give us a prophetic word of direction, or God could be leading us inwardly, and upon hearing the word, we allow fear, doubt, and human reasoning to enter our soul (mind, will, and emotions). This is what robs us of the peace of God that is intended to be a confirmation in our life. The enemy could never rob us of our peace if we would simply give ourselves to prayer, fasting, and saturating ourselves in His Word. We should tune out all invading outside forces and focus on God, on worshipping Him and giving Him thanks for creating us!

We should expect Him, in faith, to answer our call and ask Him without doubting. He will direct us. Remember, He takes pleasure in our submission and obedience to His will. It is His will that was predestined by Him and Him alone! We must continue to meditate on the Word of God that pertains to direction for our life until faith comes in that area. Don't forget that faith comes by *hearing* and *hearing* by the Word of God.

CHAPTER 25

A SPIRIT-LED LIFESTYLE

Faith for a Spirit-led lifestyle comes through meditating on scriptures pertaining to a Spirit-led life. The Word of God has been given eternal instructions by God Himself to produce after its own kind. Here are some scriptures to help you get started on your daily meditation process:

Proverbs 3:5-6 (NKJV): Trust in the LORD with all your heart, and lean not on your own understanding; in all your ways acknowledge Him, and He shall direct your paths.

Jeremiah 1:5 (NKJV): "Before I formed you in the womb I knew you; before you were born I sanctified you; I ordained you a prophet to the nations."

Ephesians 1:18 (NKJV): The eyes of your understanding being enlightened; that you may know what is the hope of His calling, what are the riches of the glory of His inheritance in the saints.

Psalm 37:23 (NKJV): The steps of a good man are ordered by the LORD, and He delights in his way.

Proverbs 11:5 (NKJV): The righteousness of the blameless will direct his way aright, but the wicked will fall by his own wickedness.

Isaiah 58:11 (NKJV): The LORD will guide you continually, and satisfy your soul in drought, and strengthen your bones; you shall be like a watered garden, and like a spring of water, whose waters do not fail.

Isaiah 30:21 (NKJV): Your ears shall hear a word behind you, saying, "This is the way, walk in it," whenever you turn to the right hand or whenever you turn to the left.

Psalm 48:14 (NKJV): For this is God, our God forever and ever; he will be our guide even to death.

Proverbs 16:9 (NKJV): A man's heart plans his way, but the LORD directs his steps.

Isaiah 28:26 (NKJV): For He instructs him in right judgment, his God teaches him.

Isaiah 42:16 (NKJV): I will bring the blind by a way they did not know; I will lead them in paths they have not known. I will make darkness light before them, and crooked places straight. These things I will do for them, and not forsake them.

It would do us justice to commit these scriptures to memory and, if we are leaders, ask our followers to do the same. This will give us a reservoir of scriptures for the Holy Spirit to use when guiding us daily. This is, by all means, a discipline that will ultimately become a way of life. Renewing of the mind is a process and will take time and consistency. This is not for lazy leadership. How can those of us who are leaders, the leadership of God, lead the masses when we cannot organize and take control of our own life? It would be like the blind leading the blind—everyone would have a ditch ministry!

Once we have the Word of God built in us, when doubt comes our way we are able to immediately cast it down before it takes root in our thinking. First the enemy comes with the thought of doubt, and if we receive that thought, rehearse, and ponder it in our mind, it becomes a belief. That belief will soon result in an action. Human nature always gravitates to its most dominant thought, and before we know it, we are being led by our carnal perceptions.

The carnal mind is enmity with God! When the Word of God is built within us, the moment we sense a thought of reasoning contrary to the Word and the dispersing of doubt, we can immediately say the scriptures we have memorized to pull those thoughts down and bring them under the captivity of Christ. Jesus dissects the process of doubt in Matthew 6:31 (NKJV):

> *Therefore take no thought, saying, What shall we eat? or, What shall we drink? or, Wherewithal shall we be clothed?*

Notice that Jesus used the two words "thought" and "saying." Once we verbalize our thoughts, they will become actions shortly. Our actions are the fruit of our thoughts. That is the reason we must put our hands over our mouth before we verbalize certain thoughts—just because we *think* something does not mean we have to *say* it! The fruit of the Spirit that places a muzzle over our mouth is temperance—the ability to control our tongue and ourselves.

Therefore, if we receive the thoughts by *saying* them; then by the same method, we must cast those same thoughts down by *saying* the opposite. Life and death are in the power of the tongue. We must guard our spirit and heart with all diligence, for out of our heart flow the issues of life.

The discipline of the tongue is the most important factor in developing a Spirit-led life. We can literally take ourselves out of the will of God with the words that we speak and by listening and consulting with people who are anything but Spirit led. When two people come into agreement, nothing is restrained. I have witnessed leaders talk themselves into a situation that was not planned for their life. The golden rule for living a Spirit-led life is this: Just say what God says, especially when we do not know what else to say!

Now that we have learned that being led by the inward witness is the basic principle of living the Spirit-led life, let's take a close look at our own life. I know that we can see the areas where we have violated the principles of God. Today, let's stop the madness, stop vacillating between two opinions, and instead follow the voice of God.

We must guard and follow the peace of God that is our divine compass and indicator. If peace is absent from our life, we need to check up on our thoughts and words. If we are continually speaking and meditating on the Word of God and are still lacking the peace of God, we should consciously listen for the Scriptures to speak to us through our spirit.

CHAPTER 26

HIS LEADING, OUR HEEDING

The Bible says that we have a more sure word according to 2 Peter 1:19. The Word of God is a very sure way of being led by the Spirit. During our daily devotion time we should practice listening to the Holy Spirit for scriptures to confirm what the Lord has been saying to us. I began to develop this practice during my early years in ministry. The Holy Spirit will most commonly speak through the Word we have already programmed into our "software," our spirit.

In other words, if we never study and meditate on the Word of God, then the Holy Spirit will be limited in His retrieval of the Word of God from our human spirit to guide us. The Holy Spirit sometimes gives me a scripture reference to turn to, and it is the very word I need to answer my question. God also has used a dream to reveal a scripture to me. When I awoke, I turned to that scripture and found it the very answer I needed for my ministry to move in a certain direction.

The Word of God is called a lamp to our feet and a light to our path. The Word and the Spirit of God will always agree. The Word shines into the dark areas of our life. Second Peter 1:19 states:

> *And so we have the prophetic word confirmed, which you do well to heed as a light that shines in a dark place, until the day dawns and the morning star rises in your hearts.*

First Thessalonians 5:21 says (NKJV):

> *Test all things; hold fast what is good.*

Let's look closely at the scriptures. The Word and the Spirit work together to confirm the will of God. We are told to prove all things by the Word of God. His Word is our schoolmaster and the chief custodian to the counsel of God. It is tried, proven, true, and will never speak contrary to His will. In judging prophecies, words of wisdom, words of knowledge, dreams, visions, or premonitions always go to the Word of God to prove their sobriety and soundness. A God-given prophecy comes from the throne of God, not from man, as Peter tells us in 2 Peter 1:20-21 (NKJV):

> *Knowing this first, that no prophecy of Scripture is of any private for prophecy never came by the will of man, but holy men of God spoke as they were moved by the Holy Spirit.*

We can judge every spiritual experience by the Word of God. If we are sensing or hearing anything that is contrary to His Holy Word, we need to *trash it!* God would never give a prophecy to a woman to become involved with a married man; He would never prophesy to a believer that He would give them something that belongs to someone else. We must never allow other people to speak words into our life that are contrary to the Word of God. God will never lead us into any prophecy that will draw us away from His sovereign will.

In the New Testament we can see Paul making several references to the prophet Isaiah. John the Baptist even quoted the Old Testament prophetic Word of God when leading the early church. David quoted the word of the prophets when leading the children of Israel. Many references are made to the prophetic Messianic promises. The Word of God is a safe compass for our life.

We should never seek prophecies as our primary way of God's leading because God does not generally lead His people by them. In the Old Testament the children of Israel were led by the voice of the prophets because they did not have the indwelling presence of the Holy Spirit to lead them. The closest leading of accuracy the children of Israel possessed was the voice of the prophets. During that time, man could only walk with God; man did not have God's Spirit working inside, working together with their human spirit as we have today. We are definitely operating under a better covenant. Hebrews 8:6 tells us:

> *But now He has obtained a more excellent ministry, inasmuch as He is also Mediator of a better covenant, which was established on better promises.*

One of these better promises is the Holy Spirit. His ministry in the earth today is to lead us with absolute accuracy. As our Heavenly Father designed the quality of life for the New Testament believer, He devised a plan that would not require us to be led externally or depend upon man to lead us. Following man's guidance makes us subject to their human frailties. The leading of the inward witness and the collaboration of our human spirit with the Holy Spirit protects us from the manipulations of man to use their gifting for filthy lucre. Let's look at the sin of Simon in Acts 8:14-20 (NKJV):

> *Now when the apostles who were at Jerusalem heard that Samaria had received the word of God, they sent Peter and John to them, who, when they had come down, prayed for them that they might receive the Holy Spirit. For as yet He had fallen upon none of them. They had only been baptized in the name of the Lord Jesus.*
>
> *Then they laid hands on them, and they received the Holy Spirit. And when Simon saw that through the laying on of the apostles' hands the Holy Spirit was given, he offered them money, saying, "Give me this power also, that anyone on whom I lay hands may receive the Holy Spirit."*
>
> *But Peter said to him, "Your money perish with you, because you thought that the gift of God could be purchased with money!"*

The safest and surest way of being led by the Lord is revealed by a caution in 1 Corinthians 14:10 (NKJV):

> *There are, it may be, so many kinds of languages in the world, and none of them is without significance.*

Many people rely upon voices that they claim to hear, but the voice of God is distinct and bears witness with the Word of God. In the beginning, God uttered His voice and it was the Word of God. The same was in the beginning; the Word of God is God Himself. He was first uttered through His voice to be written as His *logos* Word and later to be written for the purpose of uttering the *rhema* revealed Word of God. It is our safe haven. We cannot know what the Word of God says without first reading it. It is our daily bread and the bread of life.

Recently, I was in a ministers' conference and witnessed twenty to thirty ministers in the pulpit occupying the first couple of rows without their Bibles! I saw one minister become absolutely embarrassed because when the guest minister called for all to stand for the reading of the Word, he didn't have his Bible. This is sad but true—he was the host of the entire conference!

Early in ministry, I learned to observe how important it is for a leader or minister to value the Word of God; it is our gauge as to how disciplined we are as skilled warriors. How can a soldier be deployed for battle without a weapon! One of my assistants was in the military and the head of her platoon. One day while on a field exercise she lost her weapon. Her sergeant ordered her to put her gas mask back on and go back to find the weapon; she could not return until she found it. She was openly rebuked by the sergeant and embarrassed in front of the platoon she led.

I try to keep my sword near me as much as possible. That has helped me develop a relationship with the Word of God. David said in Psalm 119:11 (NKJV):

> *Your word I have hidden in my heart, that I might not sin against You!*

We must fall in love with the Word of God and make it our final authority in life. I think that we will find it most appealing and beneficial to us as we are building our character and developing a new life being led by the Spirit in every area of our life. Character building and the development of a Spirit-led life is contingent on hard work and discipline. This is why some believers find it easier to dial up a toll-free number and get an instant false prophecy than to apply themselves to developing the things of God. Believe me, I never want to make you think that becoming a believer is a passport for a nonconfrontational life of easy living. Why do you think Jesus calls us disciples? Disciples are *made* not *born.*

Once we are born again, we become an instant child of God and are on the road to becoming a disciple of God. Romans 8:16 (NKJV) tells us:

> *The Spirit Himself bears witness with our spirit that we are children of God.*

To become a disciple, we must work at it daily until we are fully conformed into the image and nature of Christ. The epitome of hypocrisy is to allow God to be headship and leader in one area of our life and not allow Him to be Lord in other dysfunctional areas of our life. God does not want us fragmented as Spirit-led believers. In 1 Thessalonians 5:23 (NKJV) Paul states:

> *Now may the God of peace Himself sanctify you completely; and may your whole spirit, soul, and body be preserved blameless at the coming of our Lord Jesus Christ.*

God desires for us to be whole in spirit, soul, and body. Remember, man is a three-part being made in the image and likeness of God.

Jesus Himself used the Word of God as His schoolmaster and defense when Satan came to Him with temptation. He combated and countered Satan's offers with the Word of God. Jesus said in Matthew 4:4 (NKJV):

..."It is written, 'Man shall not live by bread alone, but by every word that proceeds from the mouth of God.'"

If Jesus relied on the Word of God to guide Him, then so should we rely on it as His disciples. Another example of Jesus referring to the written Word was when He was making public His ministry as the anointed One in Luke 4:18 (NKJV):

"The Spirit of the Lord is upon Me, because He has anointed Me to preach the gospel to the poor; he has sent Me to heal the brokenhearted, to proclaim liberty to the captives and recovery of sight to the blind, to set at liberty those who are oppressed."

In this scripture in Luke, Jesus quoted from Isaiah 61:1-2. The security, conformation, guidance, correction, and direction that Jesus needed during His life were all in the Scriptures. Here we see that God Himself relied on the Holy Scriptures. David allowed God to teach him His Word so that he could live to follow God's paths. When we know the Word of God, we learn His ways and can more accurately follow His leadings. For example, perhaps as you are reading, you are reminded of times when you have missed God by not heeding His Word. We do not need a prophecy to confirm whether we should marry someone who is an unbeliever because God does not want us to be unequally yoked with unbelievers in our relationships. He has already told us that in His Word!

Because man is a triune being, it is imperative for us to understand how God relates to us according to how He created us. He created us to communicate with Him in Spirit and in truth according to John 4:23:

"But the hour is coming, and now is, when the true worshipers will worship the Father in spirit and truth; for the Father is seeking such to worship Him."

God is seeking those who will worship and approach Him in this manner. God always has a prescribed way of doing things. Notice this scripture in 2 Chronicles 30:5 (NKJV):

So they resolved to make a proclamation throughout all Israel, from Beersheba to Dan, that they should come to keep the Passover to the LORD God of Israel at Jerusalem, since they had not done it for a long time in the prescribed manner.

God has a specific order in the universe and in our life. He has an order with the galaxy of stars, with the rotation of the earth, and with man. He has a specific way that man enters the earth through birth. With death it is appointed unto man once to die and then after that the judgment. In like manner, God has a determined way of communicating and leading man by speaking to him Spirit to spirit.

There is only a thin line of division between the soul and spirit in triune man, composed of a spirit who has a soul that dwells in a body. The only instrument that man has at his disposal to use as a compass for dividing the two is the Word of God. The line between the soul and the spirit is so thin that only a sharp sword can divide it according to Hebrews 4:12 (NKJV):

For the word of God is living and powerful, and sharper than any two-edged sword, piercing even to the division of soul and spirit, and of joints and marrow, and is a discerner of the thoughts and intents of the heart.

As a believer, we have Paul to thank for forensically separating the process for us. The Word of God divides the thoughts and intents of the heart. The thoughts proceed from the soul, and the intentions of man proceed from the heart. This helps us to understand how to judge matters and situations in life and how to control the thoughts, voices, and intentions that we so often entertain. We are a sum total of the thoughts we have entertained during our lifetime. The Bible tells us that whatever we think within ourselves is what we are; therefore, it is important to depend upon the Word of God as our guidance and divine compass in life.

James 1:21 (NKJV) says:

> *Therefore lay aside all filthiness and overflow of wickedness, and receive with meekness the implanted word, which is able to save your souls.*

In this scripture James, the bondservant, comforts and assures us that the Word of God is the instrument that is capable of saving our souls and not our spirits. Our spirit man does not need deliverance because it cannot sin. The filthiness and wickedness does not come from the inner man. The spirit man is a new creation when we are born again according to 2 Corinthians 5:17:

> *Therefore, if anyone is in Christ, he is a new creation; old things have passed away; behold, all things have become new.*

The new created hidden man of the heart does not sin. This is seen in 1 John 3:9:

> *Whoever has been born of God does not sin, for His seed remains in him; and he cannot sin, because he has been born of God.*

Sin originates with the guilty part of the soul; it tells the body how to respond. Therefore, in developing a Spirit-led life, we must renew and reprogram our minds with the Word of God so that it can eradicate the concepts of carnality that we have grown accustomed to as a way of life. David said that God restores his soul.

Allow me to take you through the process of developing a Spirit-led life via the Word of God as an instrument of guidance. David said in Psalm 119:54 that in his pilgrimage and journey in life, the Word of God became his song as he kept the precepts of the Word of God active in his life. David also said, as he examined himself, that he thought of his ways and his way of life and God had to turn David's feet back towards the Word of God. Then the next process was the acknowledgment of the Word of God. David said in Psalm

119:105 that the very entrance of God's Word gave him understanding and light. That same Word became a light to his feet and a lamp to his path that led him and gave him direction. He began to hide that Word in his heart and meditate upon it so that he could observe to do all that was written in it. (Ps. 119:11; Josh. 1:8.)

David also told us that his tongue would speak of God's Word for all of His commandments were righteous. David learned that the Word of God restored his soul. Being restored under the Old Covenant is the equivalent of being renewed in the New Covenant. The Word of God transforms and renews our souls. It reveals to us the line of demarcation between the soul and the spirit and will eventually save our souls. Once our minds are renewed, we can now function in harmony and no longer be in enmity with God. Romans 8:7 (NKJV) tells us:

> *Because the carnal mind is enmity against God; for it is not subject to the law of God, nor indeed can be.*

This process produces a Spirit-led life by saturating our minds with the Word of God. I will add again that it is work! Every demon in hell will attempt to keep us from living a disciplined lifestyle in the Word of God.

CHAPTER 27

A VISION OF UNITY

Today we can see how God is uniting the Body of Christ. The move of God in the earth today has transcended cultural, denominational, economic, and even gender barriers. This era in church history demands that we unite and form a strong standing united front.

The blatant opposition against the church and the rising incidences of persecution in many regions of the world should force us as believers to lay aside our petty doctrinal differences and link arms together for the survival of our brothers and sisters in other parts of the world. The vision of unity is so refreshing and ministers comfort to our soul. David said in Psalm 133:1-3 (NKJV):

> *Behold, how good and how pleasant it is for brethren to dwell together in unity! It is like the precious oil upon the head, running down on the beard, the beard of Aaron, running down on the edge of his garments. It is like the dew of Hermon, descending upon the mountains of Zion; for there the Lord commanded the blessing—life forevermore.*

Recently, upon taking two assignments in denominational churches, I was faced with laying aside my normal expressions of worship and flowing with the style to which the denominations had grown accustomed. I must be honest: At first I found myself doing the natural thing of comparing their style to the one with which I had grown accustomed. I was very comfortable in the charismatic worship style in my home church. Therefore, worshipping in this service was a cathartic experience for me. I thought, *If anyone is open to different forms and styles of worship, it is me!*

Having traveled and ministered in more than 80 nations, I had experienced diversity of worship as varied as the many cultures and languages. The first assignment was in a denomination I had grown up in that had now become a barrier I had to tackle head-on. I grew up singing those same songs, so it wasn't that they were totally unfamiliar to me. I think the challenge within me was in the area of change. It is so amazing how we gravitate comfortably to what is a tradition to us. After all, the habitual repetition of doing the same thing consistently will develop strong tradition. This is how cultures and customary practices become established and often never questioned.

So there I was, the woman who preaches unity, change, and openness to God, facing the challenge in her own life. It was so subtle because there were things that I was comfortable with and other things that I found myself constantly comparing to the charismatic service I was most used to. There is no right or wrong way in our worship experiences; the dividing factor is in the area of diversity.

Instead of celebrating the diversity and embracing the awesome privilege of entering into my Father's presence in a new expression or style, I was finding myself about to become judgmental. Alone with the mix of emotions, I experienced guilt about to creep in. I knew that I had no right to judge how another person expresses their love for the same God I worship. I was immediately reminded of an incident concerning a similar situation I had experienced in Singapore. It was my first ministry trip to Singapore through the invitation of one of the pastors. He had not informed the congregation that first, I was a woman; second, that I was a Black woman; and third, that I was an American. As I entered the Sunday morning worship hour, I walked into a massive auditorium of Indians,

Chinese, Singaporeans, and Malaysians worshipping God. Some were former Hindus, Muslims, Buddhists, and traditional Catholics.

Now mind you, I was fresh out of Bible school—in Tulsa at that—the center of the day for biblical studies! I didn't find myself judging the people, but trying, with my two African American friends who accompanied me, to enter into their style of worship. The songs were sung with a nasal sound; the instruments they played were different from ones I had heard before, and their style of dancing was beautiful, yet I could not understand a word they were saying! I looked around and tried to begin entering into worship by clapping my hands, but I couldn't find the rhythm. As an African American missionary, raised as a Southern Baptist, I was waiting for the syncopated beat. I never found it, so I started trying to imitate their steps and style of dancing. I could hear the women giggling, but it didn't bother me because at this point I was on an exploration of worship. Then I thought, *Let me try this nasal thing,* so I tried to find the pitch.

Because I didn't speak the language, I began to sing in the Spirit with my heavenly language. Thank God for the Holy Ghost! Before long I had truly entered into the presence of God. With tears streaming down my face, I began to thank God for His omnipotent power and His omnipresence. He was the same in Singapore as in my home church. I began to think about what heaven would be like, and as I did, I realized I was in a training class at that particular moment. I recalled Revelation 5:9-10 and 7:9-10:

> *And they sang a new song, saying: "You are worthy to take the scroll, and to open its seals; for You were slain, and have redeemed us to God by Your blood out of every tribe and tongue and people and nation, and have made us kings and priests to our God; and we shall reign on the earth."*
>
> Revelation 5:9,10 NKJV

> *After these things I looked, and behold, a great multitude which no one could number, of all nations, tribes, peoples, and tongues, standing*

before the throne and before the Lamb, clothed with white robes, with palm branches in their hands, and crying out with a loud voice, saying, "Salvation belongs to our God who sits on the throne, and to the Lamb!"

Revelation 7:9,10 NKJV

I realized that God gets the full expression of global worship only as each tongue and tribe gives Him the praise due to His name. I began to sense how it pleases Him to see the nations give Him true worship. God Himself obviously is a culturally diverse God, and He is able to relate to every culture. Our Heavenly Father not only appreciates diversity, but He orchestrated it. The very word *orchestra* is a most appropriate demonstrative to depict God's true order of worship in eternity. Each instrument is uniquely different, giving a distinct sound, playing simultaneously, yet in perfect harmony, making melody to the Most High. The trumpet doesn't compete with the flute; the harp doesn't strive against the cymbals, and the cello does not intimidate the violin. They all need each other to make up the symphonic masterpiece.

Likewise the human body is the depiction of the Body of Christ. Paul explains this dichotomy in 1 Corinthians 12:14 (NKJV):

For in fact the body is not one member but many.

The diversified functions of the members do not separate themselves from the Body. Even so, though we are many members with different functions, we are still in Christ Jesus. God achieves this mystery by the Spirit, baptizing us all into one Body. The ethnic persuasion of a certain person does not give them entitlement—one ethnic group is not better than any other—we are all the same in God's eyes. First Corinthians 12:13 (NKJV) tells us:

For by one Spirit we were all baptized into one body—whether Jews or Greeks, whether slaves or free—and have all been made to drink into one Spirit.

Our diversity cannot dictate a different form of baptizing because, whether bond or free, we all drink from the same Spirit.

We can allow our human bodies to teach us a life lesson concerning the unified Body of Christ, according to 1 Corinthians 12:15-19 (NKJV):

> *If the foot should say, "Because I am not a hand, I am not of the body," is it therefore not of the body? And if the ear should say, "Because I am not an eye, I am not of the body," is it therefore not of the body? If the whole body were an eye, where would be the hearing? If the whole were hearing, where would be the smelling?*
>
> *But now God has set the members, each one of them, in the body just as He pleased. And if they were all one member, where would the body be?*

Though the foot is positioned at the bottom of the body, it has multiple functions. If it were to be removed from the body, it would cause major demobilization. The foot's function is vital to the balancing of all the members even though it is positioned at the bottom of the body. It comes in contact with the dirt, snow, and rain, and it also has to bear the weight of the body. Every nerve ending is in the foot, which is revealed when something is out of order in the body. Certain illnesses can be detected by examining the foot. It is impossible for the hand to say to the foot that because the foot is not a hand, it is not a part of the body.

Isn't this what we have done in the Body of Christ? One denomination baptizes in the name of Jesus only, and another part of the Body of Christ baptizes in the name of the Father, the Son, and the Holy Spirit. Each refuses to accept the other as a part of the same Body because of their doctrinal differences.

Though we may have different doctrinal perspectives, we cannot disassociate from other members of the Body. The foot needs the hand to massage it when it's in pain. The foot needs the hand to put shoes on it to protect it in the snow and rain. The foot needs the hand to wash it and care for its needs. Does the hand need the foot at all?

It would be very easy for the hand to feel important because of the services that it provides to many members of the body. Nonetheless, the hand cannot go get the lotion for the foot or go to the sink for washing if the foot doesn't take the hand. Through the function of the human body, it is apparent that we all need each other.

Paul gives an observation in the area of the connecting of the body parts, but he also gives a clear observation to the need of each body part in 1 Corinthians 12:20-21 (NKJV):

> *But now indeed there are many members, yet one body. And the eye cannot say to the hand, "I have no need of you"; nor again the head to the feet, "I have no need of you."*

From one perspective he addresses our connection one to another, then he later addresses our need and appreciation for one another. We begin to understand that the most vital parts of the body are the unseen parts; they are the less honored parts but are the most needed. First Corinthians 12:23-27 (NKJV) tells us:

> *And those members of the body which we think to be less honorable, on these we bestow greater honor; and our unpresentable parts have greater modesty, but our presentable parts have no need. But God composed the body, having given greater honor to that part which lacks it, that there should be no schism in the body, but that the members should have the same care for one another.*
>
> *And if one member suffers, all the members suffer with it; or if one member is honored, all the members rejoice with it. Now you are the body of Christ, and members individually.*

This scripture reveals to us how we must not compare ourselves and show favoritism in the Body of Christ. The parts that are seen openly gain most of our attention and pampering, while the unseen and the common parts receive fewer honors. The kidney, liver, heart, colon, and appendix are vital parts of the body that we don't give much thought to daily, but are important for the body to function.

Without them there would be no body! Little do we understand that the unseen members are what allow the visible members to function.

In the Body of Christ, we often show little appreciation to the parking lot attendants, ushers, or maintenance crew but highly exalt the ministers, elders, and deacons. As a missionary, I have experienced this firsthand myself. The frontline colleagues of mine who return home on furlough are hardly ever applauded; many have no place to stay and lack proper support. The honorariums to missionaries are never the same as to the visible television evangelists. The common response that I often hear is that no one knows who they (the missionaries) are. They are not widely seen as are others.

Does this mean that exposure merits honor above service? These are hard issues to face and to be honest with ourselves about them. The frontline missionaries take the hardest hits and are open targets to the enemy. Unfortunately, they receive by far the least honor. The Kingdom equalizer is Christ Jesus Himself. He said every man's work will become clear, according to 1 Corinthians 3:13-14 and 2 Corinthians 5:10.

> *Each one's work will become clear; for the Day will declare it, because it will be revealed by fire; and the fire will test each one's work, of what sort it is. If anyone's work which he has built on it endures, he will receive a reward.*
>
> 1 Corinthians 3:13,14 NKJV

> *For we must all appear before the judgment seat of Christ, that each one may receive the things done in the body, according to what he has done, whether good or bad.*
>
> 2 Corinthians 5:10 NKJV

On that day, there will be a rude awakening because most of what we have focused our attention on will be judged. It is not the title or name or notoriety of a person that shall guarantee the reward of their work. Christ alone will be seated as the Great Equalizer and Just Judge. No man will be exempt from any deed he has done because Paul said we all must appear. There will be no VIP line or preferred seating section. Every man will stand equally before the Christ. The honor and rewards granted to the recipient on that day will be based upon the requirement and qualification of the Judge.

Many people who have been despised, overlooked, rejected, and ex-communicated from denominational boards and religious organizations for following after the Truth will receive their just reward from the living Christ. Sadly, we will discover that some who had massive followings will not necessarily receive the most recognition and honor. This statement is not meant to reflect on any minister who has a grand following; it is simply a recommendation for self-examination.

Let us be honest with ourselves: In everyday life how often do we go out of the way to commend the seemingly insignificant servants who have laid down their lives to make sure that our vision comes to pass? Sometimes the servants who make the greatest sacrifice and labor the hardest receive the least honor. But praise be to God—there is a day of reckoning.

CHAPTER 28

GOD WANTS TO GET UP IN YOUR STUFF

Very few believers ever make the necessary changes to position themselves as vessels of distinction. Although we all come into the Kingdom as babes in Christ, we are given the entitlement of growth. Making the decision to grow up and press fervently after the things of God is a choice that we all have to make. It doesn't alter God's love for us at all. He will always love us unconditionally, and there will always be a longing in His heart to use us for His glory. Because we view it as our prerogative to grow or stagnate, we often do not sense the urgency for maturity.

After all, many of us have learned how to maintain our position of neutrality. How to keep our head above water is not the question to ponder. The thought-provoking question is, "If God has already been able to do great things through us based on our present level of surrender, how much more will He be able to do through our life if we surrender all and make ourselves totally available to Him?" What if we were to yield ourselves totally into the Master's pruning hands and willingly place ourselves on the potter's wheel? What kind of fruit would our destiny yield if we allowed God to really make us a vessel fit for the Master's use? The answer to each question lies within our decisions to make choices and grow to maturity.

We must always remember that the Father desires our growth more than we desire it. As we saw previously, John 15:16 (NKJV) states:

> *"You did not choose Me, but I chose you and appointed you that you should go and bear fruit, and that your fruit should remain, that whatever you ask the Father in My name He may give you."*

Apostle Paul said in Galatians 4:19 (NKJV):

> *My little children, for whom I labor in birth again until Christ is formed in you.*

The earnest expectation of the Father is to bring His children to a place of maturity, but regardless of how much He wills this for our life, we must determine to make a quality decision to grow and be stretched to another level or else we will remain in the stagnant position.

God expects us to bear fruit that remains. It would be profitable for us to consider and examine our present growth level. Many people entered this race at the same time we did. Some are no longer participants; some are barely moving; some are continuing at a steady and consistent pace; and some have even come up from the rear and are pressing towards the finish line. In the Kingdom of God, some people are satisfied with church as usual, and mediocrity seems to be their diet for the day.

Begin to ponder the formative stages of your walk with Christ. Recall those you have witnessed who always made themselves available and remained faithful. Such people are always the ones whom team leaders want to be on their team or committee. Those who develop and possess these qualities are the ones who rise to the occasion of leadership. They are the ones on whom everyone knows they can depend, and their word is always their bond.

The very weight that hinders us from growth is the prime target that God is daily aiming at in our life. He is the divine Vinedresser of the field and knows where to cut in order to bring to fruition the maturity in our life. The Father uses life circumstances to our advantage. It is the Word that He uses to train, prime, and develop us. We are sanctified, chastened, and washed by the water of His Word.

David declared that he hid the Word in his heart so that he would not sin against God. When we are faced with trials, life's afflictions, and the normal challenges of living life as a believer, we grow and flourish every time we adhere to the Word and allow the Word to water the situation so that much fruit can be produced. The part of our life lacking fruit is the area where the Master has the most major interest—that area of our life yet to be developed. Why? Because He wants to make us whole according to 1 Thessalonians 5:23 (NKJV):

> *Now may the God of peace Himself sanctify you completely; and may your whole spirit, soul, and body be preserved blameless at the coming of our Lord Jesus Christ.*

He desires for His light to shine in every dark place of our life. The *stuff* that He is after in our life is the *stuff* that we refuse to confront and the *stuff* that we resist! *God wants to get up in our stuff!*

Our procrastination stuff, our disorganization stuff, our unforgiveness stuff, the stuff we conceal, and the stuff we reveal. The stuff we deny and the stuff we admit—He wants to shine the light into the dark areas of our life! The stuff that we have under-spiritualized and the stuff that we have over-spiritualized, the stuff with titles and the stuff with degrees, the stuff that hinders us from becoming a yielded vessel—all this is the *stuff* that God desires to obliterate from our life!

Our Heavenly Father emphatically wants to use us! He has established our end from our beginning, and He will continually commit Himself to our development if we invite Him into the areas of our life that need maturity. As we acknowledge Him in every area of our life, He promises to direct our path according to Proverbs 3:5-6 (NKJV):

Trust in the LORD with all your heart, and lean not on your own understanding; in all your ways acknowledge Him, and He shall direct your paths.

We have this confidence that is unwavering—the Father, who began His good work in us, will complete it if we allow Him. In the place where we hide, He is already there. We have this treasure in our earthen vessel. The Master longs to complete His work in us because He knows that the light afflictions that we face are not worthy to be compared to the glory that will be revealed in our life. He woos us into His presence to prepare us to be a living sacrifice for His glory. We matter to Him—everything that concerns us, concerns Him. The feeling of our infirmities touches Him, and He is not so aloof that He can't see what we are facing.

God uses what is in our life to develop maturity in us. He cannot judge us or use us based upon another person's challenges. He uses our own life to deal with us. Our growth and Christian walk are personal and between God and us. We must understand that the challenges we are facing at this very moment are issues that demand our attention, and we shouldn't just chalk them up to coincidence.

God orders the steps of the righteous. We live a life driven by purpose, not a life driven by circumstance. We must make a conscious effort to allow our Maker to give us the grace to face our areas that need growth head-on and give attention to the detailed areas in our life that are not bearing fruit. We must refuse to accept our lack of growth as a personality flaw. We are the righteousness of God in Christ Jesus and have a God-given right to request our *Paraclete,* the Holy Spirit as Comforter,[1] to heal our infirmities. He has been assigned to help us apprehend our maturity in Christ Jesus and confront whatever has been contending against our growth.

The question to ask ourselves as we are examining and taking inventory of our life is, "Am I walking in sincerity, reliability, maximum performance, credibility, consistency, steadfastness, fruitfulness, transparency, abundance, and discipline in every area of my life?" Any area in which we are lacking one of these is a strong indication that growth is needed. Most people shy away from the confrontation of their shortcomings. The areas that we find painful or dreadful to face are the issues of growth in which God wants to assist us. There is no need to fear—our Master is near—and He is craving to help us *grow up!* We must invite Him into the *stuff* in our life and prepare for a journey that will be our greatest adventure.

It is hard to believe that many believers struggle while in the process of growth when the Lord has given us all things that pertain to life and godliness. Denial and pride prevent us from crying out for help from the Lord. This does not mean that we serve a God with a "disposable mentality" concerning His people. He is not an anti-growth type of God and does not discard us as we are endeavoring to produce fruit that remains. He knows that growth takes time, and He urges us only to purpose to mature in our Christian walk and make a commitment to walk in the godliness of redemption's purchase. For the remainder of our life, we will be growing in several areas. God is enlisting candidates for leadership in this strategic hour. The state of the church demands mature Christians in order for us to be equipped for His limitless outpouring of the Holy Spirit.

I've read statistics that reveal 25 percent of average believers never pray; 30 percent never read their Bibles; 40 percent never give to the church; and 20 percent never attend church. The average church keeps a record of members, and only 20 percent of those on the role actually attend. The ones who don't attend will tell anyone who asks that they are definitely members!

Other statistics state that 50 percent of members on the role attend special services; 60 percent have never given to world missions; and 25 percent never assume a position of leadership or devote their time to serve in any area of ministry in the church! Interestingly enough, 80 percent have never attended a midweek service; 95 percent have never led one person to the Lord in their lifetime; 97 percent have never tithed. Three percent of the Body are faithful tithers who carry the load of the God-robbers who feel that they have a prerogative not to tithe. The most intriguing fact in this entire poll is that 100 percent of all believers believe that they are going to heaven! Matthew 7:22 reminds us, "Many will say to me in that day, Lord, Lord, have we not prophesied in thy name? and in thy name have cast out devils? and in thy name done many wonderful works?" It is quite obvious that if He is Lord of one's life, the statistics will not testify against that life.

If there is ever a time that God needs an army of mature believers, it is *now!* If not now, when? If not you, then whom will He enlist? Maturity is meant to be a beautiful process, but it is not without its challenges and obstacles. Jesus said:

> *"I am the true vine, and My Father is the vinedresser."*
>
> John 15:1 NKJV

He goes on to say:

> *"I am the vine, you are the branches. He who abides in Me, and I in him, bears much fruit; for without Me you can do nothing."*
>
> John 15:5 NKJV

The joy of growth is abiding continually in the Vine. The branch cannot bear fruit of itself; the only way we can come to the maturity of bearing fruit is to seek to live in the dwelling place of the Vine. In our own strength we can do nothing; we cannot grow on our own. We need the Vinedresser. He watches over us for growth and, as we cling to Him, the same life that is in the Vine will flow into every area of our life. Proverbs 8:35 (NKJV) tells us:

> *For whoever finds me finds life, and obtains favor from the LORD.*

We are instructed to seek Him, and he who seeks Him will find life indeed.

Our Father places a demand on our growth because He desires to draw out the potential within us. The dominion given to us came from the Father, and everything that was placed inside of Adam is inside of us. Adam's dominion reached from the depth of the sea to the stars in the galaxies. The same power of authority abides in us. The only hindrances between where we are now and walking in the maximum potential are the weights and fruitless areas in our life. The greatest power in heaven and in earth is submerged beneath those weights and fruitless areas. As we grow into each dimension and gain victory over every targeted hindrance, the power of God will be released to flow out of our life more and more, pruning those fruitless areas that they may bear much more fruit. We will in turn become much more useful to our God and His Kingdom.

He desires to perfect those areas in our life that concern us. The word *perfection* is used to also express maturity. The Lord wants to mature us in the things that cause us great concern; therefore, He constantly motivates the growth process in our life because He knows what He placed inside us. Can you imagine what God must see in us and how He feels when He daily observes us struggling with things that He has given us victory over? The formula to walking in the overcoming presence and power of God is a capsule inside us! It's in *you!* It's in *you!* It's in *you!* We must meditate on the fact that God is more than enough for us.

He wants to get up in all of our *stuff* because we were created for greatness, to rule and to walk in dominion and authority. He craves to see our full potential released. There are souls held in captivity awaiting our manifestation of maturity. Remember, our growth is an ongoing project, and we must deal with each matter one day at a time—line upon line, precept upon precept. There is no "jiffy magic microwave" concept or shortcut. God is waiting to see us walk in the full manifestation of our righteousness. After all, our restoration cost the Father God the blood of His precious Son, so surely He remains committed to our growth process! Allow this time to be a beautiful experience in God as you grow from strength to strength. The process of wholeness does not have to hurt. Allow God to *get up in your stuff!*

CHAPTER 29

RUNNING WITH THE FOOTMEN

Now that you've read the previous chapters, I'm sure several challenges have come your way. Simply making a decision to come up another level is enough to make the enemy nervous. Your sheer determination to change has already positioned you to win. Follow through step-by-step with every quality decision that you have made. Refuse to allow the enemy to pull you back into mediocrity and stagnation. You were born to win and the beauty of transitioning from where you were to where you are going is the process of growing that we all must go through. Get used to it, because this process will never cease. Ask the Father to give you an appetite for excellence. Develop a palate for change and never allow neutrality to paralyze you.

There is so much potential in you. Your days of running with the footmen are over. (See Jer. 12:5.) You know in your heart that there has always been greatness in you and that you are more than a diamond in the rough. You are His workmanship created in Christ Jesus, and your inner man has been waiting to be received into your destiny. The hidden potential in you is craving to be exposed; your eternal purpose and destiny has already been self-programmed to put you on top. Everything that you need now or will ever need is already inside of you.

Running with the footmen was your former state of being, but that pull on the inside of you to go to the next level is the indicator of your potential. The power of the Holy Spirit is at work in you to give you that surge of *zoe* life, the second wind given to a runner. When you have grown accustomed to running with the footmen and God places a demand on you to run with the chariots, change is inevitable. Often there's a stirring of agitation because your human spirit craves the revealing of redemption's potential in you. You were predestined for more than you are working in right now, and it's time to tap into your undiscovered potential.

The ability to run with the chariots is well within you, and His love for you will never require of you what He has not made available to you. He who did not spare His own Son, but delivered Him up to us all, shall He not freely give us all things that we need? This is exactly what He has done for you as an individual; He personally has graciously designed a blueprint for you that will enable you to do all that He has predestined for you. You have to believe in this, personalize it, and take ownership of it. Everything that the Master has for you is for you.

There are going to be times and even days when you may not feel like you can run even with the footmen, but know this: The anointing to contend with the chariots is within you. Don't ever get into the mode of comparing yourself to others. The Bible clearly states that this is not a wise thing to do. What God has planned for your life is uniquely orchestrated for you alone. Daily seek His face and place a demand on the potential in you. Purpose to seek growth. The moment you stop growing, you will stagnate and die. Where the Father is intending to take you in this season of your life demands the anointing of a chariot runner. He elected you for this race. You didn't choose Him—He chose you. Where He's taking you does not remotely resemble where you have been or where you are now.

Get accustomed to a new way of doing things as this transition begins to prioritize your thinking. Allow Him to speak to you to do things that you have never done before that are within godly parameters—the things that you have despised dealing with such as the junk drawer, time management, and reorganizing your office structure. Establish a budget; choose to forgive the person who has wronged you; go back to school; and deal with seemingly more unspiritual things such as weight loss.

When we engage in weight-training, the weights that benefit us the most are the ones that slow us down. When runners are preparing for a race, sometimes they place weights on their ankles while running to strengthen and build up their leg muscles. But when the race draws nigh they reduce the weights so that their pace becomes faster. At the time of the race, they discard all weights. Their leg muscles are much stronger; therefore, their running is much faster and their time is much shorter.

You too must throw off every weight of sin that is hindering you from running the race of life. Throw off the weight to finish strong instead of weak. I am not saying that the runner will never finish the race with the weights on their ankles, but the objective of a race is to finish strong. Hebrews 12:1-2 (NKJV) tells us:

> *Therefore we also, since we are surrounded by so great a cloud of witnesses, let us lay aside every weight, and the sin which so easily ensnares us, and let us run with endurance the race that is set before us, looking unto Jesus, the author and finisher of our faith....*

Rest assured that there is no distraction, or attraction, that is worth the glory that the Master desires to release in your life. As we saw previously, Paul said it this way in 2 Corinthians 4:17-18 (NKJV):

> *For our light affliction, which is but for a moment, is working for us a far more exceeding and eternal weight of glory, while we do not look at the things which are seen, but at the things which are not seen. For the things which are seen are temporary, but the things which are not seen are eternal.*

The process that you are transitioning through is not permanent. Change is the only thing that is permanent because growth is inevitable. However, the circumstances in the midst of the process of change are temporary and subject to change. Therefore, it is crucial not to allow your visual perception to govern your choices. Only the God-ordained, external purposes are everlasting. This is an extremely vital key to know as you grow.

No matter what is facing you, regardless of what the things surrounding you appear to be indicating, always remember that the situation is subject to change. Things will not always be as they are right now! Through it all, you must continue to look to Jesus—the only One who can give you the strength to endure the race. You must acknowledge that the oppositions and afflictions are catapulting you towards something far greater. Do not place the opposition above the end result that will come, but rather glorify God in the midst of it. Know that the trial of your faith is also working something in you. It is working within you patience, and as long as you allow patience to have its perfect work, then you will be mature, whole, entire, and complete—lacking nothing.

Purpose in your life to confront the challenges of growth. Confronting the challenges is often easier said than done, especially in the hard, resistant areas of your life, the areas that you have become professional at avoiding. Learn to face them head-on, beginning with the most difficult ones, and the Holy Spirit will be your comforter, teacher, guide, and helper. He's waiting to see you through because on the other side of your growth in each arena is your breakthrough and your blessing.

The Father takes great pleasure in blessing His obedient children. He is longing to release the fullness of Himself without measure through you. Your growth causes you to decrease, so that He can increase in your life. You become hidden with Christ in God, and only He is seen and glorified.

Decree a perpetual decree over your life. Jeremiah 5:22 (NKJV) tells us:

"Do you not fear Me?' says the LORD. 'Will you not tremble at My presence, who have placed the sand as the bound of the sea, by a perpetual decree, that it cannot pass beyond it? And though its waves toss to and fro, yet they cannot prevail; though they roar, yet they cannot pass over it.'"

It is great that you have made a quality decision to take inventory of your life. Second Corinthians 13:5-6 (NKJV) states:

> *Examine yourselves as to whether you are in the faith. Test yourselves. Do you not know yourselves, that Jesus Christ is in you?—unless indeed you are disqualified. But I trust that you will know that we are not disqualified.*

You have made a quality decision to examine yourself and pursue excellence. You have made a decision to grow up in the areas that you've allowed immaturity for so long. Even in areas that are painful to admit and face, purpose to not make excuses but to rather simply *grow up into the full stature of Christ Jesus.* Allow the Holy Spirit to conform you into His image. You were ordained by God to run with the chariots. You were never designed to be the last runner in the race! Running in cadence with the chariots, you will finish strong. Settle into your new life, and never cease to pursue spiritual maturity. God needs you in this hour to grow up. The unreached person who does not know God, needs you. Your family and your church need you to press on to maturity!

CONCLUSION:

THE FINISHING TOUCH

I trust that this book has been life changing for you and an encouragement. Many of us begin our Christian walk with so many challenges. The beauty of the redeemed life is that we are just that: *redeemed*. We have been purchased by the blood of the Lamb. It doesn't matter how we start—what matters is how we finish.

The Word of God tells us: "...if any man be in Christ, he is a new creature: old things are passed away; behold, all things are become new" (2 Cor. 5:17). You can now walk in the newness of life in Christ Jesus. You can walk as the creature that has never existed before. All things have become new for you.

The application of these principles will be an ongoing and life-changing process. But our greatest confidence is that He who has begun this good work in us will complete it, even until the day of Jesus Christ. (See Phil. 1:6 NKJV.) God has committed Himself to our finish. He Himself is the author, the originator, the developer, and ultimately the finisher of our faith. (See Heb. 12:2.) No matter what we face or encounter in life, nothing has the power to abort the implanted work of the Holy Spirit in our life, as we yield to His unctions.

I am convinced that you have everything within you to finish strong! The grace to finish strong lies within your reach. He has given you all things that pertain to life and godliness. (See 2 Peter 1:3.) After all, He who did not spare His own Son, but delivered Him up for us all, how shall He not with Him also freely give us all things? (Rom. 8:32.) Remember, the race isn't given to the swiftest runner; rather, to the one who endures to the end! It may appear that others in life have had a better running start than you; they may seem to have taken off and left you in the shadows. Just be encouraged that this race is a marathon, and the purpose is to finish strong.

> *But that which ye have already hold fast till I come.*
>
> *And he that overcometh, and keepeth my works unto the end, to him will I give power over the nations.*
>
> Revelation 2:25,26

ENDNOTES

Introduction

[1] Micah 4:1-3 (NKJV)

Now it shall come to pass in the latter days that the mountain of the Lord's house shall be established on the top of the mountains, and shall be exalted above the hills; and peoples shall flow to it.

Many nations shall come and say, "Come, and let us go up to the mountain of the LORD, to the house of the God of Jacob; he will teach us His ways, and we shall walk in His paths." For out of Zion the law shall go forth, and the word of the LORD from Jerusalem.

He shall judge between many peoples, and rebuke strong nations afar off; they shall beat their swords into plowshares, and their spears into pruning hooks; nation shall not lift up sword against nation, neither shall they learn war any more.

But everyone shall sit under his vine and under his fig tree, and no one shall make them afraid; for the mouth of the LORD of hosts has spoken.

Chapter 1

[1] "EL (el). This is the name by which God is called in the OT—El, the God Elohim of Israel (Gen. 33:20). In prose it occurs more frequently with the modifier—El Elyon ('God Most High,' 14:18)...." Merrill F. Unger, ed. R.K. Harrison, *The New Unger's Bible Dictionary* (Chicago: Moody Press, Revised and Updated Edition, "Additional and New Material," 1988, The Moody Bible Institute of Chicago), s.v. "EL," p. 340.

Chapter 2

[1] Spiros Zodhiates, ed. Warren Baker, *The Complete Word Study Dictionary Old Testament* (Chattanooga: AMG Publishers, 1994 by AMG International, Inc.), s.v. "breath" Job 12:10, "Ruach" #7307, p. 2364.

[2] Zodhiates, s.v. "breath" Psalm 33:6, "Rauch," #7307, p. 2364.

[3] Zodhiates, "breath" Genesis 2:7, "Neshamah," #5397, p. 2343.

Chapter 3

[1] James Strong, "Hebrew and Chaldee Dictionary" in *Strong's Exhaustive Concordance of the Bible* (Nashville: Abingdon, 1890), p. 14, entry #559, s.v. "said," in Genesis 1:3,6-7,9,11.

[2] Strong, "Hebrew Dictionary," entry #559.

[3] Strong, "Hebrew Dictionary," entry #559.

[4] *Webster's II New College Dictionary* (Boston/New York: Houghton Mifflin Company, 1995), s.v. "avouch."

[5] *Webster's New World*™ *College Dictionary* 3d. ed. (New York: Macmillan, 1996 Simon & Schuster), s.v. "avouch."

[6] *Webster's New World*™ 3d., s.v. "vouch."

[7] Webster's II, s.v. "vouch."

[8] Strong, "Hebrew Dictionary," p. 98, entry #6680, "tsavah," s.v. "commanded," Genesis 2:16.

Chapter 7

[1] Strong, "Dictionary of the Words in the Greek Testament" in *Strong's Exhaustive Concordance of the Bible* (Nashville: Abingdon, 1890), p. 78, entry #5550, s.v. "time," Hebrews 5:12.

Chapter 8

[1] First Thessalonians 5:23 describes man as triune: "…your whole spirit and soul and body…."

[2] Romans 8:13 and Colossians 3:5 NKJV.

[3] Strong, "Greek Dictionary," p. 49, entry #3499: "to deaden, i.e. (fig.) to subdue," s.v. "mortify," Colossians 3:5.

Chapter 9

[1] 2 Corinthians 5:10 NASB

For we must all appear before the judgment seat of Christ, that each one may be recompensed for his deeds in the body, according to what he has done, whether good or bad.

Chapter 10

[1] *Webster's New World*™ *Thesaurus* 3d ed. (New York: Macmillan, 1997 Simon & Schuster), s.v. "contrite."

[2] *Webster's II,* s.v. "contrite."

[3] W.E. Vine, *Vine's Complete Expository Dictionary of Old and New Testament Words* (Nashville: Thomas Nelson Inc., 1984), "An Expository Dictionary of New Testament Words," p. 667, s.v. "washing," 2. "loutron."

[4] Unger, *New Unger's,* p. 49, s.v. "altar."

Chapter 12

[1] Or "Shechinah"; William Smith, LL.D., *Smith's Bible Dictionary* (Old Tappan, NJ: Spire Books, Fleming H. Revell, May 1981 16th printing), s.v. "Shechinah," p. 631.

Chapter 14

[1] *Webster's II,* s.v. "principle."

[2] Strong, "Greek Dictionary," p. 70, entry #4991, "*soteria,*" s.v. "salvation," Philippians 2:12.

[3] Strong, "Greek Dictionary," p. 70, entry #4982, "*sozo,*" s.v. "save," as in John 12:47.

Chapter 15

[1] Strong, "Greek Dictionary," p. 225, entry #2937, s.v. "creature," 2 Corinthians 5:17.

Chapter 16

[1] Vine, "New Testament," p. 608, s.v. "SUFFER," "A. Verbs," "(b) to endure suffering," "2. *pascho*…3958."

In 2 Tim. 1:12 the specific meaning is: "(II), of human 'suffering' (a) of followers of Christ."

In Heb. 5:8 the specific meaning is: "(I) of the 'sufferings' of Christ (a) at the hands of men" and "(b) in His expiatory and vicarious sacrifice for sin," "(c)…'passion.'"

[2] Spiros Zodhiates, ed., *The Complete Word Study Dictionary: New Testament* (Chattanooga: AMG Publishers, 1992 by AMG International, Inc., Rev. Ed. 1993), p. 1127, s.v. "3958."

[3] *Webster's New World*™ Thesaurus, s.v. "endure."

Chapter 17

[1] *Webster's II,* s.v. "peril."

Chapter 18

[1] 1 Corinthians 12:6-11

And there are diversities of operations, but it is the same God which worketh all in all.

But the manifestation of the Spirit is given to every man to profit withal.

For to one is given by the Spirit the word of wisdom; to another the word of knowledge by the same Spirit;

To another faith by the same Spirit; to another the gifts of healing by the same Spirit;

To another the working of miracles; to another prophecy; to another discerning of spirits; to another divers kinds of tongues; to another the interpretation of tongues:

But all these worketh that one and the selfsame Spirit, dividing to every man severally as he will.

Chapter 19

[1] Unger, *New Unger's,* p. 1124, s.v. "SANCTIFICATION."

[2] R.A. Torrey, *What the Bible Teaches* (London: Marshall Pickering, 1957), p. 342: "Sanctification—the separation of men from sin and separating them unto God—is God's own work."

[3] Torrey, p. 343: "By the giving up or the sacrifice of Himself, Christ sets the Church apart for God."

[4] Vine, "New Testament," p. 546, s.v. "SANCTIFICATION, SANCTIFY," "A. Noun," "*hagiasmos* (...38)."

[5] Zodhiates, *The Complete Word Study Dictionary: New Testament,* p. 70, s.v. "40."

[6] Zodhiates, p. 70, s.v. "40," "(I)," "(B)."

[7] Vine, "New Testament," pp. 307-308, s.v. "HOLINESS, HOLY, HOLILY," "B. Adjectives," "1," "(b)."

[8] Biblesoft's *Jamieson, Fausset, and Brown Commentary,* electronic Database, copyright © 1997 by Biblesoft, all rights reserved, "1 Peter 1:16."

[9] *Jamieson, Fausset, and Brown Commentary,* s.v. "Hebrews 10:20."

[10] Strong, "Greek Dictionary," p. 216, entry #1457, s.v. "consecrated," Hebrews 10:20: "from 1456; to renew, i.e. *inaugurate:*—consecrate, dedicate."

Chapter 20

[1] Genesis 16:13,14

And she called the name of the Lord that spake unto her, Thou God seest me: for she said, Have I also here looked after him that seeth me?

Wherefore the well was called Beer-lahai-roi; behold, it is between Kadesh and Bered.

In verse 13, the Greek word from which "God" is translated is "*el*" (Strong, "Hebrew Dictionary," p. 12, entry #410) and the Greek word for "seest me" is "*ro'iy*" (Strong, "Hebrew Dictionary," p. 106, entry #7210): "God" "(that) seeth."

Chapter 28

[1] Strong, "Greek Dictionary," p. 55, entry #3875, "*parakletos,*" s.v. "Comforter," John 14:26.

PRAYER OF SALVATION

God loves you—no matter who you are, no matter what your past. God loves you so much that He gave His one and only begotten Son for you. The Bible tells us that "...whoever believes in Him should not perish but have everlasting life" (John 3:16 NKJV). Jesus laid down His life and rose again so that we could spend eternity with Him in heaven and experience His absolute best on earth. If you would like to receive Jesus into your life, say the following prayer out loud and mean it from your heart.

Heavenly Father, I come to You admitting that I am a sinner. Right now, I choose to turn away from sin, and I ask You to cleanse me of all unrighteousness. I believe that Your Son, Jesus, died on the cross to take away my sins. I also believe that He rose again from the dead so that I might be forgiven of my sins and made righteous through faith in Him. I call upon the name of Jesus Christ to be the Savior and Lord of my life. Jesus, I choose to follow You and ask that You fill me with the power of the Holy Spirit. I declare that right now I am a child of God. I am free from sin and full of the righteousness of God. I am saved in Jesus' name. Amen.

If you prayed this prayer to receive Jesus Christ as your Savior for the first time, please contact us on the Web at **www.harrison-house.com** to receive a free book.

Or you may write to us at
Harrison House
P.O. Box 35035
Tulsa, Oklahoma 74153

ABOUT THE AUTHOR

The ministry of Dr. Pat Bailey has created tremendous impact for more than 20 years in over 80 countries around the world, bringing deliverance and salvation to countless thousands. A 1982 graduate of New Life Bible College in Tennessee, a 1984 Charter Class Graduate of Victory World Missions Training Center in Tulsa, Oklahoma, and a 1993 graduate of All Nations for Christ Bible Institute in Benin City, Nigeria, Patricia D. Bailey's journey into ministry began at the age of 21 with an invitation from the late Daisy Osborn (wife of T.L. Osborn) to travel to East and West Africa.

Dr. Bailey is a lecturer, author, and founder of Master's Touch Ministries International, a mission outreach. MTM has also founded Y.U.G.O. (Young Adults United for Global Outreach) and Sister to Sister, an international outreach to women in foreign countries. Dr. Bailey serves as a missions strategy consultant to several growing churches and has developed leadership programs around the world.

Dr. Bailey has focused her recent efforts of spreading the liberating good news of the Gospel of Jesus Christ toward the people living in the 10/40 window which includes North Africa and the Middle East, an area that is the most populated, but the least evangelized, in the world.

Master's Touch Ministries has headquarters in Atlanta, Los Angeles, and London, England. Dr. Bailey is the proud mother of a son, Karim Israel Bailey.

To contact Dr. Bailey, write:

Dr. Patricia D. Bailey

Master's Touch Ministries International

P.O. Box 3175

Alpharetta, Georgia 30023

Web site: **www.mtmintl.org**

Please include your prayer requests

and comments when you write.

COMING SOON BY PAT BAILEY

Women Risktakers

Available 2004

HARRISON HOUSE
Tulsa, Oklahoma 74153

THE HARRISON HOUSE VISION

Proclaiming the truth and the power
Of the Gospel of Jesus Christ
With excellence;

Challenging Christians to
Live victoriously,
Grow spiritually,
Know God intimately.